The Social Psychology of Aging

DATE DUE

The Claremont Symposium on
Applied Social Psychology

This series of volumes highlights important new developments on the leading edge of applied social psychology. Each volume concentrates on one area where social psychological knowledge is being applied to the resolution of social problems. Within that area, a distinguished group of authorities present chapters summarizing recent theoretical views and empirical findings, including the results of their own research and applied activities. An introductory chapter integrates this material, pointing out common themes and varied areas of practical applications. Thus each volume brings together trenchant new social psychological ideas, research results, and fruitful applications bearing on an area of current social interest. The volumes will be of value not only to practitioners and researchers, but also to students and lay people interested in this vital and expanding area of psychology.

Books in the Series

Interpersonal Processes, *Stuart Oskamp and Shirlynn Spacapan, Editors*

The Social Psychology of Health, *Shirlynn Spacapan and Stuart Oskamp, Editors*

The Social Psychology of Aging, *Shirlynn Spacapan and Stuart Oskamp, Editors*

The Social Psychology of Aging

Shirlynn Spacapan
Stuart Oskamp
Editors

 The Claremont Symposium on
Applied Social Psychology

 **SAGE** PUBLICATIONS
The Publishers of Professional Social Science
Newbury Park   London   New Delhi

For information address:

SAGE Publications, Inc.
2111 West Hillcrest Drive
Newbury Park, California 91320

SAGE Publications Ltd.
28 Banner Street
London EC1Y 8QE
England

SAGE Publications India Pvt. Ltd.
M-32 Market
Greater Kailash I
New Delhi 110 048 India

Printed in the United States of America

Library of Congress Cataloging-in-Publication Data

Main entry under title:

The social psychology of aging / edited by Shirlynn Spacapan and
   Stuart Oskamp.
      p.   cm. — (Claremont Symposium on Applied Social Psychology)
   Includes bibliographies and indexes.
   ISBN 0-8039-3555-2. — ISBN 0-8039-3556-0 (pbk.)
      1. Aged—Psychology—Congresses.   2. Aging—Social aspects—
Congresses.   3. Life change events in old age—Congresses.
I. Spacapan, Shirlynn. II. Oskamp, Stuart.   III. Claremont Symposium
on Applied Social Psychology (5th   : 1988   : Claremont Graduate
School).   IV. Series: Claremont Symposium on Applied Social
Psychology (Series)
HQ1061.S6483   1989
305.26—dc20
                                                           89-10121
                                                           CIP

FIRST PRINTING, 1989

Contents

Preface

The chapters in this volume are based on presentations given at the fifth Claremont Symposium on Applied Social Psychology on February 20, 1988. These symposia, held annually at the Claremont Graduate School, bring outstanding psychologists from various parts of North America to join in discussion and analysis of important topics and issues in the field of applied social psychology. We appreciate the generous financial support for this series of symposia from each of the Claremont Colleges (Claremont Graduate School, Claremont McKenna College, Harvey Mudd College, Pitzer College, Pomona College, and Scripps College). We are also indebted to the John Randolph and Dora Haynes Foundation of Southern California, for a founding grant for the conference as well as for a 1988 Faculty Fellowship, which enabled the first editor to work on this volume. This year, additional thanks are due to Karen Rook, of the Program in Social Ecology at the University of California at Irvine, and Jon Pynoos, of the Andrus Gerontology Center at the University of Southern California, for their help in serving as discussants of the presentations at the conference. We are also grateful to Fay Hicks, Craig Huhta, Lilian Klepa, Shawn Okuda, and Michael W. Scott for their help with proofreading and indexing, and to Mike Nichol and Catherine Cameron for their support.

In preparing the conference presentations for publication, we suggested that the contributors expand and elaborate on points that they did not have time to cover orally and incorporate material addressing some of the points raised by the audience discussion. We also encouraged the contributors to maintain some of the informal style that made the conference talks so interesting by using a personalized, narrative tone and including personal examples or anecdotal information to highlight their research findings and theoretical material. To reflect the symposium panel discussions led by Rook and Pynoos, and to provide a fuller integration of the several papers, we have written an introductory chapter summarizing some of the major themes in the social psychology of aging. Finally, we solicited an additional, concluding chapter on aging and public policy to underscore the importance to current political policy of the "leading edge" research and thought of prior chapters.

We believe this volume will be interesting and valuable to researchers and practitioners in both social psychology and gerontology, as well as to professors, students, and lay people who want to know more about this exciting and increasingly important field.

Shirlynn Spacapan
Stuart Oskamp
Claremont, CA

1

Introduction to the Social Psychology of Aging

SHIRLYNN SPACAPAN
STUART OSKAMP

There is perhaps no other developmental stage of life so full of contradictions and myths as that of old age. Common stereotypes of the elderly, for example, hold that they are in poor health, unhappy, lonely, and fearful of crime (see Butler, 1975). Less than one-fourth of the oldsters polled, however, reported experiencing these problems (National Council on the Aging, 1975), and many surveys have found that feelings of satisfaction are higher among the elderly than among young adults (Herzog, Rogers, & Woodworth, 1982). It is interesting that many older respondents did report that *other* elderly people (e.g., "the old biddy next door" or "the old fogey down the street") experience these problems, suggesting that our older population believes in, and perpetuates, some of the ageist myths. One sad result of such social devaluation, according to Aiken (1982), is the development of negative self-concepts and earlier symptoms of biological aging.

How can some of the negative symptoms of aging be eased? A rapidly developing body of knowledge suggests that there are a number of cognitive and social factors that may ameliorate the negative aspects of aging. Some of these factors—predictability, perceived control, prior expectations—are ones that environmental psychologists have studied in relation to lessening the negative impact of stressors like noise, crowding, and pollution. Other researchers have found that these same factors are effective in improving the health of elderly patients in institutional settings (Langer & Rodin, 1976). In addition, environmental psychologists have suggested ways in which the physical environment of the elderly can be altered to enhance functioning (see Simon, 1987). As Lawton, Altman, and Wohlwill (1984) have pointed out, these and other similar research areas—such as issues of age-segregated housing (Rosow, 1967)—provide information that is helpful to public policymakers.

All of the topics mentioned above—stereotypes, feelings of life satisfaction, perceived control, the physical environment, and research input to public policy—are among the dozen recurrent themes in this book. In this first chapter, after a brief outline of the volume, we will summarize these issues or themes common in the study of the social psychology of aging. Then the chapter concludes with a preview of each of the following chapters of the volume.

Outline of the Volume

The following seven chapters are framed, on either end, by chapters that present a set of challenges to researchers in the field. In the first of these, Chapter 2, Robert Hansson provides a broad overview of the challenges to basic social psychological assumptions inherent in studying old age and aging. In the closing chapter, Chapter 8, Thomas Puglisi and Larry Rickards outline roles psychologists can play and public policy changes that are needed to meet the challenges presented by our aging society.

In between these two sets of challenges, the chapters are presented in an order that roughly corresponds to some of the tasks of later life: caring for elderly parents, the retirement transition, postretirement issues, creating one's environment and maintaining positive affect, and the adaptive role of possessions in late adulthood. In Chapter 3, Melvin Lerner and his colleagues point out that, in middle age to early old age, parents' needs for their children's care and resources may result in a form of social dilemma for the siblings; and they present a theoretical framework and recent data that help in understanding the development of the dilemma. Next, Tora Bikson and Jacqueline Goodchilds report some results from a field experiment in which retirement planning and problems were analyzed in long-term task groups made up of individuals on both sides of "the great retirement divide"—individuals who were close to retirement and those who had retired within the preceding four years. In the fifth chapter, Philip Dreyer highlights the factors that may contribute to life satisfaction in later life and reports some results of two recent studies of retirees. Powell Lawton elaborates on some of the consequences of person-environment transactions, focusing on affect among aging individuals, in Chapter 6. Chapter 7 presents Laura Kamptner's discussion of the instrumental and symbolic functions of possessions and her findings on the possessions that were particularly valued by a sample of oldsters.

Themes in a Social Psychological Approach to Aging

Interdisciplinary Approach

At the outset, it is important to note that the study of aging is an interdisciplinary undertaking. This is reflected in the content of journals in the field and in the composition of major professional associations of researchers in aging. To take one example, the Gerontological Society of America brings together biological, behavioral, and social science researchers, as well as those whose backgrounds are in clinical medicine and social planning or practice. An interdisciplinary approach to the study of aging is not only appropriate but necessary, given the complex interactions between health, social competence, and cognitive functioning in the elderly. In Butler's (1975) classic book, several poignant illustrations—such as how a health problem may lead to impaired cognitive functioning, which in turn may drive away sources of social support—serve to remind us of the importance of examining these interactions. This idea is reinforced by the contributors to this volume, and constitutes a major theme throughout the chapters. In the following chapter, Hansson reviews some recent findings on the interrelationships between psychological, social, and health issues for the elderly, and suggests that social psychologists should assume a greater role in the interdisciplinary effort to understand these interactions. In discussing roles that psychologists can take in affecting public policy for the aged, Puglisi and Rickards note that such activist roles require an ability to understand and apply multidisciplinary research findings.

In addition to suggesting more activities that cross disciplinary boundaries, several authors in this volume emphasize strengthening the interface between various subdisciplines within psychology in order to make headway in understanding the process of aging. Puglisi and Rickards focus on the potential of the two subfields of health psychology and the psychology of women, urging researchers in aging to begin to incorporate the insights of these areas. Hansson describes how cognitive, personality, industrial/organizational, and other areas of psychology have gained from the added perspective provided by studying older populations, and he encourages social psychologists to do the same. He stresses that not only will they learn something about aging, but they may find their favorite social psychological assumptions and theories challenged, revised, and (in the end) enriched. One good example of this is Lawton's contribution to this volume, where he explicitly states that the general study of person-environment transactions may be advanced through exploring the motivation of elderly individuals in interacting with their environment.

It seems, then, that if a "social psychology of aging" is to flourish and make important contributions to gerontology, it will need to be more than just a "social" psychology. The interdisciplinary approach that has marked the study of aging is evident in much of the exciting new social psychological work on aging, and we note developmental and clinical psychologists as well as social psychologists as contributors to this volume.

Life Satisfaction

While "life satisfaction" is the topic of Chapter 5, the related issues of "successful" aging and the psychological well-being of the elderly are at the core of several of the chapters. This topic has also been a central concern in the field of gerontology, where "life satisfaction" is one of the oldest areas of research. As Dreyer's chapter relates, measures of life satisfaction vary, but generally include having a zest for life, resolution and fortitude, congruence between desired and achieved goals, a positive self-concept, and positive affect (see Neugarten, Havighurst, & Tobin, 1968). Theories of successful aging have ranged from prescribing *disengagement* from active social roles in order to attain higher levels of life satisfaction in old age (Cumming & Henry, 1961) to Neugarten's proposal that it is *continuity* of life-style across the life span that leads to happiness in later life (Neugarten et al., 1968). Recent work, including research by Dreyer and his colleagues (this volume), suggests that continuing one's preretirement life-style leads to more satisfaction with life after retirement.

While Lawton has developed a popular measure of life satisfaction (see Lawton, 1975), in Chapter 6 he turns his attention from global measures to the affective component of life satisfaction. Affect is also a topic addressed in Kamptner's chapter, where she delineates the function that personal possessions may play as moderators of their owner's affect. Possessions are not only sources of comfort and pleasure, she reports, but are also tied to one's self-identity and self-concept. This component of positive self-concept or self-esteem is one of the main issues that Bikson and Goodchilds investigated in their study of the retirement transition, reported in Chapter 4. In addition to highlighting this classic component of life satisfaction, their work points out that a variety of other factors—such as time spent with spouse—also contribute to one's happiness. Thus Bikson and Goodchilds, as well as Kamptner and other contributors, remind us that interpersonal ties are related to life satisfaction.

Interpersonal Processes

Interpersonal processes are the heart of social psychology. As psychologists turn their attention to the social psychology of aging, then, it is not surprising to find that interpersonal processes are discussed at every turn. This is reflected in each chapter that follows, to varying degrees. For instance, Lerner and his colleagues devote a chapter to examining the processes that produce a social dilemma for children of dependent elderly parents, while Puglisi and Rickards mention the need for research on the interactions between elderly patients, professional caregivers, and families of patients.

The importance of interpersonal processes is evident in the theoretical bases of many of the following chapters. Sometimes it is implicit, as in Lawton's application of the opponent-process model to affectivity in aging, while at other times interpersonal processes are an explicit part of key hypotheses, as in Dreyer's summary of theoretical views of healthy adjustment, which involve an individual's social role activity. Even when interpersonal aspects are not the theoretical focal point of a chapter, they are included with other key processes in aging. For example, in discussing the symbolic functions of possessions, Kamptner notes that possessions may represent their owner's relationships with others in addition to being symbols of the self or sources of comfort.

The crucial nature of interpersonal processes is evident also throughout the research findings reported in this volume. For instance, Bikson and Goodchilds's chapter reports that, contrary to expectations, retirees have relatively full social lives in comparison with their slightly younger, still-employed counterparts. As other examples, Kamptner reports that her elderly population overwhelmingly attributed interpersonal-familial meanings to their most valued possessions, and Dreyer found that continuity in socializing with one's family was one of the few factors that distinguished his group of retirees who were most happily and successfully adjusting to the changes that come with aging. Hansson's chapter stresses interpersonal processes in its coverage of a variety of traditional social psychological topics like social support, social comparison, and stereotyping—which he urges us to consider in the context of their development over the life span.

Stereotyping

Of all the various interpersonal processes discussed throughout this volume, stereotyping of the elderly may be the one most deserving of further attention. Stereotypes of the elderly abound and include the idea that they are "unteachable, disabled, poor, sexless, powerless" (Dreyer, this volume). Hansson reminds us that, unlike other groups that may be the objects of our stereotyped beliefs, we are each destined for membership in the group of "elderly." As mentioned earlier, even after joining this group, people continue to express ageist beliefs. Psychologists themselves have allowed ageism to creep into their research and theories, and the disengagement hypothesis of successful aging is one example (Rook, 1988): that is, the idea that happiness in old age accompanies withdrawal from active social lives and problem solving is based on the assumption that inactivity is synonymous with old age and that it is best to "give in and go along." Recently, various writers have pointed out that, as society is gradually leaving behind the disengagement-inactivity stereotype of the elderly, it may not be moving toward a less ageist stance, but instead may be substituting a new stereotype of the (hyper)active, athletic senior (see, for example, Anaya, 1988).

Both the causes and consequences of stereotypes have been studied by social psychologists for years. While none of the chapters in this volume focuses primarily on stereotyping, Lerner and his colleagues examine a form of biased perception, and the information in their chapter sheds light on the causes of some types of stereotyping and prejudice. The consequences of stereotyping are numerous and take varied forms: Kamptner writes that such social devaluation may damage one's self-esteem and interfere with one's competence and efficacy, while Lawton indicates that ageism results in a tendency to disempower the aged and rob them of access to a wide range of experiences that could enhance the quality of their lives. Even more chilling is the information from Puglisi and Rickards that important public policy on aging is often guided by stereotypical views of the elderly.

Heterogeneity

Stereotyping the aged, of course, involves the tendency to regard them and treat them as if they were one homogeneous group. On the contrary, in this volume the heterogeneity of the elderly population is a theme that cuts across all the chapters. Hansson sets the stage for this in Chapter 2 by listing some of the areas in which within-group variability increases with age: health, intellectual abilities, interpersonal skills, and so on. To a great extent, this increasing heterogeneity is related to the complex interactions between aspects of individuals' health and their psychological functioning, and the complexity of this relationship reinforces the importance of an interdisciplinary approach to aging.

The theme of heterogeneity is apparent at several different levels in the contributions that follow. At the most micro level, it is reflected in specific findings of research projects, such as Bikson and Goodchilds's finding that their sample of retirees was more heterogeneous in their allocation of time across activities than were the still-employed subjects. At the demographic level, some authors note that aging has different implications for different subgroups of the population. Dreyer, for instance, reviews literature indicating that retirement entails different meanings and activities for different occupational groups and different racial or ethnic minority groups. Hansson points out that older Black and White groups differ in the frequency of contact with their children as well as in the amount and type of assistance they receive from their offspring. Women, as a subgroup, are especially likely to experience aging differently than men, and the particular case of aging women constitutes another theme in this volume.

Women

To discuss older women and their particular experiences as a separate theme in aging research can be considered misleading, for many writers have remarked that the psychology of aging *is* a psychology of women, and the problems of the very old are essentially women's problems (see, for example, Dreyer or Hansson, this volume; Rodeheaver & Datan, 1988). This is due, in large part, to the simple demographic facts that women, on average, tend to outlive men substantially and to marry men older than they are. One result of these facts is that studies of negative events in old age, such as bereavement or loss of social support, turn out to be mostly studies of women. Another result of the longer life expectancy for women is seen in recent surveys indicating that women constitute almost 80% of the elderly who live alone (Kasper, 1988). Further descriptions of the life of older women may be found in Chapters 2, 5, and 8, and range from women's specific health care needs to their vulnerability to poverty.

To some extent, the particular concerns of today's elderly women are due not only to women's longevity in comparison to men but also to the socialization processes experienced by their cohort. Thus Kamptner attributes her findings—that older men imbue their possessions with somewhat different sets of meanings than do women—to the differential gender-role socialization to which each group was exposed. Other indicators that gender differences in later life may have their roots in earlier life experiences may be found in Lerner et al.'s chapter, which points out that the role of caregiver for dependent parents typically falls on the shoulders of the middle-aged daughter, or the chapter by Bikson and Goodchilds, which reports that a man's retirement may mean very different things for himself and his wife.

Health

We have already mentioned the topic of health several times in this chapter, and with good reason. Chronic illness, often due to the interaction of several health problems, is a widespread phenomenon among the elderly. Furthermore, Puglisi and Rickards report that the health-care costs of older persons come to one-third of the total U.S. health-care expenditures. Despite the amount of money that is spent on health care for our aging population, congressional investigations reveal vast unmet health needs, particularly in the area of long-term care (Select Committee on Aging, 1987; Special Committee on Aging, 1988). Older adults themselves recognize the severity of the problem, and the task forces in Bikson and Goodchilds's study identified "health" as one of the six focal issues for their discussions.

A concern for the health of the elderly is found, in one way or another, in each chapter of this volume. In the work reported by Lerner and his colleagues on caregivers, it was the deteriorating health of an older person that set the stage for the research topic. In other cases, health is tangentially related to the topic, as when Dreyer relates that good biological health is one of the predictors of postretirement life satisfaction. The relationship between physical and mental health is addressed by several authors, and Chapter 8 is noteworthy for its extensive discussion of mental health and aging. Finally, it should be noted that mental health or psychological well-being is closely intertwined with life satisfaction, a theme we have already discussed.

Financial Security

The implications of chronic health problems for one's financial status are summed up in the title of a recent publication from the U.S. House of Representatives, *Long Term Care and Personal Impoverishment* (Select Committee on Aging, 1987). The association of money with health is indirectly noted at several points in the chapters to follow: Both money and health were among the six concerns of Bikson and Goodchilds's subjects; both financial security and physical health are listed by Hansson among the losses one commonly experiences in later life. There is also a brief discussion of the poverty rate of the elderly in the chapter by Puglisi and Rickards. Thus, although financial security in old age is not a major theme of this volume, it is a theme that forms the background or context for many of the issues that are raised. Here, we echo the caution stated by Puglisi and Rickards to remember that the elderly are a heterogeneous group in this respect, as in so many others.

Personal Control

A major reason why financial security and good health are topics of such concern in the psychology of aging may be because threats to one's financial or health status also challenge one's sense of personal control or autonomy. Substantial research indicates that, at least with respect to health status, the reciprocal relationship also holds; that is, a sense of control has important beneficial consequences for one's physical health (Rodin, 1986). Evidence that a sense of control or efficacy is also conducive to good psychological health has led to the now well-accepted "principle of minimal intervention," which cautions against providing excessive levels of instrumental support for older people (see Kahn, 1975; Rowe & Kahn,

1987). In fact, the central role of personal control in the process of successful aging has resulted in entire books on the topic (see Baltes & Baltes, 1986).

In this volume, Hansson, Kamptner, and Lawton each devote sections of their chapters to the role of control in aging. Hansson reviews some of the positive consequences of a sense of control and notes that the construct of personal control has been fine-tuned as a result of being studied from a life span, developmental perspective. In explaining the instrumental functions that people's possessions serve, Kamptner includes the idea that possessions are sources of personal control for their owners. The exercise of control is one means by which we express our autonomy, and the consequences of such proactive behavior for people's positive affect form the topic of Lawton's chapter. Mention of specific forms of exercising control occur throughout this volume, as when Bikson and Goodchilds attribute their finding that retirees are happier with their use of time than are employees to data indicating the importance of the ability to vary (i.e., control) how time is spent.

A large literature has developed on other cognitive and contextual factors that, like control, may ameliorate the negative effects of some of the stressors we encounter in life (see Cohen, 1980, for a review). While a discussion of these factors is beyond the scope of this introductory chapter, several factors deserve mention as they relate to this book: *Choice* of retiring versus remaining employed appears to be an important predictor of satisfaction with retirement (Dreyer, this volume); *predictability*—or rather, the lack of it, uncertainty—is mentioned as a common concern of those facing retirement (Bikson & Goodchilds, this volume); the *expectation*, or anticipation, of retirement is much more negative than the experience warrants (Bikson & Goodchilds, this volume).

The Physical Environment

One way in which individuals can exercise a sense of control is to help shape their physical environment. In Chapter 6, Lawton mentions his previous work with older, housebound individuals, where an arrangement of furniture yielded a "control center" over the external environment, with positive results. Similarly, Kamptner points out that, in relatively barren physical environments like nursing homes and hospitals, one's personal possessions can afford an opportunity to exercise control, with positive consequences for recovery and rehabilitation. In addition to its central role in those two chapters, the physical environment is touched on elsewhere throughout the volume. As one example, Bikson and Goodchilds note that the implications of retirement for sharing space at home (losing control?) loom large among the concerns of the wives of their participants.

Public Policy

The theory and research presented in this volume have enormous implications for public policy. As one example, the stress under which filial caregivers labor (Lerner et al., this volume) suggests the opportunity for community programs to provide both training and a source of social support. Other major examples are seen in the health and mental health needs of the elderly. To date, however, most psychologists have not taken the step of translating their research findings into forms that are readily available and usable to policy makers. In the closing chapter, Puglisi and Rickards outline several ways in which psychologists could contribute to the development of sound public policies relative to aging.

Overview of Following Chapters

To complete the introduction to this volume, we present here a very brief summary of the chapters and mention key points unique to each chapter.

In order to address the question of what social psychologists might contribute to the study of aging, Robert O. Hansson begins Chapter 2 by outlining challenges inherent in the study of aging. Among these challenges to the assumptions of the traditional social psychologist are some of the themes we have already mentioned—heterogeneity; interrelationships between psychological, social, and health functioning; stereotyping; women's issues—as well as the environmental docility hypothesis, which is discussed in more detail in Lawton's chapter. Readers unfamiliar with gerontology or a developmental perspective will find a section in Hansson's chapter particularly helpful for its explanation of concepts like "social clock" and examples of gerontological research which have been useful in setting public policy. Hansson offers several models that the interested social psychologist might follow in studying the elderly, which could lead to the refinement of theory in social psychology. In this regard, he agrees with recent concerns expressed about the generalizability of a social psychology derived very largely from research on young adults (Sears, 1987).

The topic of caregiver strain, mentioned by Hansson, is the focus of Chapter 3 by Melvin J. Lerner, Darryl G. Somers, David W. Reid, and Mary C. Tierney. More specifically, they describe the stress and conflict experienced by adult children of dependent elderly parents, which results from insufficient resources to meet the parents' needs. The combination of scarce resources with the participants' biased information on the contributions each makes to the parents' well-being produces a form of social dilemma. Lerner and his colleagues trace the consequent deterioration of sibling relations from one of an identity relationship, to a unit, and then to a nonunit relationship; and they present research that supports this hypothesized sequence. Readers who are interested in intervening in the process, either to prevent the eventual deterioration of relations or to reestablish positive feelings characteristic of identity relations, will find a concluding section of this chapter particularly useful.

Family adjustment is but one of the topics of concern in Chapter 4 by Tora K. Bikson and Jacqueline D. Goodchilds. These authors hypothesized that those involved in the later-adulthood task of making the transition to the role of "retiree" might benefit from being put in contact with one another. At the outset, Bikson and Goodchilds encouraged the active involvement of their subjects by having them generate the topics of group discussion and study. Preliminary results on four topics—use of time, family and social adjustment, self-image, and the retirement planning process—are reported in this chapter, and they contain a few surprises. Among these results are the findings that retirees view retirement less as a role loss than as the addition of a new role to their repertoire, and that prior views of the retirement transition are negative whereas the adjustment is seen as relatively easy in retrospect.

While Bikson and Goodchilds examined the transition of retirement, Chapter 5, by Philip H. Dreyer, is concerned with one's quality of life several years after retirement. Two of gerontology's most-researched topics are reviewed—adjustment and life satisfaction—and three main hypotheses of healthy adjustment to old age are explained: the disengagement, activity, and continuity hypotheses. Dreyer presents selected relevant results from two recent, unpublished studies of retirees. Finally, he cautions against mistaking a "psychology of age groups" for a developmental approach to the study of aging, and he challenges social psychologists to take a life-span perspective, a challenge that complements points made by Hansson.

Chapter 6, by M. Powell Lawton, is largely theoretical in nature. Lawton augments the usual model of person-environment transactions (where such transactions are viewed as antecedents of affect) with the idea that affect may be the antecedent for changing one's behavior, environment, or person. Lawton's application of opponent-process theory (Solomon, 1980) to aging is an important contribution to the field. Through a discussion of this model, Lawton raises several questions, including whether the mix of positive-negative or novel-routine events changes in old age, and the degree of proactivity in self-regulation of affective states by older people. Practitioners will find a useful section of this chapter devoted to interventions, as well as thoughtful comments throughout the chapter on such points as creating positive events and ending habituation to negative events.

One aspect of the physical environment that has implications for affective states in later life is one's personal possessions. In Chapter 7, N. Laura Kamptner points out the dearth of psychological literature on personal possessions and their meanings beyond early childhood. Her chapter is noteworthy for its thorough review on personal possessions in late adulthood as well as for her original research. Kamptner stresses that possessions play an important role in adaptation to aging by serving a variety of instrumental and symbolic functions. For example, possessions can aid in maintaining one's identity, facilitating the life review process, and symbolizing sources of social support. Kamptner's finding that homes were frequently the "most important" possessions of her respondents supports earlier work, and has significant implications for policymakers and families of the elderly.

The volume closes with a chapter by J. Thomas Puglisi and Larry

D. Rickards, which argues that psychologists have the potential to make numerous important contributions to public policy on aging. This chapter ties together recurrent themes from earlier chapters and speaks to issues raised by other authors as it challenges us to make an impact on policymakers. To take one example within the theme of an interdisciplinary approach to aging, they urge that, as we begin to work "out" of our traditional disciplinary areas, we try to do so in a way that is intelligible to policymakers and that seizes the opportunity to affect public policy. Puglisi and Rickards discuss three areas—health policy, issues specific to older women, and in particular mental health policy—that they believe present immediate opportunities for concerned psychologists to have an impact on federal policy relevant to the elderly. This chapter should encourage and alert interested readers to consider policymaking as another avenue for the application of social psychology.

References

Aiken, L. R. (1982). *Later life.* New York: Holt, Rinehart & Winston.

Anaya, R. (1988, November). *Aging in tomorrow's world.* Keynote address presented at the meeting of the Gerontological Society of America, San Francisco.

Baltes, M. M., & Baltes, P. B. (1986). *The psychology of control and aging.* Hillsdale, NJ: Lawrence Erlbaum.

Butler, R. N. (1975). *Why survive? Being old in America.* New York: Harper & Row.

Cohen, S. (1980). Cognitive processes as determinants of environmental stress. In I. Sarason & C. Spielberger (Eds.), *Stress and anxiety* (Vol. 8, pp. 171-183). Washington, DC: Hemisphere.

Cumming, E., & Henry, W. (1961). *Growing old: The process of disengagement.* New York: Basic Books.

Herzog, A. R., Rogers, W. L., & Woodworth, J. (1982). *Subjective well-being among different age groups.* Ann Arbor: University of Michigan, Institute for Social Research.

Kahn, R. L. (1975). The mental health system and the future aged. *Gerontologist, 15,* 377-383.

Kasper, J. D. (1988). *Aging alone: Profiles and perspectives.* Baltimore: Commonwealth Fund Commission on Elderly People Living Alone.

Langer, E., & Rodin, J. (1976). The effects of choice and enhanced personal responsibility for the aged: A field experiment in an institutional setting. *Journal of Personality and Social Psychology, 34,* 191-198.

Lawton, M. P. (1975). The Philadelphia Geriatric Center morale scale: A revision. *Journal of Gerontology, 30,* 85-89.

Lawton, M. P., Altman, I., & Wohlwill, J. F. (1984). Dimensions of environment-behavior research. In I. Altman, M. P. Lawton, & J. F. Wohlwill (Eds.), *Elderly people and the environment* (pp. 1-15). New York: Plenum.

National Council on the Aging. (1975). *The myth and reality of aging in America.* Washington, DC: Author.

Neugarten, B. L., Havighurst, R. J., & Tobin, S. S. (1968). Personality and patterns of aging. In B. L. Neugarten (Ed.), *Middle age and aging* (pp. 173-177). Chicago: University of Chicago Press.

Rodeheaver, D., & Datan, N. (1988). The challenge of double jeopardy: Toward a mental health agenda for aging women. *American Psychologist, 43,* 648-654.

Rodin, J. (1986). Aging and health: Effects of the sense of control. *Science, 233,* 1271-1276.

Rook, K. (1988, February). *Social issues in aging.* Panel discussion presented at the Claremont Symposium on Applied Social Psychology, Claremont, CA.

Rosow, I. (1967). *Social integration of the aged.* New York: Free Press.

Rowe, J. W., & Kahn, R. L. (1987). Human aging: Usual and successful. *Science, 237,* 143-149.

Sears, D. O. (1987). Implications of the life-span approach for research on attitudes and social cognition. In R. P. Abeles (Ed.), *Life-span perspectives and social psychology* (pp. 17-60). Hillsdale, NJ: Lawrence Erlbaum.

Select Committee on Aging, U.S. House of Representatives. (1987). *Long term care and personal impoverishment: Seven in ten elderly living alone are at risk* (Committee Publication no. 100-631). Washington, DC: Government Printing Office.

Simon, C. (1987, December). Age-proofing the home. *Psychology Today, 21*(12), 52-53.

Solomon, R. L. (1980). The opponent-process theory of acquired motivation: The costs of pleasure and the benefits of pain. *American Psychologist, 35,* 691-712.

Special Committee on Aging, U.S. Senate. (1988). *Developments in aging: 1987* (Report no. 100-291; Vols. 1, 3). Washington, DC: Government Printing Office.

2

Old Age: Testing the Parameters of Social Psychological Assumptions

ROBERT O. HANSSON

Aging affects every one of us personally, as over a lifetime our abilities, interests, and opportunities change; our children grow and move on to lives of their own; and we experience the death of loved ones. But why should aging issues be of interest to social psychologists and relevant to the assumptions we make about the nature of the social universe?

An initial reason is that societies tend to structure themselves, using age-markers on which there is much consensus and that appear to have considerable normative impact on individual behavior and social involvement. In addition, we have witnessed in this century a dramatic increase in life expectancy, with resulting structural changes in the nature of society itself. One hundred years ago, the expected life span was about 47; it is now closer to 74. As of the 1980 census, there were more than 35 million Americans aged 60 or older, and more than 25 million aged 65 or older. Moreover, in the preceding decade the 60 and older population increased by 24%, the 65 and older population increased by 28%, and the fastest-growing group (85 and older) increased by 58% to over two million persons (Siegel & Davidson, 1984). As a result, we are beginning to note important changes in family composition and dynamics, with four-generation households expected to be common by the turn of the century, and changing patterns of responsibility, social exchange, power, and dependency within the family.

Patterns of individual involvement in social and occupational roles across the life span have also changed, with implications for economic independence, health, and self-concept. Also, the extension of life for most people to long "post-parental" and "post-vocational" periods has created a wealth of new life crises, requiring adaptation to chronic illness, to the status of retirement, to dependency, and to an increased likelihood of living alone (Schaie, 1981). Perhaps the most important development, however, has been the changing gender mix in old age, with very old age becoming, at least statistically, a women's problem (Siegel & Davidson, 1984).

Psychologists' involvement in applied fields (as aging has become) can be rewarding in that it fosters an interdisciplinary perspective. Researchers working on current problems in applied fields (e.g., health psychology, gerontology, and even industrial/organizational psychology) draw upon much the same theory and perspectives as social psychologists do, yet the populations being studied include people at the extremes—people for whom the outcomes being studied really matter. Such studies can teach us much about the limitations and utility of our approach. Basic and applied researchers concerned with aging thus have much to learn from one another, and the applied field is usually richer for the interchange. Unfortunately, the transfer of ideas and information back to the parent discipline appears to be more difficult, as David Sears (1987) noted in his recent survey of social psychology journals, which showed that only about 25% of published reports included other than college student subjects in laboratory settings. Such findings demonstrate that research and theory development in social psychology are too often decontextualized and thereby limited in value.

Older adults are important to the progress of psychological science in still another way. Experimental social psychology faces ethical and practical constraints on the nature and intensity of the experimental treatments to which human subjects can be exposed. The generalizability of its findings may thus be limited to situations of minimal stimulus intensity and duration (with respect to stress, isolation, interpersonal conflict, environmental overload, and so on). In contrast, field research on the elderly has already yielded important and reliable insights regarding coping and adaptation among people, many of whom are living "on the edge." The later years can be a time of multiple losses and declines (in physical health, sensory competence, financial security, relationships, occupational roles, and so on), which cluster into short time spans. They can also be a time of increased pressure to cope independently, as one's social support networks are strained, or as major figures in the network die, move away, or retire.

The *first* section of this chapter explores some of the implications of aging and old age for the assumptions of social psychology, and describes several pervasive themes that emerge. Topics in this section include, for example, the implications of increasing within-age-group heterogeneity in old age, the implications of increasing interactions between physical health, psychological and social functioning in old age, environmental docility, stereotyping of the elderly, and the emergence of older women's issues on the national research agenda.

The *second* section of the chapter notes some of the structural assumptions from the gerontological literature that have heuristic value for the work of mainstream social psychologists. It focuses on the concept of social clocks, on normative patterns of role involvement across the life span, and on the value of the growing data base concerned with the elderly, their problems, needs, and changing status.

The *third* section of the chapter describes several examples of how other areas of psychology (e.g., cognitive, clinical, personality) have been enriched by the study of older adults. The *fourth* section discusses some new theoretical insights by social psychologists who are working in the field, and—coming full circle—it asks, What might social psychologists have to offer to the study of aging?

Themes in Aging with Implications for Social Process

Increasing Heterogeneity

Theory in social psychology tends to focus on normative social processes (e.g., models for the prediction of attitudes and social behavior; processes by which we arrive at our impressions of other people, of the causes of their behavior, or of the degree of equity in an interpersonal relationship; normative models of social influence, social exchange, social support, loneliness, stress, coping, and so on). These efforts reflect an assumed degree of order, continuity, and predictability among members of the species due to our common genetic endowment, membership in a well-structured society, and maturational processes, tempered by the systemic influence of ethnic, cultural, gender, and socioeconomic differences.

In contrast, one of the most pervasive findings in studies of older adults is that of increasing (within-age-group) heterogeneity, such as in health and sensory status, intellectual competence, styles of problem solving, and levels of interpersonal competence and involvement. That is, studies of age-related change in such functioning do tend to show average declines, but they also show increasing variability with increasing age. Many aging individuals do indeed experience expected declines in metabolic or cognitive functioning, increased risk of osteoporosis, and the like, but many others show little or no decline (Rowe & Kahn, 1987).

This increased heterogeneity may reflect complex interactions of personal history, generational differences, and age-linked physiological changes (Baltes, Reese, & Lipsitt, 1980), but it appears also to reflect what Rowe and Kahn (1987) have termed the difference between "successful" and "usual" aging. In fact, the latter authors argue that the real story in aging is not in the average curves of maturation and decline, but in individual differences that cannot be attributed entirely to genetic influences. They point to examples of successfully retained functioning (e.g., in metabolic and cognitive functioning, and in emotional and health stability in old age) and to powerful, yet unevenly distributed, predictor variables (e.g., exercise regimen, cardiac status, autonomy, personal control, lack of stimulation, or lack of social support). They call for increased study of successfully aging individuals and a search for risk factors that make the difference, noting that many such extrinsic risk factors can be modified. The implication for social psychology is that we should participate in the interdisciplinary effort to identify and harness those factors that determine the trajectory of function with advancing age.

Interrelationships Among Psychological, Social, and Health Issues

Another important concern in studies of the elderly is the intensifying interrelationships among health, psychological, and social functioning. For example, declining health and sensory status may affect intellectual functioning, mobility, and social competence (Schaie, 1981). Similarly, age-related life events such as bereavement, retirement, or involuntary relocation may result in a decreased sense of personal control, and increased psychological and physical morbidity (Stroebe & Stroebe, 1987). A decreased sense of control is suspected as a factor in suppression of the immune system (Laudenslager, in press; Rodin, 1986). Isolation and inactivity resulting from physical disability may in turn lead to diminishing social competence, to depression, to greater difficulty in rehabilitation, and so on (Kemp, 1985). The physical health status of an elderly parent is often the most important factor in eliciting family involvement and support, and in raising a family's level of consciousness regarding aging concerns generally (Hansson, Nelson, Carver, NeeSmith, & Dowling, 1988).

As a consequence of these interrelationships, the assessment of older adults to aid in medical decisions, in forming strategies for rehabilitation and return to work after disability, in predicting level of required support within a residential facility, or simply in helping families to deal with a frail parent has become a multidimensional process. Here, gerontological researchers/practitioners have made great strides in developing assessment inventories that consider health, cognitive, and social competence simultaneously (see Kane & Kane, 1981). The OARS instrument (Duke University Center, 1978), for example, provides information across five functional domains (social resources such as number and quality of friendship and support relationships, economic resources, mental health, physical health, and capacity to perform the basic activities of daily living). Similarly, medical and rehabilitation teams now regularly adopt an interdisciplinary approach to diagnosis and treatment of the elderly (Kemp, 1985). These developments suggest that social psychologists can also assume a fundamental role in understanding the interactions between psychological, social, and health concerns in old age. There is much yet to learn about stressful life events, social transitions associated with retirement and widowhood, the determinants and effects of social isolation, and the supportive nature of personal relationships across the life course.

Social-Environmental Docility

One of the most heuristic observations about the experience of old age is what Lawton and Simon (1968) have termed the "environmental docility hypothesis." The underlying premise of the hypothesis is that older persons who are less competent (with respect to functional health, psychological, or social competence) have a narrower range of adaptability to stress. A substantial body of research has supported the hypothesis with respect to stress from the physical environment, finding that less competent older persons are more immediately distressed when housing and neighborhoods become less secure, supportive, or accessible (Lawton, 1980; Morgan et al., 1984). However, the same prediction may also apply in the case of a deteriorating, less supportive, more problematic *social* environment. In old age there is an increased likelihood of losing key members of one's social support network through death, illness, retirement, relocation, and so on, and a high likelihood that remaining members of the network will be under increased strain as an older person's needs for care become chronic and more comprehensive (Brody, 1985).

On the other hand, families and caregivers must also understand the risks of providing too comprehensive a level of care. It appears to be important to follow the principle of "minimal intervention" (Kahn, 1975) and encourage older adults to develop their own coping skills and expectations for self-help, because too much care can lead to a self-fulfilling prophecy, resulting in decreased coping, diminished self-concept, and premature decrements in cognitive and functional performance. In Kahn's research in institutions, for example, too comprehensive a level of care appeared to result in "excess disability," that is, a functional disability beyond that expected on the basis of actual physiological impairment. This presents a challenge, then, for current notions of social support. As Rowe and Kahn (1987) have pointed out, it is important for families and those who provide social support to find avenues of support (teaching, facilitating individual coping skills, and so on) that encourage a sense of autonomy and control, rather than simply "doing for" aged individuals, which encourages premature helplessness and dependency. The question of how best to accomplish this should become a central focus for social psychological research in the area of social support.

Implications of Stereotyping the Aged

Like most minority groups, older individuals are often the target of a variety of stereotyped beliefs—regarding anticipated intellectual and physical decline, negative or diminutive (e.g., "*little* old lady," "*darling* old man") personality characteristics, financial dependency, and the like. As might be expected, such beliefs have often been used to justify discrimination. They have also resulted in the elderly being discounted as credible participants in society, in the policy assumptions that they (and their needs) are all alike, and even in the conducting of less rigorous clinical assessments when the presenting complaint is considered symptomatic of old age (Butler, 1975). Considerable efforts have been expended in recent years within the gerontological professions to test such stereotyped assumptions and to educate the public more correctly. Nevertheless, concern persists regarding the practical consequences of ageist beliefs and attitudes, and it is instructive to note that, in 1986, nearly 27,000 age-discrimination cases were filed with federal and state authorities, twice the number filed in 1980. Also in 1986, one-fourth of the cases filed by the Equal Employment Opportunity Commission derived from the Age Discrimination in Employment Act (Freedberg, 1987). There is, of course, a distinct irony in people having acquired an enduring, prejudicial set of beliefs about a population that most of us are destined eventually to join, and the phenomenon has serious consequences. In fact, it provides a rationale for an important counseling/therapy strategy used with the very old (reminiscence therapy), where the most important goal is to establish or reestablish a cohort effect (i.e., a feeling of identification with one's age peers and the successes and trials and tribulations of one's generation) so that age-mates can become a credible and supportive social resource as death nears and the process of "coming to terms" with the end of life begins (Ebersole, 1978).

In the aggregate, however, the elderly have in the last decade created a quite different public perception—one that could result in a classic conflict with broad implications for social and economic policy at the national level. The sheer numbers of older people in the United States, their increased periods of dependence on social security, medicare, and long-term care assistance, combined with their highly visible political lobby—all these suggest to many observers that they may constitute a disproportionate burden on the rest of society. This premise implies a number of potential socioeconomic conflicts, some of which might be resolved by looking at the larger picture, but some not (Kingson, Hirshorn, & Cornman, 1986). The dominant theme is one of potential competition between the needs of the old and the needs of the young for scarce public health and social welfare resources, and an unfair dependency burden on a younger work force (which is itself diminishing in size relative to older populations). A secondary theme is the possibility of racial inequities and potential conflict. For example, the proportion of American Blacks and Hispanics age 65 and over is substantially lower than the proportion of Whites age 65 and over. Those percentages as of the 1980 census are as follows: Black, 7.8%; Hispanic, 4.9%; and White, 11.9% (Siegel & Davidson, 1984). This disparity reflects higher fertility rates and higher mortality rates prior to age 65 among minorities, and a substantial Hispanic immigration of primarily younger persons. It is thus understandable that younger Blacks and Hispanics, who generally hold lower-paying jobs relative to Whites, and who may expect to receive fewer retirement benefits themselves, might perceive a racial inequity in the system when they are taxed at standard social security rates ("Retiree Trends," 1988).

The gerontological community has become concerned in recent years that perceptions of "generational inequity" not diminish legitimate advances in the United States in understanding and facilitating the well-being of the elderly. One outcome has been a movement to emphasize the vast diversity among older adults, and to underscore the interdependence of the generations, focusing on (a) the high degree of reciprocity in social and economic transfers between generations (when viewed from a longer temporal perspective), and (b) the "common stake" for all parties in having a supplementary (formal) system of health and economic security in retirement. Such benefits for the older person (but also for the disabled and for dependents of a deceased breadwinner) include a "dignified and stable means of support," a stable system for insuring against the economic risks associated with disability or retirement across a lifetime, freeing younger family members from responsibility for their parents, thus permitting them to focus their resources on the needs of their children, and so on (Kingson, Hirshorn, & Cornman, 1986, pp. 12-13).

The debate continues, however; and, in such areas as health care, society is being asked to examine its most basic values in connection with the social allocation of limited resources (Clark, 1985). Here the costs will continue to increase, given more chronic illness and the possibility of living longer with chronic illness. Some have asked whether it is fair to limit older adults' access to high-tech (and astronomically expensive) medical procedures, given that they consume a disproportionate share of the national health dollar, perhaps at the expense of other needs and other segments of society. Setting aside the we-they stereotypes, society is asked to consider which criteria to use in determining the extent to which the elderly should be given access to health-care resources. Are there answers to the question of what is fair; do they reflect our values regarding human dignity, and our desire to "carry our weakest"; or should they reflect a more economic concern for return on investment (Clark, 1985, p. 123)? We will eventually have to resolve these questions. They are in part amenable to rational, ethical analysis. However, they are also embedded in a context familiar to social psychologists; competition for scarce resources is central to key social psychological topics such as prejudice, reactance, and group conflict.

The Emergence of Women's Issues in Old Age

Prior to the 1970s, the implications of gender for aging were relatively unexplored in relation to health, social, and economic policy. Yet the demographics clearly demonstrate the extent to which the emerging problems and needs of the elderly (especially in very old age) are those of women. In 1980, the ratio of males to females aged

65 and over in the United States was 68:100. For those aged 75 and over the ratio was 55:100, and elderly women continue to be the fastest growing segment of the population (Siegel & Davidson, 1984).

A 1978 conference sponsored by the National Institute on Aging (NIA, 1978) made substantial progress in defining the emerging policy issues and setting a broad research agenda. Much gerontological research had not adequately considered women; much work was needed, for example, on such health issues as osteoporosis, estrogen use, changes in the reproductive system, cancers of the breast, and so on.

Similarly, concerns were raised about the great likelihood that older women would live their later years alone, with less economic security, and in greater social isolation than men. In 1980, 51.3% of the women aged 65 or over, compared to only 12.8% of the men in that age group were widowed, and nearly 39% of the women aged 65 or over lived alone compared to only 14% of the men (Siegel & Davidson, 1984). Older women are also less likely to have access to pensions or social security which reflect a continuous lifetime of work outside the home (O'Rand, 1984), and there are substantial sex differences in the current income stream. In 1985, for example, men aged 65 and over had a median income of $10,900, whereas the median for women in that age group was $6,313 (U.S. Bureau of the Census, 1987, p. 432).

Of particular interest to social psychologists are the implications of such trends for the structure and function of the social system. The needs of older women are placing new demands on the family, which itself is in transition (e.g., four-generation families are expected to be commonplace by the turn of the century). The older members of such families for the most part remain contributing members to the well-being of the family unit. On the other hand, those elderly women who live in isolation present a challenge to their communities, with respect to the early identification of physical or mental health problems that might be reversible if diagnosed in time. Policy regarding the delivery of health and social services in the future will be challenged to adapt to these major demographic patterns of the older female population.

These emerging themes (increased heterogeneity; intensifying interrelationships among psychological, social, and health issues; social-environmental docility; ageist stereotyping and the potential for intergroup conflict; and older women's issues) provide useful examples of how an aging population may affect the theories and assumptions of social psychology. Let us turn now to a related issue, the theoretical contributions of social gerontology.

Structural Themes from Social Gerontology

With the notion of the life course, gerontologists have provided a conceptual framework and context for many of the assumptions of social psychology. They introduce time- and age-related structural elements into social psychological process. Two dominant themes exemplify this influence—the notions of "social clocks" and of normative patterns of role involvement across the life span.

For example, societies tend to divide the life span into predictable phases on the basis of age, and to have clear expectations for an individual's progress through important roles such as marriage, child rearing, occupational career, and retirement (Hagestad & Neugarten, 1985). Persons of any age thus understand their status, the roles they are expected to enter, the obligations and privileges accruing to each life phase; and they are encouraged to negotiate a social identity and self-concept appropriate to their stage of life. Indeed, the notion of life course has stimulated much theory development regarding the dynamics of adult development through the "seasons" of one's life (Levinson, 1986), and the dynamics of one's "unfolding" sense of self (Gergen & Gergen, 1987). These normative expectations may become a source of stress to an individual perceived not to be "on time" with respect to expected progress toward family or occupational milestones. There are, of course, variations; for instance, in modern (and more complex) industrial societies such as the United States, age boundaries and age-related status seem not to be as well defined, relative to less-developed countries. Similarly, within our society, socioeconomic status and gender appear to mediate the process, with minorities, groups of lower economic status, and women passing the normative milestones at earlier chronological ages. This appears to reflect a "double standard of aging" with respect to women (for whom the signs of physical aging may have earlier social consequences) and an earlier "earnings peak" for minorities and persons of lower socioeconomic class (Hagestad & Neugarten, 1985, p. 40).

There are, however, problematic aspects to age-grading across the life span. For example, sociologist Irving Rosow (1985) argues that old age is a time of general and systematic role contraction. That is, people become less involved in important functional roles that have a well defined (institutionalized) status and for which there are clear expectations and standards for role performance (e.g., occupational or family roles). However, they are likely to become more involved in roles whose status is for the most part symbolic or token, and for which there are fewer meaningful, required functions or responsibilities. Examples of such roles include retired employee, ex-husband, parent of adult children, widow, and so on. Rosow's point is that functional-role loss excludes older adults from meaningful participation in the cultural group, denying them former sources of personal reward and esteem, diminishing the degree of structure and predictability that social roles provide in their lives, and eliminating the foundations on which the social self-concept is based. A number of implications can be derived from this contraction of role involvements. The behavior of older individuals should be less "socially consequential"; thus fewer normative expectations for performance should emanate from the cultural group. Self-concept should cease to be influenced by social consensus and should, to a greater degree, reflect internal criteria. Older persons might, therefore, be expected to become less socially responsive and to place less importance on interpersonal competencies, group-valued personality characteristics, or a socially desirable identity. They might become less responsive to social reinforcers or to social stressors, and might be less likely to need or benefit from such processes as social comparison during times of personal stress (Hansson, 1986; Hansson, Hogan, & Jones, 1984; Rosow, 1985).

In a more practical vein, social psychologists can also learn much from those gerontological researchers interested in assessing needs for elderly health and social service programs, and in formulating national policy and priorities. Using large probability samples, gerontological researchers have assessed the nature and extent of social exchange processes within the family (e.g., Mitchell & Register, 1984), caregiving transactions (Shanas, 1979), caregiver strain (Cantor, 1983; Stone, Cafferata, & Sangel, 1987), determinants of changing household composition in older families (Fillenbaum &

Wallman, 1984), criminal victimization experience (Antunes, Cook, Cook, & Skogan, 1977), elder abuse (Pillemer & Finkelhor, 1988), religious involvement (Taylor, 1986), and so on. In doing so, they have provided valuable data seldom found in traditional social psychological research. That is, they provide elusive baseline data—a sense of what level and configuration of exchange, support, or other social processes typically occur in an important population.

Such studies have also helped to flesh out the picture of ongoing social process, especially within families, and have provided data on who turns to whom for what, who provides what and at what cost, how successful the transaction is, and what barriers or obstacles must be overcome. For example, there is some evidence that older White adults have more frequent contact with their children and grandchildren than do Blacks, but that Blacks are more likely to receive assistance from their children (e.g., in health or financial matters) and to take younger family members into their homes to live (Mitchell & Register, 1984).

Similarly, we have learned a great deal about caregiver strain from samples of caregivers for the noninstitutionalized elderly. A recent study, for example, found that most caregivers (over 70%) are women, 35% are age 65 or over, 32% could be described as poor to near-poor, 33% are themselves in fair to poor health, 20% had experienced a conflict between the demands of work and caregiving requiring adjustments of work load or work schedules (wives and adult daughters were more likely than husbands and sons to make such adjustments), 20% had been caring for disabled older family members for as long as five years, 25% spent three to four hours per day on caregiving activities, and another 42% spent one to two hours (Stone, Cafferata, & Sangel, 1987). It is not surprising, then, that researchers and policy analysts have investigated the likely consequences of caregiver and family strain in old age. As an example, a recent survey on elder abuse attempted to establish base rates of abuse and characteristics of abused and abuser in a large probability sample (Pillemer & Finkelhor, 1988). The authors found an overall abuse rate of 32 per 1,000 in persons aged 65 or over, with those in poor health being three times more likely to become victims. In addition, spouses rather than children (as previously believed on the basis of less representative samples) were more likely to be the abusers. Also in contrast to earlier, less representative findings, they found that elderly men were twice as likely as women to be abused (perhaps because they are more likely to live their later years with a spouse), but that women victims actually suffered more serious injuries.

Finally, studies of the elderly have also provided dramatic data regarding the scope and severity of consequences of naturally occurring life events, and in doing so have contributed substance and clarity to our understanding of the stress associated with social loss. Research of particular interest in this regard has focused on the consequences of bereavement and widowhood for morbidity, loss of control, health, and mortality (see Hansson, Stroebe, & Stroebe, in press; Rowe & Kahn 1987; Stroebe & Stroebe, 1987), and on the parallel implications of involuntary relocation (Lawton, 1980) and retirement (George, 1980).

The gerontological perspective, then, presents considerable heuristic promise for mainstream social psychologists. Its dual focus on (a) understanding the influence of age and life course and (b) mapping out the practical needs and circumstances of older adults is particularly useful in suggesting time- and age-related parameters with respect to a wide variety of social psychological assumptions.

Other Areas Enriched by
Study of Older Adults

Social psychologists can also learn from progress in other areas of psychology, where the findings of research on the elderly have fed back into the primary discipline. The most prominent examples appear to be from cognitive psychology, in particular from studies of intellectual functioning, memory, and problem solving. However, considerable progress has also been made in the fields of assessment, health psychology, personality, industrial/organizational psychology, and bereavement and loss.

Cognitive-Aging Studies

Longitudinal studies of IQ have often confirmed the multivariate nature of intelligence, for distinct intellectual abilities appear to peak at different points of the life span and then decline, each at its own rate of change. More generally, those abilities that are embedded in a context of cultural meaning (crystallized intelligence) appear to decline more slowly, whereas those nonverbal and performance abilities more related to speed of response and to physiological status (fluid intelligence) decline earlier (Schaie, 1981).

Perhaps more revolutionary, however, are the recent theoretical developments sparked by observed patterns of age-related differences in performance on current IQ tests and on cognitive problem-solving tasks. Labouvie-Vief (1985), for example, has questioned whether such differences necessarily imply cognitive deficits, or whether they might instead reflect an adaptive cognitive reorganization on the part of older adults. That is, it might be simply less relevant for older persons to perform well on abstract intellectual tasks more characteristic of the earlier life stages (e.g., the initial acquisition of skills or mastery of the knowledge of the culture). Labouvie-Vief argues that older adults, instead, appear better able to deal with cognitive problems characteristic of the demands of their current life stage, reflecting abilities important to the stability of the culture, to responsibility and dependability. Even such qualities as conservatism and rigidity may be adaptive in providing a solid platform from which to encourage the next generation of achievers. Older adults thus do better on tasks involving familiar stimuli, are more comfortable in dealing with ambiguity, more likely to seek a practical solution rather than the one correct solution, and are often able to bring different perspectives to bear. For example, they may actively involve others in a collective response to the problem, thus integrating a social dimension into the problem-solving process.

Assessment

Studies of the aged have added perspective to assessment procedures as well. As noted earlier, assessment strategies for counseling, clinical, and rehabilitation clients now reflect a greater multidimensionality, routinely taking into consideration confounding or contributing risk factors that may increase the prevalence of cognitive or emotional distress (e.g., sensory deficits, poor health, bereavement, drug interactions, malnutrition). Assessment strategies are also more sensitive now to the limitations (due to fatigue, lack of age norms, or generational bias) of many available psychological tests for older and minority populations, to age differences in how medications affect physical and psychological functioning, to the increased actual likelihood of stressful life events and the increased relationship between restricted mobility and functioning in old age, and to changing motivations during the life cycle that might inter- fere with either assessment or treatment (Kane & Kane, 1981; Kemp, 1985; La Rue, Dessonvile, & Jarvik, 1985).

Personality Psychology

The recent work of Robert McCrae and Paul Costa (1984), among others, has provided an important sense of the entirety of the life span and its relationship to personality—with growing evidence of stability of personality across the life span, and stability in the rela- tionship between personality and adjustment. In longitudinal stud- ies, for both young and old adults, test-retest correlations on objective personality scales are consistently high over periods of 6 to 30 years, and scores on both extraversion and neuroticism relia- bly predict affect and well-being over intervals ranging to over 15 years (Costa & McCrae, 1984). Moreover, cross-sectional analyses across some 50 adult years reveal very little change on such person- ality variables as neuroticism, extraversion, or openness to experi- ence, and no age-related peaks in personality scores that might suggest age-related (e.g., midlife) crises (Costa et al., 1986). These studies, which include older persons, have broad implications for developmental or life-stage theories of personality, suggesting that by early adulthood a characteristic way of dealing with the world will have formed that will be reflected in one's interactions across the life span.

Health Psychology

Much progress has been made in health psychology with respect to understanding how health behavior and status might reflect the re- lationship and communication between physician and patient, the social support resources available to the patient, the influence of socially acquired health beliefs and attitudes on seeking help or adherence to a prescribed regimen, the social determinants of helplessness, and so on. Evidence now suggests a variety of age-related influences on each of these processes.

Of particular concern, however, is the changing nature of the illness experience with aging, and the subsequent challenges to the individual, caregivers, and the health professions. Old age has become a time in which the management of chronic illness is most prevalent and when, unlike our earlier years, symptoms often reflect not a single cause (e.g., an infection or failure of a single system) but a combination of health problems in interaction. Such symptoms are thus more difficult to diagnose, and more difficult for the elderly patient to manage. Also, elderly patients may be slower to seek help for health problems because symptoms may be masked by other maladies, or the elderly interpret their symptoms to be a natural result of aging, or they believe (often correctly) that health professionals are uninterested or unable to help them (Shanas & Maddox, 1985).

The process of rehabilitation also changes for older patients, for example, by establishing therapy goals and incentives that realistically reflect their potential and circumstances at a later life stage. Similarly, the process must take into account the increased likelihood of cognitive impairment resulting from physical trauma, as well as secondary disabilities (e.g., pain, depression), less predictable drug-dosage effects, increased deleterious effects of immobility, changing symptom patterns resulting from any given illness, and so on (Kemp, 1985).

Industrial/Organizational Psychology

The issues in industrial/organizational psychology concern how best to select, develop, and manage individuals who will function productively within a given work environment. The psychologist's task involves an assessment of the individual (in a legally defensible manner) with respect to abilities, motivation, and potential, as well as an assessment of the organization's capacity to provide a safe, productive work environment, to develop employees to their productive potential, to accommodate the changing needs of a work force, and so on. Again, aging issues are central to many of these human resource functions, for the organization has to deal with policy issues for an aging work force; the relationships of health, cognitive, and motivational changes to productivity; absenteeism, turnover, and safety in the workplace; issues of developing employees with management potential, of retirement planning and benefits planning, of training and retraining older workers, and so on.

Many employers continue to harbor stereotypes about older workers, with respect to decreased productivity, safety, trainability, and the like. For example, a recent Conference Board survey of 363 American corporations asked why so many employers were unwilling to hire older workers. The most frequent responses were as follows: Older workers have too short a career potential and thus constitute a poor return on investment; they lack energy, drive, motivation, performance; they cost more in benefits; they are less flexible; they are obsolete (Rhine, 1984). However, two recent developments—repeal of a mandatory retirement age, and the high cost of being sued for noncompliance with the prohibitions of the Age Discrimination in Employment Act—have encouraged employers (and psychologists) to begin to take into account individual differences within age groups, and to demonstrate the validity and nondiscriminatory nature of all personnel decisions (see Faley, Kleiman, & Lengnick-Hall, 1984). In addition, research has begun to focus on practical age-related problems in the workplace, and the results have increased our understanding of related issues for the work force as a whole. For example, the field of human factors has been advanced considerably by investigations into those work situations or environments likely to create stress for older workers (e.g., tasks requiring bursts of energy, noisy workshop environments, tasks requiring fine visual or auditory discriminations under time pressure, and jobs whose tempo or pacing the employee cannot control; Doering, Rhodes, & Schuster, 1983). Similarly, our understanding of careers and career development has been enhanced by the incorporation of a life-span perspective. This perspective assumes the potential for development at any life stage, but also recognizes individual differences in competence, motivation, personality, and life circumstances, as well as organizational constraints, and the potential benefits (and concerns) in retraining adults to adapt to a changing workplace (Sterns, 1986). Finally, theories of employee motivation may need to be reconceptualized to take into account age- (or stage of the life cycle) related changes in individual needs or beliefs. For example, older employees are likely to place greater importance on job security and coworker relationships than on potential for personal growth. They also appear to feel greater organizational commitment, but for different reasons than younger workers; the organizational commitment in older persons may reflect more of a realization of limited mobility and a need to protect their pension than a sense of psychological commitment or loyalty to the organization (Doering, Rhodes, & Schuster, 1983).

Bereavement and Loss

Bereavement is, of course, most common among older adults. The issues involved touch on a variety of concerns important to mainstream social psychology, yet they are being addressed by researchers and practitioners from many disciplines (e.g., Hansson, Stroebe, & Stroebe, in press). In studying bereavement, much has already been accomplished in conceptualizing the psychological and physiological components of the grief reaction, and typical patterns of symptomatology and processes of recovery (Stroebe & Stroebe, 1987). Yet grief appears not to affect all persons equally. Some individuals and some classes of individuals appear to be at greater risk for poor outcomes, and many of the variables involved reflect social structure and social process. For example, older persons are more likely to experience multiple losses or deaths in a brief period of time, compounding the stress of bereavement. Also, age-related constraints on recovery from bereavement may arise, such as stereotyped societal expectations regarding acceptable options for reestablishing an independent life-style. In addition, in a heterogeneous society such as the United States, cultural or ethnic barriers to access to informal or formal support systems may occur because available services are incompatible with social norms and needs of minority populations, or because of cultural differences in the expression of grief and the function of mourning practices. Individuals' social isolation also may preclude community participation and obtaining support in the grieving process. Such isolation may reflect the interaction of old age with the variables of socioeconomic status, gender, education, and ethnicity. Still another influence on bereavement concerns traditional sex roles that foster dependency for husbands and inhibit a widow's preparation and options for resuming occupational, social, or sexual relationships. (Older women are apt to be more vulnerable to such influences.)

It seems clear from the examples in this section that our understanding of most areas of human experience could be broadened by the inclusion of older adults in the research. These examples also suggest that some of the most heuristic findings thus far have occurred in applied fields (i.e., from attempts to apply current knowledge in order to improve older persons' health outcomes, to ensure their safety and productivity in the workplace, and so on). This pattern may also prove to hold true in social psychology.

Aging and Social Psychology

To date, the aging perspective has not broadly influenced theory or research in social psychology, but a few excellent books and pockets of very interesting empirical research have appeared. For example, a recent book edited by Ronald Abeles (1987) features mainstream social psychologists adopting a life-span developmental perspective with regard to their own work. One disturbing paper in the volume (Sears, 1987), for example, discusses the implications for social psychology of a data base primarily comprising college students. Sears points out how current conceptions of social behavior and experience may have been biased by a youthful subject population, who on balance are more cognitively adept, better educated, and of a higher socioeconomic class than the majority of the population. These subjects, because of their earlier stage of life, have not entered into adult roles, and may have less crystallized social and political attitudes, a less developed sense of self, greater preoccupation with their own thoughts and feelings, a stronger need for approval resulting in increased dependency and vulnerability to peers, more unstable relationships, and greater social mobility. Sears speculates that a social psychology based on an adult (especially an older adult) subject population might be less cognitive, and as a result attitudes and behavior might be viewed as more influenced by interpersonal commitments, group dynamics, emotions, a person's stage in the life cycle, or the broader needs and interests of the community or cultural group for whom the person has assumed responsibility.

Research on older populations has also stimulated theoretical development within social psychology to account for vulnerabilities peculiar to old age or for the qualities of relationships that have endured into old age. The next paragraphs describe a few examples. First, in the context of a stress theory of bereavement and health, Stroebe and Stroebe (1987) have proposed a deficit model of partner loss. They distinguish among several domains of interpersonal loss that result from the death of a spouse (and that could presumably increase in importance with age and time): loss of instrumental, validational, and emotional support, and loss of the shared social identity and married status. As George Levinger (1976) has noted in deriving a model of the consequences of divorce, over the course of a marriage, partners tend to become more interdependent for most of their social and psychological needs, as they become more committed to the partner and allow alternative social outlets to atrophy. Thus divorce is more difficult among older individuals, and it seems reasonable to expect the aspects of interpersonal loss in bereavement also to become more complex and important in later life.

Another psychological construct that has been enriched and refined through the study of older adults is personal control. There is now much evidence regarding the positive effects on psychological and physical well-being of having a sense of control (Rodin, 1986), and Judith Rodin (1987) has noted a number of important, age-related considerations. For example, in old age life events, declining health status, and diminishing influence in social and occupational roles are more likely to force a reappraisal of one's sense of personal efficacy. Also, studies on aging may help to resolve the controversy about whether it is more useful to measure a generalized set of control expectancies or to try to distinguish among "domain-specific" measures. Rodin argues that various domain-specific control expectancies may not change uniformly with age, thus "masking" any relevant age-related changes when a global measurement strategy is used. Expectancies regarding health and intellectual functioning, she notes, may be most likely to change. She has found it useful, in her own work with older adults, to assess nine specific domains of control, including "relationships with spouse, [relationships] with immediate family members and with friends, personal safety, personal economic conditions, health, housing, transportation, daily activities, and work" (Rodin, 1987, p. 109).

Studies of the elderly have also forced us to consider age or life stage in research and theory concerned with social support. Social support, like the personal relationships upon which it depends, is in many ways quite different for the aged than for the young. It typically requires a long-term commitment, given the increased likelihood of chronic and progressive illness in old age (Brody, 1985). Moreover, the elderly are more likely to be experiencing disruptions of their social support networks, as in the case of spousal bereavement when the person at the center of the support network is the one lost. There is also some evidence that support networks for the elderly seldom rise to the occasion as an integrated team, but instead members assume responsibility in serial order, stepping forward when the primary caregiver has become burned out or unable to continue (Johnson, 1983). Also, there appear to be negative side effects of the social support process. As noted earlier, much support for the elderly may be too comprehensive, fostering a diminished sense of personal control and premature dependency, resulting in excess disability (Kahn, 1975; Rowe & Kahn, 1987). In addition, as Karen Rook (1984) has noted, accepting support in old age can often be problematic and counterproductive if the relationship involved is conflicted, in which case the costs of the relationship may outweigh its benefits.

Finally, in very old age it is often necessary to consider the aging of the support network itself. This issue is perhaps best described in Barbara Myerhoff's (1978) book, *Number Our Days*, an important anthropological study of an elderly Jewish community center in Venice, California. Myerhoff details the life of a community of Jewish émigrés, with an average age over 80, whose children and grandchildren have long since assimilated into mainstream American society and distanced themselves from the old culture, language, and orthodoxy. For these elderly people, therefore, peer-group relationships had become critical in helping each other to manage, to remain independent, and to retain dignity. Myerhoff recounts how these very old and frail people gather daily to socialize and to support one another. They provide what might be viewed as the usual benefits of relationships, but they also pay the usual costs (personal conflict, competition for attention and esteem, vulnerability to peer pressure, and so on). Among the important benefits, they provide a sense of a cohort, with a shared culture and shared contact with a potentially threatening outside world, and a support group for adaptation to the demands of aging. However, in the center Myerhoff describes, the group is itself aging, changing, and dying (with few or no replacements). So the group, which serves as the community, facilitating social interaction and mutual support, and serves as a source of identity, is itself going through adaptations affecting its own structure and survival and its ability to serve the remaining members. Consequently, the initially full-service social organization must gradually redefine it goals and scope of activities in recognition of the decline and loss of its members and friends. There are, of course, unique aspects to Myerhoff's narrative. However, these processes may be repeated in every older neighborhood in America, in garden clubs, bridge clubs, and friendship circles, as the last remaining elderly members of a changing community complete the course of their lives.

Conclusions

Several main points should be emphasized from the preceding discussion. First, older adults are an important and growing segment of the population. They are the survivors, and they have much to teach us regarding their experiences during their turn in society's roles of power, responsibility, and leadership. They are the first to reach their age in great numbers (their own parents having lived considerably fewer years). They provide the substance of adult psychology. Yet, as a group, they face a number of problems that may have been unanticipated, and that may become the dominant social and economic issues of the next half century.

Second, it has become clear that the study of aging and its implications requires an interdisciplinary effort, and that social psychologists can contribute to that effort. We can learn much along the way—about what we are to become, and about parameters affecting the assumptions of our field.

Third, it is important to consider how social psychologists might most effectively begin to address aging issues in their own work. There are several models. For example, it may be useful to emulate

Rodin's approach for investigating personal control, questioning whether it acquires more complex, domain-specific properties in later years, some of which may be more susceptible than others to threat or change. It may also be useful to assess whether certain social psychological phenomena (e.g., social conformity, social facilitation, strategic self-presentation, the centrality of sex-role schemas to self-concept, concern over equity in relationships, the perceived similarity-attraction phenomenon, and so on) can be better understood within the context of a life-stage model. That is, these phenomena may assume greater or lesser importance during a particular life stage, and in response to the "life-tasks" characteristic of that stage of the family or occupational life cycle. It would also be useful to investigate the utility or stability of our constructs across the life span, as Costa and McCrae (1984) have done with personality characteristics. In this connection, Sears (1987) has noted that a social psychology of mature adults might not be so cognitive but instead might be more influenced by emotions, interpersonal commitments, and group dynamics.

Finally, more immediate progress might result from the involvement of social psychologists in applied problems that affect older adults. Social psychologists, of course, have a history of involvement in applied problems and social issues, because of a widely shared concern for others, but also because the "real world" has always provided the more interesting questions and the more interesting tests of our assumptions. There are many applied research problems that may eventually lead researchers to consider how aging issues fit into their models or analyses.

References

Abeles, R. P. (1987). *Life-span perspectives and social psychology.* Hillsdale, NJ: Lawrence Erlbaum.

Antunes, G. E., Cook, F. L., Cook, T. D., & Skogan, W. G. (1977). Patterns of personal crime against the elderly: Findings from a national survey. *Gerontologist, 17,* 321-327.

Baltes, P. B., Reese, H. W., & Lipsitt, L. P. (1980). Life-span developmental psychology. *Annual Review of Psychology, 31,* 65-110.

Brody, E. M. (1985). Parent care as a normative family stress. *Gerontologist, 25,* 19-29.

Butler, R. N. (1975). *Why survive? Being old in America.* New York: Harper & Row.

Cantor, M. H. (1983). Strain among caregivers: A study of experience in the United States. *Gerontologist, 23,* 597-604.

Clark, P. G. (1985). The social allocation of health care resources: Ethical dilemmas in age-group competition. *Gerontologist, 25,* 119-125.

Costa, P. T., Jr., & McCrae, R. R. (1984). Personality as a lifelong determinant of wellbeing. In C. Z. Malatesta & C. E. Izard (Eds.), *Emotion in adult development* (pp. 141-157). Beverly Hills, CA: Sage.

Costa, P. T., Jr., McCrae, R. R., Zonderman, A. B., Barbano, H. E., Lebowitz, B., & Larson, D. M. (1986). Cross-sectional studies of personality in a national sample: 2. Stability in neuroticism, extraversion, and openness. *Psychology and Aging, 1,* 144-149.

Doering, M., Rhodes, S. R., & Schuster, M. (1983). *The aging worker: Research and recommendations.* Beverly Hills, CA: Sage.

Duke University Center for the Study of Aging and Human Development. (1978). *Multidimensional functional assessment: The OARS methodology.* Durham, NC: Duke University.

Ebersole, P. P. (1978). Establishing reminiscing groups. In I. M. Burnside (Ed.), *Working with the elderly: Group process and techniques* (pp. 236-254). North Scituate, MA: Duxbury.

Faley, R. H., Kleiman, L. S., & Lengnick-Hall, M. L. (1984). Age discrimination and personnel psychology: A review and synthesis of the legal literature with implications for future research. *Personnel Psychology, 37,* 327-350.

Fillenbaum, G. G., & Wallman, L. M. (1984). Change in household composition of the elderly: A preliminary investigation. *Journal of Gerontology, 39,* 342-349.

Freedberg, S. P. (1987, October 13). Forced exits? Companies confront wave of age-discrimination suits. *Wall Street Journal,* p. 37.

George, L. K. (1980). *Role transitions in later life.* Monterey, CA: Brooks/Cole.

Gergen, K. J., & Gergen, M. M. (1987). The self in temporal perspective. In R. P. Abeles (Ed.), *Life-span perspectives and social psychology* (pp. 121-137). Hillsdale, NJ: Lawrence Erlbaum.

Hagestad, G. O., & Neugarten, B. L. (1985). Age and the life course. In R. H. Binstock & E. Shanas (Eds.), *Handbook of aging and the social sciences* (2nd ed., pp. 35-61). New York: Van Nostrand Reinhold.

Hansson, R. O. (1986). Relational competence, relationships, and adjustment in old age. *Journal of Personality and Social Psychology, 50,* 1050-1058.

Hansson, R. O., Hogan, R., & Jones, W. H. (1984). Affective processes and later life changes: A socioanalytic conceptualization. In C. Malatesta & C. Izard (Eds.), *Emotion in adult development* (pp. 195-209). Beverly Hills, CA: Sage.

Hansson, R. O., Nelson, R. E., Carver, M. D., NeeSmith, D. H., & Dowling, E. M. (1988, July). *Adult children with frail elderly parents: When to intervene?* Paper presented at the Fourth International Conference on Personal Relationships, Vancouver, Canada.

Hansson, R. O., Stroebe, M. S., & Stroebe, W. (Eds.). (in press). Bereavement and widowhood [Whole issue]. *Journal of Social Issues.*

Johnson, C. L. (1983). Dyadic family relations and social support. *Gerontologist, 23,* 377-383.

Kahn, R. L. (1975). The mental health system and the future aged. *Gerontologist, 15,* 24-31.

Kane, R. A., & Kane, R. L. (1981). *Assessing the elderly: A practical guide to measurement.* Lexington, MA: Lexington.

Kemp, B. (1985). Rehabilitation and the older adult. In J. E. Birren & K. W. Schaie (Eds.), *Handbook of the psychology of aging* (2nd ed., pp. 647-663). New York: Van Nostrand Reinhold.

Kingson, E. R., Hirshorn, B. A., & Cornman, J. M. (1986). *Ties that bind: The interdependence of generations.* Washington, DC: Seven Locks.

Labouvie-Vief, G. (1985). Intelligence and cognition. In J. E. Birren & K. W. Schaie (Eds.), *Handbook of the psychology of aging* (2nd ed., pp. 500-530). New York: Van Nostrand Reinhold.

La Rue, A., Dessonvile, C., & Jarvik, L. F. (1985). Aging and mental disorders. In J. E. Birren & K. W. Schaie (Eds.), *Handbook of the psychology of aging* (2nd ed., pp. 664-702). New York: Van Nostrand Reinhold.

Laudenslager, M. L. (in press). The psychobiology of loss: Lessons from humans and nonhuman primates. *Journal of Social Issues.*

Lawton, M. P. (1980). *Environment and aging.* Monterey, CA: Brooks/Cole.

Lawton, M. P., & Simon, B. B. (1968). The ecology of social relationships in housing for the elderly. *Gerontologist, 8,* 110-115.

Levinger, G. (1976). A social psychological perspective on marital dissolution. *Journal of Social Issues, 32*(1), 21-47.

Levinson, D. J. (1986). A conception of adult development. *American Psychologist, 41,* 3-13.

McCrae, R. R., & Costa, P. T., Jr. (1984). *Emerging lives, enduring dispositions.* Boston: Little, Brown.

Mitchell, J., & Register, J. C. (1984). An exploration of family interaction with the elderly by race, socioeconomic status, and residence. *Gerontologist, 24,* 48-54.

Morgan, T. J., Hansson, R. O., Indart, M. J., Austin, D. M., Crutcher, M., Hampton, P. W., Oppegard, K. M., & O'Daffer, V. E. (1984). Old age and environmental docility: The roles of health, support, and personality. *Journal of Gerontology, 39,* 240-242.

Myerhoff, B. (1978). *Number our days.* New York: Simon & Schuster.

National Institute on Aging. (1978). *The older woman: Continuities and discontinuities* (NIH Publication no. 80-1897). Bethesda, MD: U.S. Department of Health and Human Services.

O'Rand, A. M. (1984). Women. In E. Palmore (Ed.), *Handbook on the aged in the United States.* Westport, CT: Greenwood.

Pillemer, K., & Finkelhor, D. (1988). The prevalence of elder abuse: A random sample survey. *Gerontologist, 28,* 51-57.

Retiree trends point to racial strains. (1988, June 14). *Wall Street Journal,* p. 33.

Rhine, S. H. (1984). *Managing older workers: Company policies and attitudes.* New York: Conference Board.

Rodin, J. (1986). Aging and health: Effects of the sense of control. *Science, 233,* 1271-1276.

Rodin, J. (1987). Personal control through the life course. In R. P. Abeles (Ed.), *Life-*

span perspectives and social psychology (pp. 103-119). Hillsdale, NJ: Lawrence Erlbaum.

Rook, K. S. (1984). The negative side of social interaction: Impact on psychological well-being. *Journal of Personality and Social Psychology, 46,* 1097-1108.

Rosow, I. (1985). Status and role change through the life cycle. In R. H. Binstock & E. Shanas (Eds.), *Handbook of aging and the social sciences* (2nd ed., pp. 62-93). New York: Van Nostrand Reinhold.

Rowe, J. W., & Kahn, R. L. (1987). Human aging: Usual and successful. *Science, 237,* 143-149.

Schaie, K. W. (1981). Psychological changes from midlife to early old age: Implications for the maintenance of mental health. *American Journal of Orthopsychiatry, 51,* 199-218.

Sears, D. O. (1987). Implications of the life-span approach for research on attitudes and social cognition. In R. P. Abeles (Ed.), *Life-span perspectives and social psychology* (pp. 17-60). Hillsdale, NJ: Lawrence Erlbaum.

Shanas, E. (1979). The family as a social support system in old age. *Gerontologist, 19,* 169-174.

Shanas, E., & Maddox, G. L. (1985). Health, health resources, and the utilization of care. In R. H. Binstock & E. Shanas (Eds.), *Handbook of aging and the social sciences* (2nd ed., pp. 696-726). New York: Van Nostrand Reinhold.

Siegel, J. S., & Davidson, M. (1984). *Demographic and socioeconomic aspects of aging in the United States* (Series P23, no. 138). Washington, DC: U.S. Bureau of the Census.

Sterns, H. L. (1986). Training and retraining adult and older adult workers. In J. E. Birren, P. K. Robinson, & J. E. Livingston (Eds.), *Age, health, and employment* (pp. 93-113). Englewood Cliffs, NJ: Prentice-Hall.

Stone, R., Cafferata, G. L., & Sangel, J. (1987). Caregivers of the frail elderly: A national profile. *Gerontologist, 27,* 616-626.

Stroebe, W., & Stroebe, M. S. (1987). *Bereavement and health: The psychological and physical consequences of partner loss.* Cambridge: Cambridge University Press.

Taylor, R. J. (1986). Religious participation among elderly Blacks. *Gerontologist, 26,* 630-636.

U.S. Bureau of the Census. (1987). *Statistical abstract of the United States, 1988.* Washington, DC: Author.

3

A Social Dilemma: Egocentrically Biased Cognitions Among Filial Caregivers

MELVIN J. LERNER
DARRYL G. SOMERS
DAVID W. REID
MARY C. TIERNEY

In our society, it has become normal for people to reach the age when they can no longer maintain themselves. Eventually, chronic illness or physical and mental deterioration force them to depend upon others to meet at least some of their basic needs. When this occurs, most elderly turn to members of their immediate families for the required aid and, typically, family members accept the responsibility for meeting those needs (Brody, 1978, 1985; Cantor, 1983; Lieberman, 1978; Neugarten, 1979; Shanas, 1979; Springer & Brubaker, 1984).

AUTHORS' NOTE: The research reported in this chapter was supported by Social Sciences and Humanities Research Council of Canada Research Grant no. 410-85-0489 to M. J. Lerner, D. Reid, and M. Tierney, and a Social Sciences and Humanities Research Council of Canada Reorientation Grant (Population Aging) to M. J. Lerner.

In this chapter, we first briefly outline the effects of this crisis upon the lives of the dependent parents' children. Then, after describing the common explanation for the conflict-generated stress experienced by these filial caregivers, we present our theoretical model of the deterioration that can occur in close relations when the members are functioning under conditions of insufficient resources. Finally, we discuss recent findings regarding reactions of siblings who, as filial caregivers, are functioning in this increasingly common form of a scarce-resource social dilemma.

Parental Dependence, Stress, and Conflict

It has been well documented that the main responsibility for providing care for the dependent elderly is shared by the spouse and their children (Cantor, 1980, 1983; Marcus, 1978). Although it is typically a daughter who becomes either the primary care-manager/caregiver or the source of support for the spouse who has temporarily assumed the caregiver role (Brody, 1978, 1985), the parent's dependency is a source of stress for virtually all the members of the immediate family. The complexity of the psychological demands experienced by the children in this family crisis is revealed most vividly in the finding that the extent of their stress is not determined primarily by the amount of aid they provide to meet their parent's needs. Rather, it is the extent of those needs, regardless of whether the children meet them or not, that determines how severely they are stressed by their parent's situation (Cantor, 1980; Cicirelli, 1981; Lieberman, 1978; Maddox, 1975; Neugarten, 1979; Robinson & Thurnher, 1979).

The most familiar explanation of the stress experienced by the children points to conflict over desired resources (Marcus, 1978). As individuals, the children must deal with the internal conflicts created by the parents' need for their personal resources: their time, emotional and physical energy, and possibly financial resources as well. Typically, these newly imposed demands on the children's resources occur at a time in their lives—usually middle age to early old age—when their resources are already fully committed, if not oversubscribed (Brody, 1978, 1985). To the extent that they meet their filial obligations to help their parents, it will be at the expense of commitments to their spouses, children, and their own plans for

that time in their lives. Because meeting one set of demands must occur at the cost of scanting the others, as the sum of demands on their resources increases, the net effect is greater guilt or frustration and resentment.

As each of the children attempt to cope with this essentially unresolvable internal conflict, it is not surprising that it can eventually affect their relations with one another. Because they each suffer from insufficient resources to meet all their expectations, goals, and obligations, it is natural for them to hope the others will take responsibility for a large enough share of their common burden so that their own personal conflicts can be managed. Typically, the participants in such dilemmas recognize that, given their common desire to minimize costs at the inevitable expense of the others, the most stable solution is one that is fair to all concerned (one where they each accept an equal or equitable portion of the costs). However, the issue of fairness usually provides the arena for their competitive maneuvering rather than a solution. The research literature seems to support the obvious hypothesis that all the participants attempt to justify the particular arrangement that minimizes their own personal costs (Cook & Messick, 1983; Greenberg & Cohen, 1982; Walster, Walster, & Berscheid, 1978). In addition, they often take advantage of opportunities to renegotiate and alter the arrangement so it becomes even less costly to themselves, while purportedly becoming more fair.

As a result, the participants in this form of social dilemma typically become increasingly distrustful and guarded in their relations with one another, and they may eventually assume a competitive orientation out of a perceived need to protect their own interests from the expected exploitative behavior of the others (Kelley & Stahelski, 1970). Apparently, even the most intimate and enduring relationships are not immune to this conflict-inducing process if the participants are functioning under extended periods of scarce or insufficient resources (Berscheid & Campbell, 1981; Holmes, 1981; Kelley, 1979).

A Natural History of Close Relations Under Conditions of Scarcity

Although this portrayal of the internal and interpersonal conflicts provides a generally accurate description of the stress exhibited by filial caregivers and their siblings, there is considerable reason to question the explanation of the underlying processes. For example, the internal conflicts experienced by the filial caregivers are assumed to be a consequence of the insufficiency of resources available to meet all of the demands; that is, meeting their obligations to their parents must occur at the expense of other desires and commitments. Although it is true, in the literal sense, that allocating a resource to another person occurs at a cost to the allocator and must reduce the allocator's pool of available resources, the psychological costs of allocating or gaining resources may follow very different rules.

The evidence suggests that allocating a resource may be experienced as a rather neutral event or possibly a benefit, depending upon the allocator's judgment of who is entitled to that resource (Adams, 1965; Berger, Zelditch, Anderson, & Cohen, 1972; Homans, 1961; Lerner, 1975; Walster et al., 1978). In effect, keeping a resource to which one does not feel entitled often will be experienced as more costly than allocating that resource to deserving others.

The central role that considerations of entitlement play in people's lives has been well known by social scientists. Sociologists and political scientists have observed that people can live under very minimal conditions of desired material resources, and even with some degree of continuing suffering and pain, without feeling seriously deprived or demoralized. These objectively deprived people will not be resentful if they believe that what they are experiencing is their fair lot in life—that is, what they are entitled to have (Crosby, 1976; Suls & Miller, 1977). There is also evidence, although less systematically documented, that there are virtually no conditions of affluence or abundance that will prevent people from feeling resentful, cheated, or even demoralized by their unjust fate. An extended strike by physicians in Ontario a few years ago clearly illustrated this (Gee, 1986). Although by most standards the doctors were extremely well-off, they were willing to incur serious risks to their own well-being and to the health of their patients in order to protest the unfairness of their pay. Presumably, most of them genuinely believed they deserved, and were thus entitled to, considerably more affluence then they already possessed; and to avoid the demoralization of feeling unjustly treated, they were driven to extreme acts.

These observations suggest that, although there may be many rather direct sources of stress for filial caregivers, one, if not the most important, source of stress is tied to their judgments of what they are entitled to keep for themselves and their immediate families and what their parents are entitled to have from them. Transferring a resource, whether it is time, energy, or money, to their parents will not be experienced as a cost or a stressor if the children genuinely believe, considering everyone's needs, that the parents are entitled to that resource. However, the decision as to what is appropriate for them to contribute to their parents' welfare will be shaped to a great extent by their perceptions of the obligations and contributions of their siblings (Walster et al., 1978). The failure of the siblings to meet their responsibilities by contributing their fair share, or their imposition of unfair demands, can be a source of stress for the filial caregiver. It is also reasonable that feeling unfairly treated and alienated from one's siblings can elicit a defensive strategy as a protection from their seemingly exploitative behavior (Deutsch, 1973; Kelley & Stahelski, 1970).

The stress and deterioration in relations experienced by filial caregivers can be best understood as a sequence of events that might be expected to appear in virtually all close relations existing under continuing conditions of insufficient resources. This sequence of personal and interpersonal events results from natural errors in the siblings' information processing that produce apparent conflicts in their own and the others' entitlements.

Identity Relations:
Justice Reactions to the Crisis

The theoretical scenario in this "natural history" begins with the onset of a crisis. In this case, the crisis is the serious threat to the well-being of the parents, with its attendant emotional effects on the children. Possibly one of the parents has had a serious stroke or heart attack but no longer needs hospitalization. Or, more commonly, Alzheimer-based deterioration has made one of them delusional or so forgetful that he or she needs continual supervision. Typically, the crisis initially elicits in the participants a sense of compassion and caring for each other that is characteristic of an *identity relation* (Hoffman, 1982; Lerner, 1975, 1981). As a result, it seems natural that their pool of common needs dictates what everyone does. All the involved family members attempt to reduce everyone's suffering. Their siblings' stress and burdens are as important as their own in determining how they attempt to help each other and their parents. There is, of course, the assumption that the others are responding similarly. One might say that the family members' reactions, as is often the case when a natural disaster strikes a community, are psychologically similar to the honeymoon stage of an intimate relationship—that is, the participants become fully identified with one another's welfare.

From then on, the course of events in this natural history is directed by the parents' continuing, if not increasing, needs, which create demands for the children's already committed resources. In this form of insufficient-resource social dilemma, the most salient factors are the participants' costs and contributions, because there are relatively few benefits or rewards to consider. Each participant has more information about his or her own costs and contributions than about those of the siblings. As an inevitable consequence of this differential availability of relevant information, the siblings each develop an egocentrically biased assessment of their own costs in comparison with the costs of others (Ross & Sicoly, 1979). As a result, each sibling will arrive, sooner or later, at the judgment that the others are not giving the same consideration to his or her costs, contributions, and needs as he or she is giving to theirs.

This surprising set of events requires further explanation. According to the available research literature, people in an identity relation will initially attribute what appear to be self-serving acts by the others to external factors that are temporarily or chronically impinging upon them (Kelley, 1979). They will think: "It is not my sweet sister's fault she is ignoring my needs; it is her terrible husband forcing her not to contribute her share to our parents." Or, "It is the stress of my brother's job that forces him to act in ways that are inconsiderate." As a consequence of this kind of attribution, and because each child is identified with the others' needs, the children forgive, accept, and accommodate these failings of the others. This can create a fairly stable set of circumstances, but eventually the children can no longer adapt, either because their resources are almost exhausted or because the stability of their own families is threatened. In this situation of insufficient resources, it is not unusual eventually to reach the point of virtually exhausting all available resources.

Unit Relations:
The Democratic Solution

Although the initial reaction of identifying with one another was elicited by the compelling cues of common suffering, the next stage, following exhaustion or threat, arises out of a more consciously guided search for a solution. That solution is guided by the need for children to explain why their siblings seem not to recognize their true needs. The answer that usually arises is that, although the siblings have a great deal in common, they are also separate individuals with their own lives. The problem that the children must deal with—the dependency of their parents—makes salient what they have in common—how they are similar in important ways. This perception of similarity elicits the psychology of a *unit relation* (Lerner, 1975, 1981). What emerges naturally is a definition of the situation in which, as independent but essentially similar people, each child should be treated equally. Thus there should be equal, or at least equivalent, contributions and costs. It is interesting to note that this usually tacit form of contract is typical of the posthoneymoon stage described in much of the literature on couples and close relations. After the first glow of being united fades, a couple realizes that they are basically separate people, partners with equal rights and privileges, entitled to equal treatment and outcomes (Holmes, 1981).

This solution, although it appears natural and stable, is in fact a very unstable arrangement. The participants are virtually entrapped by the conflict between the apparent correctness and appropriateness of this solution and the insidious effects of their continuing egocentrically biased assessment of relevant contributions. Because each of the siblings is still arriving at assessments of relative contributions based upon considerably more information about their own costs than they have about their siblings' costs, it eventually becomes evident, that what initially appeared to be a fair solution was actually a bad bargain, or that the others are not now contributing their fair share. Even sincere attempts to adjust the arrangements based upon one's own reassessment of what would be more fair for all concerned are often met with unexpected and clearly unfair counterproposals from the others.

Nonunit Relations:
The Defensive Reaction

At this point, given the others' apparent violation of the rules of equality and fair treatment, and the inappropriate defensive accusations they now make about each others' motives, an internal attribution is most likely—especially given the consistency over time in the others' "violations" of the rules of fairness (Kelley & Michela, 1979). The conflict is now attributed to the siblings' enduring traits, and each one thinks his or her siblings are lazy, devious, defensive, neurotic, and/or selfish—as they "always were," even as children. But the siblings remain tied to one another because of their parents' need for help. From then on, however, they perceive the others in a *nonunit relation*—that is, they see each other as different from themselves in important ways. Thereafter, the involved participants will develop defensive strategies to protect themselves from what appear to be the selfish, if not exploitative, acts of the others— "them" (Kelley & Stahelski, 1970).

In this fashion, the natural history of the siblings' relations progresses from *identity* to *unit* to *nonunit*; from feeling compassionate toward and fully identified with one another, to emphasizing similarity, to becoming convinced of essential differences. This progression of events is driven not by selfish motives but by egocentrically biased assessments of relevant contributions and costs, and the consequent attributions.

The Research Project and
Relevant Findings

This process and the various hypotheses are being examined in two research projects, begun at approximately the same time. One, with David Chiriboga and Philip Weiler, studies a sample of filial caregivers of Alzheimer patients from the areas around Davis and San Jose, California (Chiriboga, Weiler, & Lerner, 1985). The other project, with David Reid and Mary Tierney as coinvestigators, is centered in Toronto, Canada, and employs an opportunistic sample of filial caregivers of dependent elderly parents, whose degree and cause of dependency were intentionally allowed to vary (Lerner, Reid, & Tierney, 1984). This chapter describes some of the findings from the first wave of Toronto data.

The design of the Toronto study called for a two-stage panel of interviews one year apart. The sample was selected and interviews conducted by a survey research firm, Canadian Facts, employing instruments and an interview schedule designed by the Toronto and California research teams. The criteria for inclusion in the Toronto sample were chosen in order to select middle-aged or older adults who had elderly parents with serious needs that they could not meet on their own, and whose dependency created a problem for the children. To be included in this sample, these filial caregivers had to have a sibling in the same geographic area who was also involved in helping the parents. In addition, the parents could not be either in an institution or living with a member of the family, and English had to be the primary language in their home. The final requirement for inclusion was the willingness of both siblings to be interviewed about their involvement with their parents.

The total sample of the first wave consisted of 140 pairs of siblings: 12 pairs of brothers, 56 brother-sister pairs, and 73 pairs of sisters. The income, religious affiliation, and education level of the participants were comparable to the general population in the Toronto area for that age category. We interviewed the participants concerning their costs and contributions, the benefits they received from helping their parents, their relationship to their siblings (identity, unit, or nonunit), their attitudes toward their siblings, their level of stress, and their sense of well-being. We also assessed their perceptions of each of these items for their siblings, that is, the siblings' costs, contributions, benefits, and so on.

Although the second wave of interviewing has not been completed at the time of this writing, there are data from the first wave that indicate whether one of the central factors presumed to be generating the process is operating among the siblings in this sample. The underlying dynamic in this "natural history" is driven by the participants' (siblings') egocentrically biased assessments of their relative costs and contributions. Therefore, in order for the proposed theoretical analysis of the siblings' internal conflict and eventual interpersonal conflicts to be supported, we should find the siblings' biased assessments in the initial interview. They should overestimate their own costs, contributions, influence, and even their benefits or satisfactions in the situation. To test these predictions, we considered 15 comparisons of the respondents' descriptions of their own inputs and outcomes—costs, contributions, and benefits—with their reports of their siblings' inputs and outcomes.

Egocentric Biases
Among Sibling Caretakers

The six pairs of items in Table 3.1 are the most direct assessments of the respondents' views of how costly the parents' dependency has been for themselves and for their siblings. For example, the S-LIFE item: "Overall, thinking about what your life was like before your parents needed help, consider to what extent your parents' problems have made your life better or worse." Contrary to our expectation, there was no significant difference between the respondents' estimation of how much their own lives had become better or worse and their response to the same question (O-LIFE) concerning their siblings' lives. The overall mean of 3.00 on this item's five-point scale indicated that, on the average, the respondents experienced "no change" in their lives.

This pattern of generally accepting the situation and reporting no significant perceived discrepancy between their own and their siblings' costs in this crisis was borne out by the other items measuring the direct impact of the parents' dependency. For example, the S-GIVEN/O-GIVEN item asked, "Please tell me how much you have (your brother or sister has) given up to help your parents." These respondents reported that their costs were no greater than their siblings' costs, and that the arrangements were very fair to them and their siblings (S-FAIR and O-FAIR). The only egocentrically biased response was that the respondents reported they themselves received greater satisfaction from helping their parents than did their siblings (S-SATIS and O-SATIS).

At this point we considered whether the description of these people as the "caught generation" (Marcus, 1978) was a myth, or whether the sample was so self-selected we would find nothing but positive reactions, or whether our interview schedule and interviewers were eliciting only socially acceptable reactions. However, when we examined the reactions to the other nine items that focused on

Table 3.1
"Direct Impact" Items Tested for Egocentric Bias

Self/Sibling Item Codes	Item	Means for S	for O	t (df ≥ 276)
S-LIFE/O-LIFE	Consider to what extent your parents' problems have made your life better or worse.	2.99	3.02	.38
S-GIVEN/O-GIVEN	Please tell me how much you have given up to help your parents [9 individual items summed to single index].	16.92	17.43	1.50
S-INTER/O-INTER	To what extent has helping your parents interfered with your personal life?	3.23	3.14	.81
S-FAIR/O-FAIR	How fair would you say the present arrangements are to you?	5.27	5.18	.96
S-SATIS/O-SATIS	Overall, then, how satisfying is it to you, personally, to help your mother/father at this time?	3.67	3.44	5.33*
S-STRESS/O-STRESS	Overall, how stressful have the problems with helping your parents been in your life, up to now?	2.70	2.63	1.15

*$p < .001$.

specific aspects of the participants' and their siblings' contributions to their parents, seven of the nine items revealed significant self/sibling discrepancies that conformed to the expected egocentric biases.

The S-HELP item (see Table 3.2) is a standard measure of extent of helping that lists 14 possible needs the parent may have (e.g., homemaking, home health care, transportation, psychological support). The respondents rated the extent of their parents' needs, then how often they personally met or directly arranged to meet those needs, and finally how often their siblings did so (O-HELP), on a

Table 3.2
"Contribution" Items Tested for Egocentric Bias

Self/Sibling Item Codes	Item	Means for S	for O	t (df ≥ 276)
S-HELP/O-HELP	How often do you do, or directly arrange for someone else to do, each of these things [14 individual categories summed to single index]?	35.27	32.86	4.06***
S-INPUT/O-INPUT	How much personal influence did you have in determining (i.e., setting up) the present arrangements for helping your parents?	2.66	2.38	3.74***
S-CHGS/O-CHGS	If it became necessary to you, how easy or difficult would it be for you to make changes in your contributions to helping your parents?	2.43	2.52	1.46
S-CHOICE/O-CHOICE	To what extent do you feel you have any choice in deciding whether to continue to help your parents?	2.63	2.81	2.67**
S-GIVES/O-GIVES	Would it be more fair to everyone if you contributed [less/more]?	3.04	3.16	2.23*

*$p < .05$; **$p < .01$; ***$p < .001$.

scale from 1 (never) to 6 (always). Here we found that the respondents claimed to do more than their sibling on virtually every need and, of course, on the overall composite of all the activities added together.

Similarly, the respondents described themselves as having more influence than their sibling (S-INPUT/O-INPUT). Though the S-CHGS and O-CHGS items produced no significant differences between the respondents' self-estimates and their perceptions of the sibling's position, on S-CHOICE/O-CHOICE they reported believing they had less choice and were more trapped than their sibling. In addition, the respondents generally believed it would be more fair to everyone if their sibling contributed more and if they contributed relatively less (S-GIVES and O-GIVES).

Overall, then, the participants reported that they contributed more to meeting their parents' needs than did their siblings, had more influence in setting up the present arrangements, felt more trapped by their parents' needs, and felt things would be more fair to everyone if their siblings contributed more than they currently were.

Table 3.3 shows the respondents' reactions to questions comparing their own views of what was happening with what they believed was their sibling's view of the respondent's situation. For example, comparing the S-GIVES and O-SGIVES items shows whether the respondents believed their sibling agreed with them concerning who should do more or less in order for the arrangement to be more fair to everyone. On the first two items, the respondents expected a significant amount of disagreement between their own view of what their contribution should be and what their sibling would say.

Table 3.3
"Reflected Contribution" Items Tested for Egocentric Bias

Self/Sibling Item Codes	Item	Means for S	for O	t (df ≥ 276)
S-GIVES/O-SGIVES	Would it be more fair to everyone if you contributed [less/more]?	2.63	2.81	2.31*
S-OGIVES/O-GIVES	Would it be more fair to everyone if your brother/sister contributed [less/more]?	3.15	3.08	1.75*
S-OMORE/O-OMORE	If it seemed necessary to you, how easy or difficult would it be to get your sibling to make more of a contribution?	2.87	3.06	2.80**
S-OQUANT/O-OQUANT	How much do you think your brother/sister contributes to the caregiving?	8.23	7.55	1.54

*$p < .05$; **$p < .01$.

Generally, the findings reported in Tables 3.2 and 3.3 suggest the expected bases for conflict, unless, of course, the respondents thought it would be easy to get the siblings to alter their contributions. That was not the case, however, as revealed by responses to the S-OMORE and O-OMORE items (see Table 3.3). The respondents thought it would be difficult to get their siblings to change, but that their siblings thought that they (the respondents) could more easily be persuaded to change their contribution. However, there appeared to be little room for change, according to the reactions to the S-OQUANT and O-OQUANT items. Generally, both siblings believed they were close to doing "all that is reasonable and possible." Thus, overall, we found considerable evidence of egocentrically biased perceptions of the contributions made to the parents, and some awareness of disagreements concerning the appropriateness of those contributions.

The Accuracy of Sibling Perceptions

In trying to understand the origins and consequences of these biased perceptions, there are various questions to consider. For example, beyond the mean differences or systematic discrepancies, correlation coefficients can show how similar or different were the respondents' *perceptions* of their siblings' responses and how similar or different were the two individuals in fact. The "perceived similarity" column of Table 3.4 shows that (comparing each respondent's rating of him- or herself with his or her rating of the sibling), respondents believed their siblings were relatively similar to themselves in terms of their costs, contributions, and perceptions of the situation, except that they differed on the issue of whose increased contribution would make the situation more fair (S-GIVES and O-GIVES). The second column shows that, comparing the actual self-ratings of a respondent and his or her sibling's self-ratings (e.g., their answers to "How much is *my* life better or worse?"), there was virtually no correlation—that is, no more similarity between the two siblings' self-reports than one would expect to find between any two strangers. Finally, the intraclass correlations in column three show the degree of agreement between respondents' self-ratings and the siblings' description of the respondents.

Table 3.4
Selected Examples of Correlations Assessing the
Correspondence of Siblings' Responses

Item	Perceived Similarity with Sibling (n = 280)	Actual Similarity with Sibling (n = 140)	Agreement with Sibling about Impact (n = 280)
S-LIFE/O-LIFE	.46**	−.07	.14
S-INTER/O-INTER	.39**	.05	.24**
S-SATIS/O-SATIS	.36**	−.01	.20*
S-HELP/O-HELP	.45**	.06	.33**
S-CHGS/O-CHGS	.49**	.11	.18*
S-GIVES/O-GIVES	−.22**	.01	−.01
S-OGIVES/O-OGIVES	.27**	−.03	−.10
S-OQUANT/O-OQUANT	.20*	−.04	−.07

*$p < .01$; **$p < .001$.

It is interesting that this column shows there was a significant amount of agreement with the sibling on some items (how often the other one helps, how much the situation has interfered in the other's life, satisfaction in helping, and the ease with which one could contribute more).

Apparently, these respondents believed that their sibling was reacting very much as they were to their parents' dependency, whereas, in fact, that similarity was no greater than between any two people who had dependent elderly parents. There was some agreement concerning specific reactions that each one was experiencing, but (as indicated in Tables 3.2 and 3.3) the siblings generally had egocentrically biased evaluations of who was doing more and who should contribute more to meet their parents' needs.

Correlates of the Siblings'
Egocentric Biases

There are other possible factors that may correlate with these systematically biased perceptions. For example, we considered how close the respondents felt to their siblings, how much contact they

Table 3.5
Correlations Between Possible Mediating Variables

Variable	1	2	3	4	5	6
1. Closeness	—					
2. Liking	46***	—				
3. Frequency of contact	−.51***	−.27***	—			
4. Parents' needs	−.09	.00	−.07	—		
5. Subjective difference	−.35***	−.55***	.34***	−.04	—	
6. Resources contributed	.05	−.02	−.13	.10	.01	—
7. Gender	.13*	.01	−.11	−.12*	.00	.17**

**p < .05; **p < .01; ***p < .001.*

had with them, the amount of liking for the sibling, the extent of parental need, the amount of contributed resources, and gender. The correlations among these possible mediating variables, in Table 3.5, indicate that feelings of being close to the other, of liking, and reported amount of contact were intercorrelated, as one would expect. (The subjective difference variable was computed using Osgood, Suci, & Tannenbaum's, 1957, distance measure.) It is interesting that both gender and the resources contributed to the parents as well as the parents' needs were somewhat independent of the liking and contact cluster, and they were slightly correlated with one another. Women contributed more resources.

The correlations in Table 3.6 show that the most consistent correlates of egocentric bias were gender (especially for the direct impact items), the amount of resources devoted to parents, the subjective difference measure, and the liking for the sibling. Regression analyses revealed that two of the most consistent predictors of the extent of egocentrically biased assessments were the extent of liking for the sibling and the amount of resources contributed to the parents' welfare. Less liking for the sibling and more resources expended were associated with a greater probability that the respondents saw the sibling as contributing less than they—less than his or her fair share—and greater belief that it would be difficult to get the sibling to change his or her contributions, but that the sibling believed it to be relatively easy for the respondent to change.

Of course, with cross-sectional data based on one interview, it is difficult to infer the direction of causation and the extent to which

Table 3.6

Selected Examples of Correlations Between Possible Mediating Variables and Egocentric Bias

Item	Closeness	Liking	Frequency of Contact	Parents' Needs	Subjective Difference	Resources Contributed	Gender
S-LIFE/O-LIFE	.03	-.04	.02	.03	.05	.05	.02
S-INTER/O-INTER	-.02	.09	.02	.12*	-.10	-.20**	-.22***
S-SATIS/O-SATIS	-.13*	-.30***	.02	.05	.13*	-.02	.03
S-HELP/O-HELP	-.07	-.25***	.08	-.08	.16*	.23***	.22***
S-CHGS/O-CHGS	.08	.07	-.08	-.17**	-.01	.01	.05
S-GIVES/O-GIVES	.12*	.26***	-.10	.11	.23***	-.24***	-.12
S-OGIVES/O-OGIVES	-.15*	-.28***	.12*	-.04	.23***	.17**	.02
S-OQUANT/O-OQUANT	.13*	.28***	-.07	-.02	-.12*	-.17**	-.14*

*p < .05; **p < .01; ***p < .001.

motivational or informational processing generated these egocentrically biased reactions to the situation. Does less liking for a sibling lead the respondent to perceive that sibling as contributing less than would be fair, or does the perception of lesser contribution elicit less liking for the sibling? Does the quantity of resources one expends on one's parents lead to overestimating one's contributions, or are those comparative judgments actually relatively veridical perceptions for at least some of the respondents? By and large, however, the findings are quite consistent with the proposed theoretical model of the causes of the siblings' conflicts.

Differences Between Direct and Indirect Assessments

Even with these generally supportive data, an anomalous set of findings needs to be examined. When asked directly, most participants reported that everything was fine and fair and that they had not been particularly stressed or overloaded. Even more surprising, the participants claimed that helping their parents had been no more costly for them than for the sibling. How can we understand this seeming contradiction between their reactions to the direct questions of costs and the later questions concerning relative contribution and changes that would make the arrangements more fair?

The first thing to consider is the possibility of an artifact of the instrument or data-gathering situation. For example, was it easier or was there more demand for the respondents to self-monitor or disguise their true feelings in response to the direct questions, but more difficult for them to disguise their reactions to the explicit contribution questions? Because the direct questions came earlier in the interview, were the respondents less comfortable and more wary of the interviewer than they were when responding to later questions? These explanations seem implausible because the participants were willing to claim greater satisfaction from helping than they attributed to their siblings, and they claimed to have more influence in deciding upon the present arrangements.

If we take all of these findings at face value, we can see how they might fit within the initial theoretical hypotheses. Two related aspects of our sample become important for these considerations. Our respondents not only agreed to participate in this study, they also agreed to identify a sibling living nearby who was also one of the primary caregivers, and that sibling had to agree to be interviewed as well. It should be no surprise, then, to discover that in terms of our theoretical model the vast majority of our respondents reported, as part of the interview, that they felt either an identity or unit relation with their siblings.

In order for the respondents to be able to make informed judgments about their type of relation with their siblings, each respondent was given short prototypical descriptions of the three relations. The identity relation included statements like, "What seems to typify our relation with one another is the recognition that each other's welfare is as important to us as our own." The unit relation included statements such as, "What typifies our relation are feelings of independence and mutual respect. . . . We each take responsibility for our own lives." Nonunit relations were described by statements like, "Although we are both members of the same family, and thus share some things in common, we are essentially different kinds of people. We differ . . . in important ways."

Given the predominance of identity or unit relations with the sibling, it would be reasonable to expect that the respondents believed they were meeting their own and their siblings' needs, minimizing or equalizing everyone's costs as much as possible. One item revealed that the respondents believed they and their siblings were doing about as much as was reasonable, given everyone's present circumstances. Conceivably, then, our direct questions tapped these general thoughts and feelings. But when we began asking more specific questions concerning their own and their sibling's contributions, and whether it would be more fair for the sibling to contribute more and for them to contribute less, we required them to examine explicitly the details of the present arrangement. Their responses to that inquiry about relative contributions revealed the presence of the expected egocentric biases. This was clearly confirmed by almost every item of the frequency-of-helping list of activities, as well as the overall index. We thus found consistent evidence for the expected potential source of conflict based upon the respondents' assessment that they were contributing more than their siblings, more than was fair to everyone, and that their siblings disagreed with them.

The common scenario that we believe has been revealed here is that, as in any common crisis among people who have a history of a close relationship, our caregivers initially, and for as long as was possible, tried to meet everyone's needs—manifesting an identity relation, that was eventually replaced by the unit relation, but still focused on similarity of costs. However, at the same time, genuinely held beliefs emerged, based upon their processing of the systematically biased available information. These beliefs were that they were contributing more than their siblings and that their siblings did not appreciate this sufficiently. It makes sense, according to the theoretical model presented here, that most of the respondents then would be in some state of transition: most between identity and unit, some between unit and nonunit, perceptions of their siblings.

Egocentric Bias in Identity, Unit, and Nonunit Relations

This analysis would be supported, at least in part, if we found that those siblings who already arrived at (or possibly began with) the nonunit phase of this natural history reported the greatest egocentric bias in their perceptions of relative contributions and disagreements concerning who should contribute more. That appears to be the case, for some items reveal a significant relationship between the reported phase (identity, unit, nonunit) and the self/sibling discrepancies. A first look at these data (see Table 3.7) revealed relatively little egocentric bias among those respondents who maintained the identity or unit relation, while those in the nonunit relation most clearly manifested these biases. For example, the nonunit respondents saw themselves as having given up a great deal for their parents, much more than their siblings. They also believed that their siblings found helping their parents considerably less satisfying, and that it would have been more fair to everyone if their siblings contributed more. To test whether liking for the sibling was a mediator of these results, rather than perceived similarity or commonality, a separate set of analyses was performed removing the influence of liking. The egocentric biases remained, however, even when liking for the sibling was statistically partialed out. It appears, then, that the essential component is the perception that the sibling and the respondent are different in important ways.

Table 3.7
Selected Examples of Significant Egocentric Bias Effect Means for Identity, Unit, and Nonunit Relationships Between Siblings

Item	Identity	Unit	Nonunit	p
S-GIVEN	16.88a	16.53ab	19.08b	.01 (.01)
O-GIVEN	17.98a	17.09a	16.36a	
S-SATIS	3.74a	3.60a	3.56a	.01 (.01)
O-SATIS	3.53a	3.42a	2.84b	
S-GIVES	3.04a	3.04a	3.08a	.002 (.005)
O-GIVES	3.03a	3.15a	2.84b	

NOTE: Parentheses indicate probability with liking for the sibling covaried out of the analysis. Means with different letters differ significantly at *p* < .05.

Although these findings are consistent with the theoretical hypotheses, longitudinal panel data are required to test the underlying processes. Therefore, we will examine these siblings' reactions a year after the first interviews to determine antecedent predictors of the dominant relationship, the kinds of biases, and how these are related to the amount of stress experienced by the filial caregivers. One hypothesis is that, regardless of the present relationship and amount of liking for the siblings, the extent of the latent egocentrically biased perceptions will be the best predictor of the subsequent feelings toward the sibling and the amount of stress induced by the potential conflict. It will be important to find out if, in fact, the amount of unfairness experienced by the participants will be determined by these biased assessments and, in turn, if that experience mediates the stress with which they must cope.

Some Final Thoughts and Caveats

The natural history of close relations under conditions of continuing scarcity or insufficient resources that we have described is not an inevitable or invariant process. Not all interpersonal relations will deteriorate from identity to unit to nonunit relations and certainly not at the same rate. There are theoretically predictable events that would presumably cause the relationships to stabilize at a given point or even reverse themselves. For example, the relationship might stabilize at the initial identity stage if one of the participants is able and willing, alone, to provide sufficient resources to meet the parent's needs. That person, for various reasons, may have a relative abundance of the resources required, or fewer competing demands for these resources. Then, even though she perceives the sibling to be less sensitive to her own needs than she is to the sibling's, she will nevertheless maintain the identity relation by making an external, situational attribution for the aberrant, insensitive behavior (e.g., it is her sister-in-law who is to blame for her brother's relative self-centeredness or failure to be sufficiently considerate), and she will stabilize the relationship by providing the needed resources herself. We use the feminine pronoun here because it is usually one of the daughters who, very early in such situations, takes on the primary caregiver role (Brody, 1978). Why her? Even in this era in our society, as our data illustrate, the normatively based obligations associated with the status role of "middle-aged daughter" make it seem more appropriate and legitimate to all concerned for a daughter to care for the parents. As a result, it is probably demonstrable that even she will experience these contributions as less of a personal cost. However, that will not continue if and when her own immediate family refuses to cooperate and reasserts their demands for her time and energy. In any case, this solution of female caregiving seems increasingly unlikely with each succeeding generation.

A more common solution taking place in our society is for the participants, usually at the unit relation stage in the process, to attempt to eliminate the conditions of insufficient resources by pooling their economic resources on an equal or equitable basis to purchase virtually all the caregiving resources needed by the parents. Whether or not this arrangement stabilizes the relations among the siblings depends, we think, upon the same set of factors described in the natural history. Certainly there are good theoretical reasons and empirical evidence that the equality or equity solutions for allocating desirable resources are the least stable and most amenable to the influence of the participants' biased sampling of relevant information (Holmes, 1981). For example, how does one decide what monetary contribution is truly equal or fair, given differences in participants' family size, economic affluence, age composition of their children, and the inevitable changes in circumstances that will affect each participant's need for money or his or her relative affluence? What was fair at one time may be obviously unjust at another. What happens then— especially if the family members seem to one another to have obviously subjective and seemingly self-serving, biased perceptions of their own and others' costs and contributions? After all, regardless of one's level of affluence in our society, it is common for money to become a scarce resource sooner or later. There is just not enough to meet the demands.

Given that the participants in this social dilemma are members of the same family, a situation that keeps them in relatively close and continual communication, there are events that can predictably reverse the course of deterioration in the relations. For example, the identity relation may be reestablished for some period of time if one of the members indicates that he or she is in a period of crisis or serious deprivation. Something harmful may have happened or be threatening a member of the extended family. On the other hand, there are also wonderful things that can happen to a sibling or his or her family that elicit a sense of positive identity in the other siblings—a wedding or birth, for example.

Also, many families have traditions and rituals that reestablish the sense of belonging to the same unit or being identified with one another. For example, families may come together for family dinners on regular occasions such as religious or public holidays, graduation ceremonies, and so forth. It is no surprise that successfully married couples often have traditions and rituals for reestablishing and making salient their common bonds of similarity, even of identity.

Unfortunately, however, there is a high probability that the natural history will proceed to the terminal and relatively stable stage of the nonunit relation unless one of two things occurs. Either the situation must change from one of insufficient resources to one of abundant resources available to all the participants, or the members must somehow no longer engage in biased sampling of the relevant information about their own and the others' relative costs and contributions. Ross and Sicoly (1979), by refocusing the participants' attention to relevant aspects of the others' contributions, were able to reduce but not completely eliminate this biased assessment in an experimental situation. Theoretically, it should be possible to accomplish this with siblings caught in the social dilemma of parents' dependency by using some of the techniques devised by marriage counselors to help partners gain a clearer, more complete picture of one another's costs and benefits (Messick & Brewer, 1983).

The main impediment to successfully maintaining the siblings' relations at some level prior to the distrusting, nonunit relationship is the naive psychology that is prevalent in our society. Most of us have been socialized into believing that people try to maximize their own profits or benefits—to make the best deal for themselves in all encounters, including those among intimates in long-term relations (Lerner, 1981, 1986; Messick & Sentis, 1983). As a result, it is commonly believed that the reason people are good, kind, or caring is because they think such apparently altruistic behavior promises the most benefit and least cost to themselves, either immediately or in the long run (Schwartz, 1975; Walster et al., 1978). Couples believe that the reason they stay together is because the relationship is the best deal they have available (Berscheid & Campbell, 1981).

What is most ironic about the acceptance of this economic, or exchange, model of human relations is that, although it clearly reflects the assumptions extant in our economic, legal, and even religious institutions, it is probably not a valid description of the way people actually function. There is a considerable amount of research now available that documents the popular acceptance of this myth at the verbal and public level of discourse (Lerner, 1986). It is the way people think to themselves and talk to others about what motivates people and guides their behavior. However, there are much more powerful scripts, agendas, or motives that actually direct people's acts—including, in particular, the basic drive to create an environment in which people get what they deserve, and get what they are entitled to have by virtue of who they are or what they have done (Lerner, 1980, 1986; Lerner, Miller, & Holmes, 1976; Miller, 1975).

If the findings of this research provide additional confirmation and support of the theoretical hypotheses, we will be in a much better position to design methods for preventing or eliminating the deterioration in relationships that often occurs when people are required to function under conditions of insufficient resources. Typically, those who have sought to generate constructive solutions to avoid the "tragedy of the commons" (Hardin, 1968) have been guided by the assumption that it was necessary to provide additional incentives, both positive and negative, for people to overcome their naturally self-serving strategy and engage in the required cooperative efforts. Our interpretation of the evidence, both that available in the scientific literature and our own research findings, suggests that the self-serving strategy is neither a "natural" nor an inevitable human response. It will only appear in those situations where people believe they are in a nonunit relation with the others, that is, that they are interacting with people who are "different" from them in important ways (Campbell, 1986; Keil & McClintock, 1983). Those differences then lead to the anticipation of their engaging in exploitative or competitive acts under conditions of interdependence and insufficient resources (Greenberg, 1981). However, it is just as human and natural for people's behavior to be guided by considerations of everyone's welfare (identity relation) or equality in contributions and outcomes (unit relation).

The importance of the present research with filial caregivers is that we have been able to isolate one, if not *the*, pathogenic process that leads to the deterioration of relations between people who have to work together on common concerns. Simply because each knows much more about his or her own costs and contributions than about those of the other in this social dilemma (e.g., the sibling), each develops a systematically biased view of his or her relative contributions to the common problem. Given these biased assessments, it is inevitable that people eventually become surprised by the seemingly self-centered or selfish behavior of others. In the process of trying to understand the others' apparently self-serving behavior, they are gradually forced to the dispositional attribution that the others are, in fact, "that kind" of person.

Once having identified and confirmed this process, we can hope to design procedures that will enable the participants—in this case, the siblings—to become aware of this pathogenic process and put in place corrective devices that will enable each of them to avoid the systematically biased sampling of their inputs and outcomes. Under most circumstances, such interventions should be sufficient to enable them to continue dealing with their common problem while protecting one another's welfare or maintaining a relationship of equality. It is only when the participants have reached that point where they see the others as "them" that we will need to resort to external sanctions, at least on a temporary basis (Holmes, 1981). With some additional factors, we should be able to extend this model to the behavior of people in all forms of social dilemmas. Identifying those factors and generating the relevant research are the next steps in applying this social psychological theory to the search for constructive solutions to important societal problems.

References

Adams, J. S. (1965). Inequity in social exchange. In L. Berkowitz (Ed.), *Advances in experimental social psychology* (Vol. 2, pp. 267-300). New York: Academic Press.

Berger, J., Zelditch, M., Anderson, B., & Cohen, B. P. (1972). Structural aspects of distributive justice: A status-value formulation. In J. Berger, M. Zelditch, & B. Anderson (Eds.), *Sociological theories in progress* (Vol. 2, pp. 119-146). Boston: Houghton Mifflin.

Berscheid, E., & Campbell, B. (1981). The changing longevity of heterosexual close relationships: A commentary and forecast. In M. J. Lerner & S. C. Lerner (Eds.), *The justice motive in social behavior: Adapting to times of scarcity and change* (pp. 209-234). New York: Plenum.

Brody, E. M. (1978). The aging of the family. *Annals of the American Association of Political and Social Science, 438*, 13-27.

Brody, E. M. (1985). Parent care as normative family stress. *Gerontologist, 25*, 19-29.

Campbell, D. T. (1986). Rationality and utility from the standpoint of evolutionary biology. *Journal of Business, 59*, S355-S364.

Cantor, M. H. (1980, November). *Caring for the frail elderly.* Paper presented at the meeting of the Gerontological Society, San Diego.

Cantor, M. H. (1983). Strain among caregivers: A study of experience in the United States. *Gerontologist, 23*, 597-604.

Chiriboga, D. A., Weiler, P. G., & Lerner, M. J. (1985). *Adult child caretakers of dependent parents: A process study* (Grant no. 1 9460 36 494 A1). Washington, DC: U.S. Public Health Service.

Cicirelli, V. G. (1981). *Helping elderly parents: The role of adult children.* Boston: Auburn House.

Cook, K. S., & Messick, D. M. (1983). Psychological and sociological perspectives on distributive justice: Convergent, divergent, and parallel lines. In D. M. Messick & K. S. Cook (Eds.), *Equity theory: Psychological and sociological perspectives* (pp. 1-12). New York: Praeger.

Crosby, F. (1976). A model of egoistical relative deprivation. *Psychological Review, 83*, 85-113.

Deutsch, M. (1973). *The resolution of conflict: Constructive and destructive processes.* New Haven, CT: Yale University Press.

Gee, M. (1986, June 23). A bitter doctor's strike. *Maclean's*, p. 19.

Greenberg, J. (1981). The justice of distributing scarce and abundant resources. In M. J. Lerner & S. C. Lerner (Eds.), *The justice motive in social behavior: Adapting to times of scarcity and change* (pp. 289-316). New York: Plenum.

Greenberg, J., & Cohen, R. L. (1982). Why justice? Normative and instrumental interpretations. In J. Greenberg & R. L. Cohen (Eds.), *Equity and justice in social behavior* (pp. 437-469). New York: Academic Press.

Hardin, G. (1968). The tragedy of the commons. *Science, 162,* 1243-1248.

Hoffman, M. L. (1982). Development of prosocial motivation: Empathy and guilt. In N. Eisenberg (Ed.), *The development of prosocial behavior* (pp. 281-313). New York: Academic Press.

Holmes, J. G. (1981). The exchange process in close relationships: Microbehavior and macromotives. In M. J. Lerner & S. C. Lerner (Eds.), *The justice motive in social behavior: Adapting to times of scarcity and change* (pp. 261-284). New York: Plenum.

Homans, G. E. (1961). *Social behavior: Its elementary forms.* New York: Harcourt Brace.

Keil, L. K., & McClintock, C. G. (1983). A developmental perspective on distributive justice. In D. M. Messick & K. S. Cook (Eds.), *Equity theory: Psychological and sociological perspectives* (pp. 13-46). New York: Praeger.

Kelley, H. H. (1979). *Personal relations: Their structure and process.* Hillsdale, NJ: Lawrence Erlbaum.

Kelley, H. H., & Michela, J. L. (1979). Attribution theory and research. *Annual Review of Psychology, 31,* 1-89.

Kelley, H. H., & Stahelski, A. J. (1970). Social interaction basis of cooperators' and competitors' beliefs about others. *Journal of Personality and Social Psychology, 16,* 66-91.

Lerner, M. J. (1975). The justice motive in social behavior: An introduction. *Journal of Social Issues, 31*(3), 1-19.

Lerner, M. J. (1980). *The belief in a just world: A fundamental delusion.* New York: Plenum.

Lerner, M. J. (1981). The justice motive in human relations: Some thoughts on what we know and need to know about justice. In M. J. Lerner & S. C. Lerner (Eds.), *The justice motive in social behavior: Adapting to times of scarcity and change* (pp. 11-38). New York: Plenum.

Lerner, M. J. (1986). Integrating societal and psychological rules of entitlement: The basis task of each social actor and fundamental problem for the social sciences. *Social Justice Review, 1,* 107-125.

Lerner, M. J., Miller, D. T., & Holmes, J. G. (1976). Deserving vs. justice: A contemporary dilemma. In L. Berkowitz (Ed.), *Advances in experimental social psychology* (Vol. 9, pp. 134-162). New York: Academic Press.

Lerner, M. J., Reid, D., & Tierney, M. (1984). *Family response to the dependency needs of the aging parent: A social-psychological investigation* (Grant no. 410-85-0489). Ottawa: Social Sciences and Humanities Research Council of Canada.

Lieberman, G. (1978). Children of the elderly as natural helpers: Some demographic differences. *American Journal of Community Psychology, 6,* 489-498.

Maddox, G. L. (1975). Families as context and resource in chronic illness. In S. Sherwood (Ed.), *Long-term care: A handbook for researchers, planners, and providers* (pp. 317-347). New York: Spectrum.

Marcus, L. (1978). *The situation of the elderly and their families: Problems and solu-*

tions. Paper presented at the National Symposium on Aging, National Bureau on Aging, Ottawa, Canada.

Messick, D. M., & Brewer, M. B. (1983). Solving social dilemmas: A review. In L. W. Wheeler & P. Shaver (Eds.), *Review of personality and social psychology* (Vol. 4, pp. 11-44). Beverly Hills, CA: Sage.

Messick, D. M., & Sentis, K. (1983). Fairness, preference, and fairness biases. In D. M. Messick & K. S. Cook (Eds.), *Equity theory: Psychological and sociological perspectives* (pp. 61-94). New York: Praeger.

Miller, D. T. (1975). *Personal deserving versus justice for others: An exploration of the justice motive.* Unpublished doctoral dissertation, University of Waterloo.

Neugarten, B. L. (1979). The middle generations. In P. K. Ragan (Ed.), *Aging parents* (pp. 258-265). Los Angeles: University of Southern California Press.

Osgood, C. E., Suci, D. J., & Tannenbaum, P. H. (1957). *The measurement of meaning.* Urbana: University of Illinois Press.

Robinson, B., & Thurnher, M. (1979). Taking care of aged parents: A family cycle transition. *Gerontologist, 19,* 586-593.

Ross, M., & Sicoly, F. (1979). Egocentric biases in availability and attribution. *Journal of Personality and Social Psychology, 37,* 322-336.

Schwartz, S. (1975). The justice need and the activation of humanitarian norms. *Journal of Social Issues, 31*(3), 111-136.

Shanas, E. (1979). Social myth as hypothesis: The case of the family relations of old people. *Gerontologist, 19,* 3-9.

Springer, D., & Brubaker, T. H. (1984). *Family caregivers and dependent elderly: Managing stress and maximizing independence.* Beverly Hills, CA: Sage.

Suls, J. M., & Miller, R. L. (Eds.). (1977). *Social comparison processes: Theoretical and empirical perspectives.* Washington, DC: Halsted-Wiley.

Walster, E., Walster, G. W., & Berscheid, E. (1978). *Equity: Theory and research.* Boston: Allyn & Bacon.

4

Experiencing the Retirement Transition: Managerial and Professional Men Before and After

TORA K. BIKSON
JACQUELINE D. GOODCHILDS

Very recently (in historical terms) our society has changed so that more and more employed men expect to, are able to, and elect to retire from the paid labor force (see Hansson, this volume). The proportion of the male population financially and physically able to withdraw from paid employment

AUTHORS' NOTE: The research presented here is part of a larger study (still in progress) supported through a grant from the John and Mary R. Markle Foundation, a nonprofit organization whose two programmatic interests are aging/adult development and social uses of media. A more complete report of the research can be obtained from Tora K. Bikson, the RAND Corporation, P.O. Box 2138, Santa Monica, CA 90406-2138. We thank Dr. Linda Garnets, who served as the task force facilitator; Dr. Leonie Huddy, who supervised the data collection; and Carolyn Funk, Laurie Skokan, and Sherry Schneider for their assistance in data collection and interpretation. We also thank the Los Angeles Department of Water and Power for its willing and skillful cooperation throughout the project.

at an age when—given current longevity projections—they can expect to live healthily for up to 20 additional years has increased to the point where it is clearly a normative life-span experience. The average retirement age for men is approximately 58, and less than 20% of men over 65 are in the paid labor force (Parnes et al., 1985). Of those who keep working, some continue as a matter of monetary necessity and some because they cannot imagine voluntarily withdrawing (Hayward & Hardy, 1985). It is that choice, now posed to the working adult population—whether to stay or leave, and how to accomplish such a voluntary change of state—that constitutes a major question of interest for social psychologists.

Accordingly, we designed the present research to study a group of men comparable in age and work background and relatively free from financial and health impediments, and to involve them in an exploration of the social psychological factors in the transition from worker to retiree status. We selected the sample so that approximately one-half of our participants would be men who had fairly recently made the shift from working to retired status and one-half would be men who, although eligible to do so, had not yet chosen to leave the workplace. We were particularly interested in how the experience of the retirement transition (the good things, the bad things, the issues in general) would be described if these two categories of people were brought into interaction with one another—individuals on either side of the "great retirement divide."

We had three major hypotheses. First, we supposed that people who had retired might suffer from the loss of contact with colleagues with whom they had developed meaningful social relationships, so that putting them back in touch with former work friends could itself be an interesting and positive experience (Larson, Mannell, & Zuzanek, 1986; Lee & Ishii-Kuntz, 1987). Second, we believed that those still employed but nearing retirement might benefit from involvement with the already retired, because the employed face an uncertain future—they might be worried about retiring and in doubt about what it might entail (Evans, Ekerdt, & Bosse, 1985; Fretz, Kluge, & Merikangas, 1986). Preretirement planning classes and workshops have proliferated and are readily available, but overwhelmingly they tend to focus on estate planning, financial concerns, medical coverage, and the like (Palmore, 1982). Though this focus is appropriate, in practice it has meant that the social psychological aspects of the process get short shrift from professionals in the retirement planning field. We expected, in contrast, that men facing this change might profit from exposure to a different sort of expertise—that found in people just like themselves who had recently undergone the retirement experience. The interchange among them would be likely to raise, and perhaps to help resolve, the social psychological issues of greatest concern.

Finally, because we thought that communication between peers in this general situation might be extremely important, we wanted to investigate what role, if any, new information and communication media that are computer-based could play in the retirement transition. Previous RAND research has explored the role of electronic communication among members of intact work groups in organizational settings (e.g., Bikson, 1987; Bikson, Eveland, & Gutek, in press; Eveland & Bikson, 1987, in press). These studies suggest that, for ongoing tasks, computer-based communications help overcome spatial and temporal barriers to effective interaction. However, because the studies did not involve random-assignment research designs, it was unclear to what degree the results were dependent on self-selection or extant task-group norms rather than the capabilities afforded by new electronic media. Further, no previous research has attempted to create links among retirees and employees. And—most important to our interest—we wanted to learn whether these new technologies might help in maintaining social networks, not simply task networks.

Procedures and Processes

The search for a research setting centered, for reasons of convenience, on our own locale, the greater Los Angeles area. We sought to draw all our participants from one workplace so that they would share, at least to some extent, a communication culture and common work experiences (Markus, 1987), which meant that we required a relatively large organization. Large size was also required in order to provide sufficient numbers of retired and close-to-retirement potential participants and to ensure that they did not already know each other well. Our search was successful, and the selected site met all desirable specifications beautifully.

The Los Angeles Department of Water and Power (DWP), established in its present form in 1925, is the largest municipal utility in the United States, employing about 12,000 people. Although administratively directed by a Board of Commissioners appointed by the mayor and city council of Los Angeles, it is financially self-sustaining and operationally separate from any other political jurisdictions. Its function is to provide water and electric service to all customers within the approximately 500-square-mile area of the city of Los Angeles—a responsibility that, in a semiarid and earthquake-prone region, has critical importance. Its domain of responsibility encompasses a vast geographic area ranging from the entire Owens Valley east of the Sierras (source of 80% of the water supply) to the Hoover Dam on the Colorado River (75% of the facilities of which are operated by DWP). The headquarters or general office building (familiarly dubbed GOB) is an attractive, modern high-rise office structure located in a downtown area that has recently undergone extensive urban redevelopment. All project participants either worked in or had retired from the GOB work setting.

Solicitation of participants was done by mail; all contact with the worker group utilized the GOB address, and the retired group was contacted through their home addresses. For a targeted sample size of 80 (20 per cell), we sent out an initial mailing to 200 prospects and a second solicitation about one month later to an additional 200. The solicitation list was compiled from the employing organization's records as a random selection among all those deemed eligible.

Eligibility criteria were that participants had to be male, and neither at the top executive levels nor at the nonexempt or blue-collar levels of the organization. The gender restriction was (regretfully) imposed because there were very few women in this situation, and their involvement in the work experience had been less lengthy, less continuous, and less psychologically central than for men in this cohort. The limitation of participants to the middle level of employment was dictated by two concerns. First, we wanted men who would have had some experience with committee or task-force activities and thus would be relatively comfortable in that setting. Second, we decided to avoid those accustomed to and experienced with being always "in charge"—those of singularly high status relative to other participants. From the list of those defined as eligible, we selected every third name among the retired, working chronologically backward by date of retirement; among the employees, we selected by moving chronologically forward by date of initial eligibility for retirement.

The solicitation letter set forth an additional requirement for participation: We hoped to recruit individuals who, if working, did not intend to retire during the project year, or who, if retired, did not intend to relocate out of the area soon. The solicitation letter was accompanied by a supportive letter from the DWP Retirement Plan Office and read, in part, as follows:

The study will focus on RETIREMENT—thinking about it, planning for it, and adjusting to it in a time when U.S. policies and organizational practices are also undergoing changes.

The unusual and, we hope, exciting aspect of the study is that we are looking to you as someone directly involved to provide the issues and explore their implications. What do you envision as the goods and bads, the major unknowns, the unexpected pitfalls and delights in retirement planning today? We ask you to consider joining us and other DWP colleagues in this effort. . . .

We are forming two retirement task forces. Members, half retired and half actively employed, will work together over the course of a year. Their task will be to consider, deliberate, probe, and develop a set of recommendations about preretirement planning—recommendations that can be addressed to persons nearing retirement, to organizations (including but not limited to DWP), and to professionals involved in preretirement planning. To realize this goal, the task force participants may meet, form subgroups, correspond, work hard, play a little, or whatever you decide will best accomplish our joint purpose.

Additionally, members of one of the two task forces will have the option of communicating with each other and conducting their business with the aid of computers. Each member of this electronic group will have access to a microcomputer. Because we are interested in the possible advantages and disadvantages of ELECTRONIC communication compared with more STANDARD media, we will randomly appoint task force volunteers to either group. We want you to consider participating whether or not you have used a computer before.

Task Force Formation

From those indicating interest, 79 men (39 employees, 40 retirees) were enrolled; each was randomly assigned to either the Standard or the Electronic Task Force. To assist the groups in getting under way, we scheduled a start-up meeting at GOB and a second about one month later for each task force. There was a third "booster" meeting for each group about halfway through the project year, as well as a closing reception for the two task forces together, to which each participant could bring a guest (many wives attended). At each of the scheduled gatherings we involved a clinical psychologist with expertise in organizational development to serve in the role of facilitator.

The first group meetings were convened in February 1987 and the closing reception was held in April 1988. These events defined the formal beginning and end of the project for participants, and they also bounded the data collection schedule. Detailed, highly structured interviews were conducted at baseline, at the end of the project, and at two interim points (the first in the summer, the second in late fall). Interviews with retired people were carried out at their homes while employees were interviewed at GOB. Four interviewers, all graduate students in UCLA's psychology department, were assigned approximately equal numbers of interviewees, distributed fairly evenly among the four cells of the research design. These four waves of data collection provided information about what project participants did with their time, the kinds of social and familial relationships in which they took part, how they viewed the adjustment to retirement, and their experiences with and perceptions of the project itself. Sociometric items were included in interview protocols to learn about emerging social structures within the task forces, while standardized psychological scales were administered at the project's beginning and end. This chapter primarily focuses on baseline data, because analyses of subsequent waves of data were not complete at this writing. However, for items of special interest to this volume, we have included some preliminary findings from later data collection efforts.

Participants

We will begin with general descriptive information about the 79 participants. Differences between retired and still-working individuals were so rare that only one need be acknowledged: The average

age of employees was 60.1, and of retirees, 62.8. Although statistically this is significant ($p < .01$), we think it is a trivial difference; the sample overall was a group of men aged 61½ (range 55-71). At the start of the study, of those still working, 12 (31%) had no retirement date in mind. Of the other 27, the average expected time to retirement was 2.3 years, with 12 (nearly half) of them intending to retire in the immediate poststudy year (1988). As of January 1987, the retired people had on the average been out of the work force two years, with a range from one month to four years.

Task force members constituted an exceedingly stable group, not necessarily representative of any other population. They were largely Anglo (66%—with 16% Asian, 10% Black, and 8% Hispanic) and Protestant (62%—with 22% Roman Catholic, 10% Jewish, and 6% "other or none"). All but four were native-born, including 37% native Angelenos. Only one man reported no education past high school, and fully 25% had received postcollege graduate training. Not surprising for this cohort, 85% had served in the military (78% during World War II, the remainder during the Korean War), for an average of two and a half years; a majority had served overseas. Nonetheless, these were largely local people—of those not born in Los Angeles, about 80% had moved to the area by 1952, and the most recent arrival located here over 20 years ago. Over half the men had lived in the same house more than 20 years—a surprising fact in the context of a rapidly changing metropolitan area which has more than tripled its population and, in major ways, altered its character during this same period.

Along with a generally stable demographic profile, we also observed an interpersonally stable profile. Five participants were divorced, one was recently widowed, two had never married; the remaining 90% were currently married and living with spouse. Of these 71 marriages, 82% were first marriages with an average duration of 35.3 years. Of the 13 for whom this was not a first marriage, the average duration of the current alliance was 21.5 years. Thus, in total, 90% of our participants had been in a current marital relationship for an average of 32.8 years (range 1-48). Eight participants were childless while the other 90% had had an average of 2.7 children (range 1-6); grandchildren had arrived for 70% of those who had been fathers, averaging about five per grandfather (range 1-13). One final indication of the strength of the Los Angeles connection for this sample was the fact that 92% of their adult children resided in California (86% of those within Los Angeles itself), as did a full 76% of their grandchildren.

Of greater project relevance was employment history. Here also the participants demonstrated singular stability. On average, these men began their first full-time employment at age 22 and worked steadily thereafter (until retirement for those who had retired). There were 11 (14%) whose only employment was with DWP; they began their DWP careers either immediately on completion of their education or on termination of military service. The other 86% had held an average of 2.7 jobs elsewhere for 10.1 years before securing employment with DWP. For the group as a whole, the number of years worked at DWP averaged 32 in 1987 (range 10-45 years).

As a check on our selection procedures—because two crucial concerns for people considering retirement are money and health —we obtained a self-assessment of these two factors from subjects in the initial interview. Asked to indicate which statement "best describes your ability to get along on your income," 56% chose "I always have money left over," and another 30% chose "I have enough, with a little extra sometimes." Only 14% of the sample assessed their financial situation as barely or not quite adequate. Objectively, all our indicators place these people, whether retired or still employed, in the middle or upper-middle strata socioeconomically. As to health, only five participants (6%) stated that their health was a matter of some concern; the others indicated that their present physical situation was either excellent (46%) or included "a minor chronic condition which is under control" (48%).

Finally, to check on the success of random assignment to the two experimental conditions, we asked subjects at baseline to let us know which among a number of electronic technologies they currently used. Their responses (see Table 4.1) showed prior computer experience to be much the same across conditions. About half in each task force had had some sort of contact with batch-processing mainframe computers at work, and about a quarter had tried using a small home computer, typically for games. None had ever used computer-based communications. The responses, moreover, failed to support popular views that retired people—or older adults in general—are reluctant to adopt new technologies as they enter the marketplace. Perhaps Kamptner's research (this volume) on favorite possessions of older men helps explain these counterstereotypic findings.

Table 4.1
Percentage in Each Group Who Use Various Technologies

Technology	Retired	Employed	Standard	Electronic
Calculator	93	100	97	95
Cable TV	56	41	41	56
VCR	80	74	74	80
Compact disc player	10	8	8	10
Phone answering machine	37	36	31	41
Automated teller machine	59	51	56	54
Computer video games	22	18	15	24
Computer at work (ever used)	54	54	54	54
Computer at home (ever used)	33	18	24	27

Task Development

How did this rather singular group of men undertake to accomplish the task we assigned to them? Recall that one-half the workers and one-half the retirees were randomly placed in what became known as the "Electronic" and the "Standard" Task Forces. (The one group with 19 rather than 20 members was the employed half of the Standard Task Force, and there were no differences on any of the demographic background variables between the members of the two task forces). At the initial meeting of each Task Force, the following written statement of the Task Force charge was provided to each participant:

> The above-named task force, convened in February 1987, is charged to attempt within the ensuing year to accomplish the following goals: Identify, consider, and explore any aspects of pre-retirement planning which might constitute issues or problems for persons approaching retirement;
>
> Develop a set or sets of policy recommendations to ease the transition to retirement—recommendations addressed to persons anticipating retirement, to employing organizations, and to professionals specializing in pre-retirement planning.

After the introductory presentation of the project and its rationale (which also was the occasion for the collection of signed consent forms), we received instant confirmation of our notion that the retirement transition importantly involves social psychological issues. Independently in both task forces, one of the first questions coming from the participants was "Why aren't there any women here?" We reiterated our reasons (noted above) for the exclusion, adding that the task force could if it wished include in its work any additional people it considered to be central to the project task. Statements were made and strongly affirmed in both groups to the effect that retirement is not an individual but a family decision and process. With the permission and eager endorsement of our participants, we have recently collected independent data in the form of a mail-in questionnaire from those among the 71 spouses who wished to volunteer their input ($n = 49$, 69% of the total).

Further corroboration of the importance of social psychological dimensions of retirement was more direct. At the first task force meeting, members were asked to proffer some examples of retirement issues of the sort that should be addressed by the group in its work, and they generated lists that included the issues in Table 4.2. In the month between the first and second meetings, each task force planned and collected a "Retirement Issues Questionnaire" from its members as a vehicle for prioritizing and grouping the issues. When collated and examined, the survey results and discussion led both task forces to conclude that six categories would encompass the topics of concern: health, finances, use of time, family and social adjustment, self-esteem or self-image, and the retirement planning process itself.

Accordingly, at the second meeting each task force established an organizational structure involving six study groups; for each group, one member was elected to be chair. The six designated chairs then constituted a Task Force Steering Committee, with one of its number designated by the group as the overall Task Force Chair. With this structure in place, the participants were on their own.

Table 4.2
Initial Retirement Issues Generated by the Task Forces

Health	Sexuality
Finances	Letting go of the job
Understanding and timing retirement	Attitudes toward retirement
Family adjustment	Housing, relocation
Time management and use	Mortality, religion
Self-impact	Continuing education
Recreation, hobbies, leisure	Community resources, information
Social adjustment	Part-time work, volunteer work

There was one quite notable structural difference between the two task forces. Study group membership was by self-selection in both, so that individuals chose to associate with a topic area they found most interesting, felt most knowledgeable about, and/or considered most problematic. In both task forces also, each study group's membership was roughly half workers and half retirees—in the Standard Task Force by design, in the other by happy accident. But one thing was not accidental at all; at the second task force meeting, as study group assignments were being worked out in the Electronic Task Force, the question of multiple study group membership arose and was answered in the affirmative. Thus, on average, the study group size was larger in the Electronic than in the Standard Task Force (10 versus 6), as a consequence of the fact that 42% of its members chose to involve themselves in more than one study group (most commonly in two). One intriguing possibility is that the prospect of electronic media availability shaped expectations of what one might be able to do and with how many people one might be able to communicate effectively.

One other preliminary item indicates the participants' situation at the start of the project. At the first interview we asked individuals the open-ended question: "Why did you agree to participate in this year-long study?" The most frequently cited reason was either that they wanted to give information about the transition to retirement or to get information about it. Fortunately, it was the retired people who were in the former category and those who had not yet retired in the latter. Some also reported their motivation as plain curiosity, either about the RAND Corporation or about the research process. There were also some who said they participated because they were hoping to be in the Electronic Task Force and use a computer. It turned out that about 10% of the people assigned by chance to the Standard Task Force had volunteered because they wanted a computer, compared with less than 5% in the Electronic group. Nevertheless, the research experience was compelling enough to sustain everyone's interest, for attrition was zero.

Results and Discussion

Because social psychological issues involved in the transition to retirement form the focus of this research, we have organized the findings under four of the issue categories devised by the participants themselves: use of time, family and social adjustment, self-construct, and retirement planning processes. (Although health and financial matters also emerged as important, they fall outside the scope of this research.)

That social psychological concerns figured explicitly in their thinking about retirement was shown in the initial interview responses of retired participants to the open-ended question: "What has been the best thing about retirement? And what has been the worst?" Examples of common responses to these questions are shown below:

Best Things:

- Being creative (my wife says it's another name for being bad)
- No daily routine—not stagnating
- Being your own boss
- No pressure
- Relief of responsibility
- No obligations, except to yourself and your family
- Palm Springs!

Worst Things:

- Nothing bad about it!
- Miss the work
- Miss my friends at work
- My wife is worried about the money
- Wife's criticism of my activities
- Getting my wife to do things
- Making up my mind what I'm going to do tomorrow

It is interesting that the modal response to the negative question was "nothing bad about it," with nearly 40% of retirees giving this reply; the most common advantage of retirement, cited by over 50%, was not having to live with an imposed schedule. But whether participants cited positive or negative experiences or both, social psychological themes dominated their descriptions of the transition to retirement.

Use of Time

One key theme was the use of time. While retirement removes job pressures and frees employees from their daily routines, it may at the same time reduce opportunities for meaningful activity—

Table 4.3
Mean Satisfaction with How Time Is Spent

Item	Retirees	Employees	df	F
Use of time	4.0	3.6	1,77	3.28*
Time spent with spouse	4.8	4.1	1,70	12.36**
Time spent with close friends	4.2	4.1	—

NOTE: 1 = very dissatisfied, 5 = very satisfied.
*p < .05; **p < .001.

particularly for people whose time has long been structured by regular work commitments (Ekerdt, 1986). Our research, therefore, sought to learn how project participants—both retirees and employees—regarded their use of time. The initial interviews collected fairly detailed reports of daily schedules for a "typical" weekday and weekend during the two weeks prior to the research visit. Interviewees were also asked to indicate how satisfied they were with their use of time in general, and with time spent with their spouses and with close friends in particular (see Table 4.3).

We found that retirees were significantly more satisfied than employees with their overall use of time—and especially so for time spent with a spouse. There were no differences between groups in satisfaction with time spent with close friends.

An examination of activity records led us to believe that differences in satisfaction favoring retirees might result more from their ability to vary how their time was spent than from differences in the kinds of things they did. For example—contrary to what many of them had anticipated—retired individuals did not systematically spend more time than their employed counterparts in activities such as reading, sports, or home and yard tasks. For a more thorough analysis of activity patterns of both groups, see Bikson, Goodchilds, Huddy, Eveland, and Schneider, (1989).

More noteworthy were differences in within-group variability among retirees across activity categories. Tests of homogeneity of variance showed retirees, as a group, to be significantly more heterogeneous in their distribution of time across the activities we studied than the employees in our sample, and this was true for both weekdays or weekends. Initially we had supposed that weekend activities for the two groups would be more similar, given the absence of work constraints. However, it appears that the need to reserve parts of Saturdays and Sundays for tasks that don't readily fit into the work week limited the range of weekend activities for employees as well.

Similar comparisons generated similar patterns of findings about whom people spend time with during a typical week. In general, retired men spent significantly more time with their wives than employed men did ($F(1,70) = 3.77, p < .05$), particularly in the afternoons. However, the two groups did not differ regarding the amount of time they spent with other family members, with current or former work colleagues, or with other friends. Rather, differences in the variability of how time was distributed among social partners were far more salient; again, retirees as a group were substantially more diverse, as evidenced in tests of homogeneity of variance.

Finally, while such variation characterized the retirees in our study at one point in time, we think it reflects within-individual variations among retirees over time. In response to questions about whether their schedules had undergone major changes in the past year and whether they were likely to undergo major changes in the coming year, retirees were significantly more likely than employees to answer both in the affirmative.

Family and Social Adjustment

As noted above, the retired men in this study were more satisfied with their use of time—especially time spent with a spouse—than were employed men. An important question for family adjustment, however, is whether more time spent with the spouse contributes to a happy marital situation. From the male perspective, at least, the answer was definitely yes. That is, those who reported a greater proportion of time spent with their wives tended to perceive themselves more as part of a pair ($r = .72, p < .0001$) and were significantly happier with their marital arrangements than were others, regardless of employment status ($t = 2.94, p < .005$; see also Funk, 1988).

Representative of this view was one retiree's answer in response to an interview question: "I'm enjoying being with my wife—we're together all the time." While we do not have comparable data from wives, we were able to solicit their open-ended comments using a mailed form. The typical responses below suggest that wives may view the adjustment to retirement somewhat differently:

- I think it's hardest on the women who don't work and then all of a sudden they have this man sitting around all day, day in and day out.
- Many people make the mistake of moving to a smaller house, and then they have no space of their own—they get on each other's nerves.
- Lack of space—I have a need for my own space and he has a need for his.
- We allow each other "free space."
- Have days when he leaves the house, to do—whatever.
- Before my husband retired, I would have the radio on most of the day while I did my work. . . . My husband does not like the radio playing—so now I have a tiny radio in my pocket and wear earphones. (It works fine.)

It is interesting that many of the spouses of project participants seemed to think about adjusting to retirement in terms of its implications for shared space rather than shared time. However, both may be reflections of what Powell Lawton (this volume) has called the "dialectic of autonomy and security." As one retiree's wife wrote, "After this siege of earthquakes, weather, and fire, I am very happy to be married to such a lovely man. I hate the loss of some of my independence, but sure like the fact that I have someone to help care about me."

To get an overall assessment of how such differences have or will be worked out, we asked married participants—both retired and employed—two questions: "How did [will] your wife adjust to your retirement?" and "How did [will] you adjust?" Responses, summarized in Table 4.4, suggest that after a year or more in retirement, the adjustment was regarded as a relatively easy one by retirees—both for themselves and for their wives. Those who had not yet retired viewed the adjustment as more difficult—marginally so, in their own case, and significantly so for their spouses. These findings

Table 4.4
Mean Assessment of the Retirement Adjustment

Item	Retirees	Employees	df	F
Wife's adjustment to your retirement	4.3	3.6	1,70	9.16*
Your adjustment to your retirement	4.3	3.9	1,77	2.72

NOTE: 1 = very difficult process; 5 = very easy process.
*$p < .01$.

suggest that family adjustment to retirement may be more difficult in anticipation than in actuality.

In addition to change in the relationship to a marriage partner, we also expected to see adjustments in the broader social contacts of the participants across time. The initial interview, therefore, also collected information about "close friends," defined as people (other than spouses) to whom participants felt especially close or with whom they spent a lot of time. In each of the subsequent data collection periods, interviewees were asked to update the information by describing any new close friends. Additionally, all interviews included a series of items tapping relationships among task force members—whether or not they recognized one another at least by name or face, whether they knew one another, and whether they had been in contact during the two weeks prior to data collection.

At the first meeting, participants on average recognized over a third of the other members of their task force but knew only about 10% of them. Very few instances of actual contact were reported. In accord with our initial assumptions, we found marked differences between employed and retired members of both task forces. Measures of recognition, knowing, and (especially) contact were substantially lower for retirees than for those still employed. Further, derived measures of sociometric centrality showed retirees in both the task forces to be relatively peripheral.

On the other hand, we did not expect—and we did not observe—differences in the total number of individuals named by retirees or employees as close friends. We did find interesting differences in types of friendships reported. We had hypothesized that retirees would tend to lose contact with people they had gotten to know through work; this view received partial confirmation from open-ended comments about the "worst things" in retirement and from the sociometric analyses mentioned above. But we supposed, in contrast, that retirees would tend to make more friends in their neighborhoods. What we learned, first, was that retirees appeared to stay in touch with close friends from work: this category—friends that one initially met at work, that is, colleagues—accounted on average for 34% of the close friends named by retirees and only 17% of those named by employees ($F(1,77) = 5.2, p < .05$) in the initial interview.

We also learned that, during the project year, retirees made more new friends than their employed peers did, both in the neighborhood and among colleagues (see Table 4.5). These data led us to wonder how good the workplace is, after all, as a place to make friends. Informal observations suggest that employees are quite busy with task-driven interactions and may not have time for developing close friendships—at least not in comparison to the time available to retirees, whose social worlds are relatively richer.

To support this interpretation, we examined responses to another question that had been repeated throughout the project. In each interview, we asked, "How satisfied are you with the amount of contact you have with [other] retired people?" We had expected that their answers would show initial dissatisfaction, reflecting retirees' loss of contact with colleagues; and we had hoped, as a result of the task force intervention, to see positive change—especially among retired respondents.

We also asked retirees to answer a second question: "How satisfied are you with the amount of contact you have with employees?," initially assuming that employees had more than ample opportunity

Table 4.5
Mean Number of New Friends at Project's End

Variable	Retirees	Employees	F
Number of new friends added	1.40	.73	2.37
Number who are colleagues	.50	.08	5.61*
Number who are neighbors	.13	0	3.64*

NOTE: *df* = 1,77 for each comparison.
*p < .05.

Table 4.6
Mean Satisfaction with Contact with Retirees

Group	Time 1	Time 2	Time 3	Time 4
Retirees	3.8	3.9	3.8	3.9
Employees	3.6	3.5	4.1	4.2

NOTE: Higher means indicate greater satisfaction on 1–5 scale.
F for time: $F(3,219) = 2.58, p < .05$. F for time $\times$ status: $F(3,219) = 4.21, p < .01$.

Table 4.7
Mean Satisfaction with Contact with Employees

Group	Time 1	Time 2	Time 3	Time 4
Retirees	3.9	3.9	3.8	3.9
Employees	—	4.0	4.3	4.4

NOTE: Higher means indicate greater satisfaction on 1–5 scale.
F for time: $F(1,74) = 4.74, p < .05$. F for time $\times$ status: $F(1,148) = 3.37, p < .10$.

to remain in touch with one another. In the second and subsequent interviews, we included the latter question in the employee protocol as well. As the means in Table 4.6 illustrate, retirees reported a relatively high and stable level of satisfaction with their contact with one another. However, employees reported increasing satisfaction about contact with retirees over the course of the project, reflected in the highly significant time-by-status interaction term. This pattern of results was found again in Table 4.7. That is, employees seemed to derive substantial social benefit from interactions with other employees as well as with retirees.

Self-Construct

As described above, project participants had a long, stable history of participation in the work force and in DWP employment. Both researchers and participants wondered how, if at all, the transition to retirement might affect the way such individuals thought and felt about themselves.

We explored this issue in a number of ways: by administering psychological scales to measure relevant constructs such as self-esteem (Rosenberg, 1965), morale (Lawton, 1975), loneliness (Russell, Peplau, & Cutrona, 1980), and the like; by asking standardized interview questions designed to tap identification with one's occupation and organization as well as the perceived centrality of work; and by providing opportunities for open-ended comment. Like Dreyer (this volume), we found little variance on the psychological scales, which were highly intercorrelated. The range of scores was much like what would be obtained from any normal adult sample, and initial means did not differentiate retirees from employees (see Bikson et al., 1989, for more details). The following paragraphs focus on data that are more closely related to work identity.

To learn about extent of involvement in work roles, initial interviews asked participants to assume they were introducing themselves to a stranger and inquired:

How likely is it that you would describe yourself as a/an "[occupational title]"?

How likely is it that you would describe yourself as a "DWP man"?

And how else might you introduce yourself?

Responses to the first two items were given on five-point scales; responses to the third question—if any—were recorded verbatim. We also asked interviewees to judge how central a role work had played in their lives and the extent to which it was separate from, or intermingled with, their social lives.

First, here are some open-ended answers from retirees about how they would describe themselves, to illustrate the varied social identities they held in addition to those defined by their major employment:

• Recycled teenager
• Investor
• Racehorse owner
• Churchgoer
• Grandparent
• Collector

- Air Force man
- Screenwriter
- By name, of course!

These responses should not, however, be taken to mean that retirees have ceased to identify themselves with work roles and devalued their importance. On the contrary, as the data in Table 4.8 indicate, retirees and employees did not systematically differ with respect to the prominence of work roles or the degree of their integration into social life. Both retirees and employees, however, were less likely to identify with specific occupational roles than with the employing organization ($F(1,77) = 23.75$, $p < .0001$). Finally, within the retired group, those most likely to claim the "retiree" identity were those most strongly identified with the organization for which they formerly worked ($r = +.54$, $p < .001$). Retirement for these men, then, seems to represent the addition of another role to one's social repertoire rather than the loss of previously meaningful roles. (This interpretation is consistent with findings about social adjustment in retirement discussed in the prior section.)

Retirement Planning Processes

When this experiment began, there was general agreement among participants that careful advance planning of retirement is likely to yield positive results. Moreover, retirees believed there was information to give, and employees believed there was information to get, that would be helpful in managing this transition. In view of our

Table 4.8
Mean Ratings of Involvement with Work

Item	Retirees	Employees	F
Identification with the organization	3.9	3.9	—
Identification with the occupation	2.8	3.2	1.25
Centrality of work in your life	4.0	3.7	1.27
Social life separate from work life	3.3	3.7	2.04

NOTE: **Higher numbers mean greater amounts, on 1–5 scales;** *df* **= 1,77 for each comparison.**

discovery that retirement seemed to be more negative in anticipation than afterward, we were particularly interested in what retirees and employees had to say about retirement planning processes.

In the initial interview, a number of questions addressed these processes, either retrospectively or prospectively. Additionally, we asked whether project participants regarded themselves as planful people on the whole, and how much they did or would look forward to retirement. We also encouraged mailed-in comments from wives of married participants about the planning process.

Qualitative information from spouses illustrated the differences in perspective before and after the transition. For example, wives of two retired participants made comments that showed diverse orientations toward planning but comparably positive outcomes:

> I pre-read everything I could. Took the classes on retirement—twice. Attended classes at Pasadena City College on "Sex after Sixty." Articles in *Modern Maturity* were very helpful. We started at least 5 years before. If we are not doing the things we love, we learn to love the things we do.

> We didn't do too much planning, and we've been surprised at how smoothly it's going. We're never bored.

Wives of two employed participants, in contrast, made comments suggesting that even to approach the planning process can be quite difficult:

> It's the biggest puzzle of our lives. We're in a total state of confusion.

> My husband refuses to talk about retirement.

Quantitative data collected from task force members themselves tended to mirror this pattern (see Table 4.9). These data, like prospective and retrospective assessments of adjustment (see Table 4.4) suggest that retirees saw themselves as somewhat more planful and regarded their planning as more adequate than employees expect theirs will be.

When we examined intercorrelations among the items of Table 4.9, we found a significant positive association ($r = .44, p < .0001$) between planning adequately for retirement and looking forward to it (see Evans et al., 1985). To explore whether advance planning leads to positive views of retirement or whether the reverse is more

Table 4.9
Mean Responses to Retirement Planning Items

Item	Retirees	Employees	F
Are you a planner?	3.4	3.0	2.56
Adequacy of your retirement planning	3.8	3.0	2.71*
Do/did you look forward to retirement?	3.75	3.4	2.2

NOTE: **Higher numbers mean greater amounts, on 1–5 scales; *df* = 1,77 for each comparison.**
*p < .10.

likely to be true (i.e., that positive views of retirement facilitate the planning process), we studied the employee group in more detail.

About one third of the employees in the project had made a decision to retire in 1988. Another third of this group had set a date between 1989 and 1993, while the final third had not yet set a retirement date. We treated this derived variable, "retirement imminence," as a three-level ordinal measure; employees who had decided to retire within a year were given a value of 1 on this measure and those who didn't know when they would retire were given a 3, with the others receiving a value of 2. We found that this variable was negatively correlated with looking forward to retirement ($r = -.51$, $p < .001$); that is, employees who were least settled on a retirement date were those who viewed that transition least positively.

Looking in more detail at the employees, we found that within this subgroup the correlation between looking forward to retirement and planning for it adequately was higher ($r = .55$) than for the participants as a whole. Further, within this subset, we found significantly negative associations between the length of time individuals had been working for DWP and both planning for ($r = -.33$, $p < .05$) and looking forward to ($r = -.32$, $p < .05$) retirement. This was true in spite of the fact that age of the employee and years in the work force were positively related ($r = .51$, $p < .001$). It is not surprising that a similar negative association characterized years in the work force and self-assessed ease of retirement. Although the subset of employees was small ($N = 39$) and the findings inconclusive, the general consistency of the patterns leads us to believe that unwarrantedly negative views of the retirement transition may interfere with employees' planning processes.

Conclusion

As we indicated at the beginning of this chapter, final data analyses have yet to be carried out, and so conclusions drawn here must be tentative and subject to modification in the light of future findings. Additionally, it is important to keep in mind the uniqueness of the subject population—managerial and professional male employees of one corporate setting, all of whom demonstrated long-standing commitment to one geographic location and truly exceptional stability in life-style and interpersonal/family relationships. With these caveats in mind, it is worth revisiting the main questions that guided this research in order to review what we have learned.

Both the quantitative and qualitative data discussed above testify to the substantial part that social and psychological issues play in the retirement experience. It appears that the process can be viewed as a role transition rather than a role loss, and that the adjustments to be made are not especially negative ones. However, the transition appears to be negative in anticipation—and more so, for employees who have invested the most time in the organization.

If this is true, then, interaction among individuals on both sides of the retirement transition might be expected to help alleviate employee concerns. That, in fact, is what we found when we looked at responses at the end of the project to the question posed in the beginning: How much did/do you look forward to retirement? As Table 4.10 shows, retirees' responses were unchanged; employees, however, gave significantly more positive responses at the end of the task force year.

Table 4.10 also sheds light on the third major research question —whether computer-based networks can foster effective communicative interactions among employees and retirees. While all employees showed increasingly favorable attitudes toward retirement over time, the effect was more marked in the electronic condition (as evidenced by the interaction effect for work status and experimental condition.)

Sociometric data obtained in interviews suggested that, while computer-based communications did not replace other types of interaction, they served to increase the total number of contacts that task force members had with one another and facilitated group activity. While level of name or face recognition had increased within both

Table 4.10
Mean Rating of Anticipation of Retirement

Group	Time 1	Time 4
Retirees		
electronic	3.6	3.6
standard	3.9	3.9
Employees		
electronic	3.6	4.2
standard	3.2	3.5

NOTE: Higher numbers, on the 1–5 scale, indicate the respondent looks forward to retirement more.
F for time: $F(1,75) = 4.48$, $p < .05$. F for time × status: $F(1,75) = 5.57$, $p < .05$. F for condition × status: $F(1,75) = 3.23$, $p < .10$.

task forces over the year, for instance, recognition measures had increased to over 90% for retirees in the electronic condition, whereas, initially, these individuals had only been recognized by about 10% of the other participants (see Figure 4.1). The same trends were even more striking in contact measures (see Figure 4.2). As a result, retirees were far more central in the sociometric structure of the Electronic Task Force by the project's end than were retirees in the Standard Task Force, who remained relatively peripheral.

Project participants themselves made similar judgments about the facilitative role of electronic networks. When asked to assess the extent to which their experimental group assignment helped or hindered their task force, the electronic group found its condition substantially more beneficial in the long run than did the standard group (see Table 4.11). While the assigned experimental condition most profoundly affected retirees, the interaction of time and experimental condition was noteworthy among employees as well.

While we cannot yet draw any definitive conclusions, we believe the findings to date support the value of bringing individuals on either side of the retirement transition into contact with one another. We also believe that new electronic technology may contribute to the development and maintenance of social networks that bridge this divide.

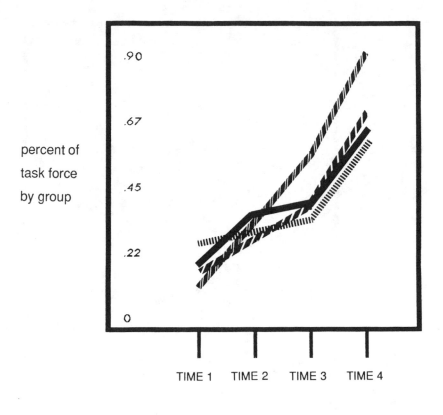

percent of
task force
by group

TIME 1   TIME 2   TIME 3   TIME 4

GROUP LEGEND: electronic employees
electronic retirees
standard employees
standard retirees

Figure 4.1. Extent of name or face recognition by other task force members.

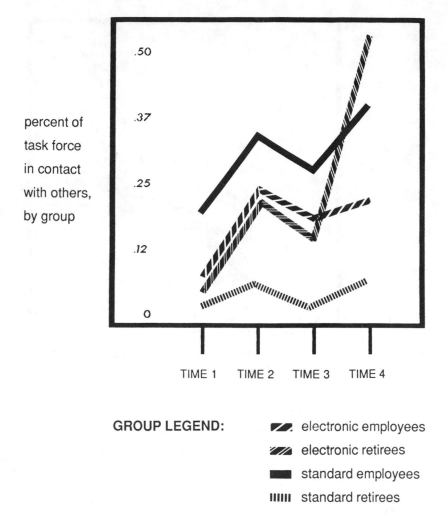

Figure 4.2. Extent of contact with other task force members (prior two weeks).

Table 4.11
Mean Rating of Impact of Experimental Manipulation

Group	Time 2	Time 3	Time 4
Retirees			
electronic	3.9	4.0	4.6
standard	3.1	2.9	2.7
Employees			
electronic	3.3	3.5	3.9
standard	3.8	4.1	3.7

NOTE: Higher numbers, on the 1–5 scale, mean the condition was perceived as more helpful.
F for condition: $F(1,70) = 7.58$, $p < .001$. F for condition $\times$ status: $F(1,70) = 16.51$, $p < .001$. F for condition $\times$ time: $F(2,140) = 10.32$, $p < .001$.

References

Bikson, T. K. (1987). Understanding the implementation of office technology. In R. Kraut (Ed.), *Technology and the transformation of white collar work* (pp. 155-176). Hillsdale, NJ: Lawrence Erlbaum.

Bikson, T. K., Eveland, J. D., & Gutek, B. A. (in press). Flexible interactive technologies for multiperson tasks. In M. Olson (Ed.), *Computer support for work group collaboration*. Hillsdale, NJ: Lawrence Erlbaum.

Bikson, T. K., Goodchilds, J. D., Huddy, L., Eveland, J. D., & Schneider, S. (1989). *Introducing interactive technology in the retirement transition: A field experiment* (Research Rep. no. R-3706-MF). Santa Monica, CA: RAND.

Ekerdt, D. J. (1986). The Bush ethic: Moral continuity between work and retirement, *Gerontologist, 26,* 239-244.

Evans, L., Ekerdt, D. J., & Bosse, R. (1985). Proximity to retirement and anticipatory involvement: Findings from the Normative Aging Study. *Journal of Gerontology, 40,* 368-374.

Eveland, J. D., & Bikson, T. K. (1987). Evolving electronic communication networks: An empirical assessment. In *Office technology and people* (pp. 103-128). Amsterdam: Elsevier Science Publications.

Eveland, J. D., & Bikson, T. K. (in press). Work group structures and computer support. *ACM Transactions on Office Systems*.

Fretz, B. R., Kluge, N. A., & Merikangas, M. W. (1986). *Correlates of preretirement anxiety in the near and remote phases*. Unpublished manuscript, University of Maryland, College Park.

Funk, C. L. (1988). *Perceptions of marital togetherness and companionship: A study of older men's marital relationships* (Research Rep. no. P-7456). Santa Monica, CA: RAND.

Hayward, M. D., & Hardy, M. A. (1985). Early retirement processes among older men. *Research on Aging, 17,* 491-515.

Larson, R., Mannell, R., & Zuzanek, J. (1986). Daily well-being of older adults with friends and family. *Psychology and Aging, 2,* 117-126.

Lawton, M. P. (1975). Philadelphia Geriatric Center morale scale: A revision. *Journal of Gerontology, 30,* 85-89.

Lee, G. R., & Ishii-Kuntz, M. (1987). Social interaction, loneliness, and emotional well-being among the elderly. *Research on Aging, 4,* 459-482.

Markus, M. L. (1987). Toward a "critical mass" theory of interactive media: Universal access, interdependence, and diffusion. *Communication Research, 14,* 491-511.

Palmore, E. B. (1982). Preparation for retirement: The impact of preretirement programs on retirement and leisure. In N. J. Osgood (Ed.), *Life after work* (pp. 330-341). New York: Praeger.

Parnes, H. S., Crowley, J. E., Hauvin, R. J., Less, L. J., Morgan, W. R., Mott, I. L., & Nestel, G. (1985). *Retirement among American men.* Lexington, MA: D. C. Heath.

Rosenberg, M. (1965). *Society and the adolescent self image.* Princeton, NJ: Princeton University Press.

Russell, D. L., Peplau, A., & Cutrona, L. E. (1980). The revised UCLA loneliness scale: Concurrent and discriminant validity evidence. *Journal of Personality and Social Psychology, 39,* 472-480.

5

Postretirement Life Satisfaction

PHILIP H. DREYER

This chapter focuses on two venerable topics of study in the field of social gerontology: "life satisfaction" and retirement from work. In studying such topics, it is important to approach them in a truly developmental manner, so the chapter begins with a discussion of the developmental approach in research. And as a prologue to that discussion, I offer a brief "life review" of my own professional development, which led me to an interest in these topics.

A life review is a process of reminiscence, reevaluation, and reconstruction by which we strive to make sense of our lives (Erikson, 1959)—in my case it represents the personal side of my professional activities. I was introduced to the study of aging by my graduate school mentors, Bernice Neugarten and Robert Havighurst, at the University of Chicago during the tumultuous years of the late 1960s. However, at that time I was committed to the study of children and adolescents and did not specialize in the area of adult development and aging. My conversion to the study of old people and the process of aging began while I was teaching at Emory University, which was then starting up a graduate program in developmental psychology. I found myself vigorously defending a life-cycle approach, which would have to include courses on adulthood and old age, and as a result I was drafted to teach those courses.

I was pleasantly amazed in those years to find how much of the gerontological literature I had absorbed by osmosis during my years as an assistant to Bob Havighurst. Later I began to participate in the discussions of the so-called West Virginia group of psychologists, who espoused a "life-span" point of view and considered "development" as an organic process involving both continuities and changes across the entire span of development. They paid relatively less attention to the unique events of the first 12 years of life and more attention to those early behaviors and psychological patterns that held up over the long stretch of adulthood. Thus childhood was not seen as the determining period in life, but as the first of several phases, each of which built on earlier ones with its own special emphases, developmental tasks, and psychosocial characteristics (e.g., Schaie, 1970).

On top of this professional socialization, my ultimate conversion to the field of gerontology was strengthened by my experiences teaching in an Elderhostel program at Pitzer College. There I had the pleasure of offering a course on "The Family" to two very bright women, aged 80 and 84. I brought them the basics of family sociology, family systems, and family therapy, while they presented me with their personal experiences and special wisdom. The result was electrifying and humbling and delightful.

The Development Approach

From my professional experience I have concluded that it is very important how we operationally define the term *developmental*. There is a crucial conceptual difference between studying the processes of aging or development and what I will call the "psychology of age groups." In the latter enterprise, one studies a particular age group and describes its peculiarities and potential in detail—for instance, as Arnold Gesell (1928) did so well in his descriptions of young children. In the developmental approach, by contrast, the detailed description of an age group is ignored in favor of investigating the processes of change that make this age different from periods that came before it. This is the kind of research that Piaget (1951,

1954; Piaget & Inhelder, 1969) did in his studies of young children, where his goal was to find the "logical invariants" in children's ways of understanding the world. Ideally, the developmental approach is longitudinal, following individuals for many years over the course of their lives, although useful insights can also be obtained from well-constructed cross-sectional studies of several different age groups at one point in time. The important issue here is to distinguish between research that is descriptive of a particular age group and research that attempts to understand the processes of continuity and change. While both approaches can be informative, in my view only the latter are truly "developmental."

Often psychologists who come from a human learning or social psychology background assume that, by recording the ages of their subjects and testing for a main effect of age, they are conducting developmental research. The classic case of this, which occurs far too often, is the researcher who has specialized in studying the minds of college sophomores and who then learns that a research grant can be obtained if he or she adds old people to the study and tests for age differences. Often, in this situation, researchers use exactly the same instruments and procedures with the older people as with the younger, claiming that scientific control requires such consistency.

The results of such research miss two basic points. First, subjects of different ages have lived in historically different social and physical environments and, therefore, have had different life experiences, which may alter their responses to experimental procedures. Thus differences in statistical results may not reflect age or developmental differences so much as differences in historical backgrounds—a "cohort effect" (Schaie, 1970, 1977). Second, whatever the results of the study, there is no way to understand the causes of such differences or lack of differences. The results stand alone, out of context, lacking in ecological validity and meaning. However, a naive investigator, committed to a particular test or concept, may not be concerned about the process of aging or about how subjects' performance may be influenced by developmental processes, and may interpret statistically significant results as being an "age effect."

My goal here is to point out the fallacy of believing that developmental processes are ones that are simply correlates of age, and to caution against mistaking the "psychology of an age group" for "developmental psychology." Thus, when the social psychology of old people is studied, there may be phenomena that are unique to a particular group of old people and are very interesting, but that are not relevant in helping us understand the developmental processes of change over time.

Many of these research issues may best be approached by social psychologists, because the real conundrum in research about aging is how to unravel the person-environment interaction. To date, the biological sciences have had a predominant influence in our study of aging. The assumption has been that the biological processes of growing older exert a major influence upon an individual's psychological state, and we have looked upon social behavior largely as coping strategies that people use to deal with the infirmities and changes of an aging body. It is time for us to reconsider these effects and to begin a conscientious study of how social factors influence the psychological state of a person independent of health.

For example, why is it that some old people are truly laid low by their physical health problems, while others seem to ignore and even transcend them? Another question is this: What are the advantages and disadvantages of social group membership for older people? Today we tend to put older people together in group living arrangements, usually to make nursing care more efficient, to increase security, and to provide companionship. What research is there on the effects of such living arrangements? Might it be that the social behavior of older people is a more important factor in psychological functioning than even health? Also, what is the effect upon individuals of sharp changes in social roles and responsibilities brought about by such life events as retirement from work or death of a spouse? To what extent are age-graded norms important in people's lives, and to what extent have we reached a point in the United States where the elderly have become a true subculture with its own distinctive lifestyle, language, norms, customs, and social structure—what Margaret Mead (1978) might call a "postfigurative" culture?

In attacking these many questions, the opportunities for social psychological research seem particularly promising. To illustrate this potential, the rest of this chapter focuses on the key topics of life satisfaction and retirement from employment. Tying these topics together, I will discuss life satisfaction as a variable in research on retirement, review data illustrating the changing nature of retirement, and present some recent research findings about how measures of life satisfaction seem to be related to events and behavior in retirement.

The Measurement and Meaning of Life Satisfaction

While the field of gerontology is little more than four decades old, the concepts of "adjustment" and "life satisfaction" have been two of the field's oldest and most popular research topics. The concept of personal adjustment was delineated by Cavan, Burgess, Havighurst, and Goldhamer (1949) in a volume called *Personal Adjustment in Old Age* as the changes that an individual experienced in response to changing conditions in the environment. For those researchers, in that time, the primary changes involved the shift from rural to urban living environments and the relinquishing of work roles as a result of retirement.

> Personal adjustment to ageing, or to other changes in one's self or one's environment, may be defined as the individual's restructuring of his attitudes and behavior in response to a new situation in such a way as to integrate the expression of his aspirations with the expectations and demands of society. This definition stresses the fact that adjustment represents an integrated reaction of the person as a member of society to a new situation. (Cavan et al., 1949, p. 11)

Some of the first studies of these constructs in the lives of old people were the Kansas City Studies of Adult Life conducted by scholars from the University of Chicago during the mid-to-late 1950s in Kansas City, Missouri (Cumming & Henry, 1961; Neugarten & associates, 1964; Williams & Wirths, 1965). This research focused on the question: What are the changes in personality associated with chronological age in the second half of life? Two sets of data were collected: The first set was cross-sectional data from 700 men and women aged 40 to 70 who came from all social status levels, while the second set was longitudinal data from 300 people aged 50 to 90 who were interviewed at regular intervals over a six-year period (Neugarten, 1973).

Several other studies also were conducted during the late 1950s and throughout the 1960s in an attempt to measure such constructs as "adjustment," "mental health," and "morale." Researchers at Duke University, for example, studied "social adjustment" in older people as part of an interdisciplinary longitudinal study of middle and late life beginning in 1955 (Maddox, 1968; Maddox & Eisdorfer, 1962; Palmore, 1970, 1974). In the 1960s, scholars at the Langley Porter Neuropsychiatric Institute and the University of California Medical School studied the "mental health" of old people and its relationship to social behavior (Clark & Anderson, 1967; Lowenthal, 1964; Lowenthal, Berkman, et al., 1967; Simon, Lowenthal, & Epstein, 1970). And psychologists at the Philadelphia Geriatric Center looked at "morale"—including such factors as self-perceptions of mood, adjustment, and well-being—as a correlate of social behavior (Lawton, 1975).

In all these efforts to advance understanding of the social psychology of old people, perhaps the most famous measure was the one called "life satisfaction," which emerged from the Kansas City studies. As part of this work, Neugarten, Havighurst, and Tobin (1961) devised the Life Satisfaction Rating (LSR), a clinical rating based on an interview, and the Life Satisfaction Index, Forms A, B, and Z (LSIA, LSIB, and LSIZ), which are paper-and-pencil measures that were developed from clinical ratings. The concept of life satisfaction was defined according to five primary characteristics:

(1) *zest*—having energy to participate in several areas of life, liking to do things, being enthusiastic;
(2) *resolution and fortitude*—not giving up, taking good with bad and making the most of it, accepting responsibility for one's own personal life;
(3) *congruence* between desired and achieved goals—feeling that one has accomplished what one wanted to;
(4) *positive self-concept*—thinking of oneself as a person of worth; and
(5) *mood tone*—showing happiness, optimism, and pleasure with life (Neugarten, Havighurst, & Tobin, 1961, 1968).

Table 5.1 provides recent data about correlations between the Life Satisfaction Index, Form Z, and other measures of psychological well-being, social desirability, self-esteem, and locus of control. These data indicate that the Life Satisfaction Index, Form Z (LSIZ), correlates very highly with the two other measures of adjustment, the Philadelphia Geriatric Center Morale Scale ($r = .74$) and the Memorial University of Newfoundland Scale of Happiness ($r = .85$), and significantly with a semantic differential measure of self-esteem ($r = .40$). While these results seem to offer evidence of the

Table 5.1
Correlations of Life Satisfaction Index (LSIZ) with Other Psychological Measures

Measure	r
Philadelphia Geriatric Center Morale Scale (PGC)[a]	.74**
Memorial University of Newfoundland Scale of Happiness (MUNSH)[a]	.85**
Marlowe-Crowne Social Desirability Scale (MCSDS)[a]	.21*
Edwards Social Desirability Scale (ESDS)[a]	.58**
Semantic differential measure of self-esteem[b]	.40**
Adult Nowicki Strickland Locus of Control Inventory (ANSIE)[b]	−.10

a. Kozma and Stones (1987), $N = 75$.
b. Dreyer, unpublished data, $N = 148$.
*$p < .01$; **$p < .001$.

concurrent validity of the LSIZ, the data also show that the LSIZ correlates significantly with two measures of "social desirability," the Marlowe-Crowne Social Desirability Scale ($r = .21$) and the Edwards Social Desirability Scale ($r = .58$), leaving us with a question of the degree to which life satisfaction ratings of older people merely reflect what they think researchers want them to say when they fill out such questionnaires. Finally, the data indicate that the LSIZ is not significantly related to the Adult Nowicki Strickland Locus of Control Inventory, although there is a trend for people who feel that they are in charge of their lives ("internals") to score higher in life satisfaction than people who feel that their lives are in the hands of such factors as fate, luck, and chance ("externals").

Theories of Ideal Aging

In the 1960s, the focus on "personal adjustment" and "life satisfaction" produced one of the most exciting and important controversies in the field of social gerontology, the argument over what Cumming and Henry (1961) called the *disengagement hypothesis* about ideal aging. Briefly stated, Cumming and Henry's analysis of the data from the Kansas City studies (Neugarten et al., 1961, 1968) led them to hypothesize that optimal human aging involved the mutual withdrawal of the individual from society. With increasing age, society expected less and less of the individual, and people who aged "successfully" adjusted to this forced retirement by disengaging from social roles, adopting a more passive problem-solving style, and becoming more self-centered. Thus disengaged old people were felt to be better adjusted and higher in life satisfaction than those individuals who resisted retirement from work and from other previous social roles.

The ink had hardly dried on Cumming and Henry's book when their colleagues took vigorous exception to this disengagement hypothesis, offering quite different explanations of what "ideal" aging might be. George Maddox and Carl Eisdorfer (1962) of Duke and Robert Havighurst (Havighurst, Neugarten, & Tobin, 1968) of Chicago became advocates of the *activity hypothesis* of ideal aging. In this view, maximum life satisfaction was predicted by the extent to which a person's postretirement role activity matched his or her preretirement role activity. In other words, people who had been highly active during middle age and who continued that level of social role activity during the later years could be expected to have high levels of life satisfaction, while people who had been active before retirement and who disengaged during old age should have low levels of life satisfaction—the opposite of Cumming and Henry's (1961) prediction.

Bernice Neugarten (Neugarten et al., 1968) proposed a similar point of view, which became known as the *continuity hypothesis* of ideal aging. From her perspective, the issue was not so much absolute levels of social role activity, such as Havighurst described, but the continuity in life-style and personality attributes that a person maintained across the life cycle. Thus a person who had been what she called "integrated" in early and midlife would have high life satisfaction in old age if he or she maintained that same "integrated" life-style. In the same vein, she pointed out, old people who enjoyed sitting in a rocking chair all day had probably spent most of their lives in rocking chairs. Both the activity and the continuity explanations of ideal aging argued that individuals who disengaged from active social roles and the complexities of everyday life would most likely experience low levels of life satisfaction, if not clinical depression and anomie, unless they happened to be individuals who had never been socially active at any point in their lives.

The Nature and Meaning
of Retirement

In this excitement over the nature of ideal aging and factors that led to high levels of life satisfaction, the issue of what retirement was and what it meant was seldom debated. The common assumption was that retirement was a "normative life crisis," which involved the loss of an individual's work roles and the sense of occupational self that was defined by those roles. Thus retirement was the most serious example of society's disengagement from the individual and the most obvious evidence that society had little use for the elderly, who were expected to fend for themselves in a world where they were considered obsolete, unteachable, disabled, poor, sexless, powerless, and unnecessary. The main question in the social psychological literature was how a person was supposed to adjust to this changing environment and the shock of retirement.

This general notion of the meaning of retirement began to change when good research finally emerged in the 1970s. One of the best studies was the Cornell Study of Occupational Retirement, carried out by Streib and Schneider and published in 1971. Their findings, based upon a longitudinal study of 1,486 men and 483 women nearing retirement in the 1950s, revealed the following:

(1) Men and women who had higher incomes, higher levels of education, and higher-status occupations tended to postpone retirement as long as possible.

(2) In general, women tended to resist retirement more than men, and single or married women retired earlier than divorced or widowed women.

(3) Despite the fact that over half of the subjects reported a postretirement decrease in income of about 50%, most considered their retirement incomes to be "adequate."

(4) There was no perceptible change in self-concept from pre- to postretirement status. Retired subjects did not consider themselves to be "old" and did not feel "useless."

(5) Feelings of "satisfaction with life" did not change from pre- to postretirement years, although people who retired "early" expressed higher life satisfaction than those who retired "late."

Thus the findings of the Cornell study did not support the widespread notion that retirement is a negative life event that leaves retirees with a sense of lost identity and a diminished sense of self-worth and satisfaction with life.

These results have generally been supported by other studies of retirement. Kimmel, Price, and Walker (1978), for example, found that the only significant predictors of postretirement life satisfaction were good biological health, positive preretirement attitudes, and being able to retire voluntarily rather than being forced to retire. Another finding that has emerged is that successful adjustment to retirement is greatly enhanced by preretirement planning, no matter what the individual's attitude is about such preretirement planning (Glasmer & DeJong, 1975; Green, 1969; Hunter, 1968). In other words, planning for retirement helps ease the transition whether the person likes the planning program or not.

In the past 20 years, some new trends in the patterns of retirement of Americans have emerged. The first of these is that the average age of retirement has decreased steadily since 1960 until it is now well under 58 years of age (Kimmel, 1980). One indication of this is the declining percentages of men and women in the U. S. labor force, as shown in Tables 5.2 and 5.3. Here the data indicate that fewer women than men continue working outside the home into old age, a finding that appears contrary to the Cornell Study of Occupational Retirement, which was done in the 1950s (Streib & Schneider, 1971). One irony of the shift toward earlier retirement is

Table 5.2
U.S. Labor Force Participation Rates by Sex and Age, 1970 to 1990 (percentages)

| | | Year | |
Group	1970	1980	1990 (projection)
Men			
55–64	83.0	72.1	65.5
65+	26.8	19.0	14.9
Women			
55–64	43.0	41.3	41.5
65+	9.7	8.1	7.4

NOTE: Adapted from U.S. Bureau of the Census (1984).

Table 5.3
U.S. Labor Force Participation Rates by Sex, Age, and
Marital Status, 1960 to 1984 (percentages)

| | Year | | | |
Group	1960	1970	1980	1984
Men, aged 45–64				
Married	93.0	91.6	84.8	81.8
Single	74.4	66.6	65.2	66.5
Divorced/Widowed	78.1	75.9	69.9	72.5
Men, aged 65+				
Married	37.1	30.2	20.4	17.3
Single	24.3	21.0	20.0	16.7
Divorced/Widowed	18.2	16.5	13.0	12.6
Women, aged 45–64				
Married	34.2	44.1	46.9	48.9
Single	75.1	67.8	62.8	66.9
Divorced/Widowed	58.3	60.7	59.5	61.0
Women, aged 65+				
Married	5.9	7.9	7.2	7.3
Single	21.6	17.6	12.0	11.5
Divorced/Widowed	11.0	9.9	8.6	7.6

NOTE: Adapted from U.S. Bureau of the Census (1984).

that its direction is opposite to the 1979 change in the age for mandatory retirement in most occupations from 65 to 70. Thus, while the age at which Americans must retire has been increased by federal law, the age of actual retirement has decreased as a result of federal social security, taxation, and medicare policies. As a result, the retirement process today is not so much a "normative life crisis" imposed upon people by a society that wants them to disengage but a new developmental phase or transition that individuals control to a large degree.

Subgroup Differences in Views of Retirement

As a result of this change, we are rapidly reaching the point where overall generalizations about the meaning and nature of retirement must be abandoned in favor of considering the retirement situation for specific occupational, sex, and racial subgroups of the population. For example, there appear to be important differences in the ways members of different occupational groups view retirement and its meaning. Blue-collar factory workers, for example, tend to look forward to retirement, plan excitedly for it, and retire early with heartfelt satisfaction. On the other hand, white-collar professionals, such as university professors, tend to resist retirement, are likely not to plan for it, and often retire reluctantly with a fair amount of resentment about having to abandon their job tenure and university life-style (Kellams & Chronister, 1987).

One issue in this process is the extent to which an individual's work is a central part of what Erikson (1959) calls his or her "identity." For those individuals whose work is central in defining their sense of "self"—who they are and what social roles give meaning to their lives—occupational retirement is resisted as long as possible. However, people who define themselves in terms of their family, community, or leisure involvements and who view their work simply as a means to some other end (such as providing the money to engage in family and leisure pursuits) usually look forward eagerly to occupational retirement. In our society, those who view work as a central aspect of their identities are likely to be professionals or skilled craftspeople, such as physicians, clergy, scholars, athletes, judges, and lawyers, although it is possible for individuals in any occupation to see their work as central to their self-concept and self-esteem. The key issue, therefore, is not the occupation or type of work itself, how much time it takes or money it pays, but how the individual in that work role views the meaning of his or her work.

With regard to sex differences, it is becoming clear that women's work histories and life expectancies are different enough from men's so that retirement has a different meaning. As reported above, women in the paid work force seem to retire earlier than do men and are more likely than men to plan their retirement around their spouses' plans. In addition, as shown in Table 5.3, a woman's marital status has implications for her retirement and the meaning it has in her life. A married woman who is not in the paid work force, for example, tends to define retirement according to her husband's work status, while her own work life changes little as long as she has a home to maintain and meals to prepare. A married woman who is in the paid work force, however, may find herself in conflict with her husband as to when each will retire and how they will spend their time subsequently. For single women, most of whom work, retirement tends to be defined very much the same way as it is for men, and they face the same economic and personal decisions as their male peers (Liang, 1982).

Finally, sex differences in attitudes toward retirement are also affected by the different life expectancies and health statuses enjoyed by women and men. In this instance, average life expectancy tables for men and women can be highly misleading, because they are based on the probability that a baby will survive to old age. The more relevant data for understanding the meaning of retirement are an individual's life expectancy once he or she has already survived to age 65. As shown in Tables 5.4 and 5.5, for a woman at age 65 there is an excellent chance that she will live at least 18 more years and, if she is married, that she will spend the last 17 of those years as a widow; while for a man at age 65, the chances are that he will live 14 more years and will remain married for that entire time. Such biological realities are part of the individual's life space and become important factors in how individuals approach retirement and how they feel about postretirement satisfaction.

The meaning of retirement also seems to differ for members of different ethnic and racial minority groups. A recent study by Gibson (1987), for example, reports that for many Blacks retirement is not a clear transition between life time and old-age work patterns, but is more likely to include the need for continuing

Table 5.4
Life Expectancy for Americans at Birth and at Age 65

Age	Men	Women
At Birth	71	78
At Age 65	79	83
At Age 65, if in TIAA/CREF[a]	83	87

NOTE: Adapted from National Center for Health Statistics (1981) and Teachers Insurance Annuity Association.
a. Members of TIAA/CREF are predominantly college and university faculty.

Table 5.5
Median Age at Time of Key Life Events for Women in the United States in 1890, 1966, and 1980

Event	1890	1966	1980
Marriage of last child	55	48	49
Death of husband	53	64	66
Own death	68	78	83
Years from end of parenting to widowhood	– 2	16	17
Years from beginning of widowhood to own death	15	14	7
Years from end of parenting to own death	13	30	34

NOTE: Adapted from Glick, Heer, and Beresford (1963) as cited in Neugarten and Datan (1973). Figures for 1980 are extrapolations made by this author based on the 1890 and 1966 figures, using 1980 U.S. Bureau of the Census data.

occasional work well into late life. Furthermore, for Black elderly there seem to be more benefits that accrue from the status of being disabled than from that of being retired. While these results are intriguing, it seems clear that we need much more research about racial and ethnic differences in how people approach retirement and what it means for them.

Thus the nature and meaning of retirement appear to be changing rapidly at this time and must be considered carefully within the context of specific life spaces, especially for different occupational groups, for women, and for racial and ethnic minorities, where variations in work histories across the life span give retirement a different meaning than for White male professionals.

It seems clear that we must focus our ideas about what retirement is and how it affects people by taking into account the meaning of work for specific subgroups in our population. This means that we must revise some of our former theories of the social psychology of aging to take into account the great diversity of people's lives and the variations that can occur with such a common life event as retirement.

Some Recent Research into
Postretirement Life Satisfaction

One of the ways my students and I have attempted to meet this challenge is by studying the relationship between retirement and life satisfaction among some of the specific occupational groups who live in several local retirement communities. Two of these studies are reported briefly here, primarily to illustrate some of the complexities and surprises that emerge in this area of research.

A Study of Christian Workers

The first study was an investigation of factors influencing successful aging conducted by Jean Albaum (1985). The participants in the study were 61 American retired Christian workers, all of whom had given at least 20 years to professional service as ministers, missionaries, YMCA or YWCA directors, or teachers of religion. Representing 10 mainline Protestant denominations, all had spent a minimum of three years overseas. Ten of the participants described themselves as conservative in religious beliefs and the remainder as liberal. All of them had at least enough income to meet their needs, and all lived in independent homes on the grounds of a retirement community in Southern California. The 42 women and 19 men ranged in age from 66 to 96 and had been retired from six months to 29 years. All of the women had held paying positions for at least a portion of their lives.

The highly unique status of the participants of this study automatically controlled for a number of factors and provided additional, interesting dimensions for the data analysis. For example, all of the participants subscribed to a religious faith that assumes a belief in life after death. All possessed at least a bachelor's degree; more than two-thirds possessed graduate degrees; and all had traveled extensively both before and after retirement. All lived in a highly rated retirement community that assured attractive housing, adequate food, and complete medical care. The participants also maintained very active lives, contributing to a wide variety of community service, educational, and church-related projects. High status was ascribed to residency in this retirement community, and the role of "retired Christian worker" was generally well-received in the surrounding city.

The five dimensions of life satisfaction proposed by Neugarten, Havighurst, and Tobin (1968) were used to represent the variable of "successful aging." They were measured by the Life Satisfaction Index, Form A (Neugarten et al., 1968), which incorporates the characteristics mentioned earlier—zest, resolution and fortitude, congruence between desired and achieved goals, positive self-concept, and mood tone—and the Inventory of Psychosocial Maturity (Constantinople, 1969). The latter was designed to measure both successful and unsuccessful resolutions of Erik Erikson's first six stages of development, and it provides two scores for each psychosocial stage. It was first developed using college undergraduates but has proven useful for studying noncollege adults as well as older people. Constantinople (1969) reported a six-week retest reliability coefficient of +.70 for 952 college-age subjects as well as a moderate pattern of increasing maturity over the four years of college. A retest coefficient of reliability over a five-month time span for 25 of the retirees in this study was +.89, and for all participants the Pearson correlation coefficient between the Inventory of Psychosocial Maturity and the Life Satisfaction Index scores was +.60 (see Wood, Wylie, & Sheafor, 1969).

A total "successful aging" score was computed for each participant by adding the Life Satisfaction Index score and the Inventory of Psychosocial Maturity score. This yielded a total score with a possible range of 198 points. A total score test-retest Pearson correlation of +.90 was found, indicating good reliability. The mean for all 61 participants was 93.8 with a standard deviation of 39.2, while the median was 100. Using these data, participants were divided into two groups, the "average" and "high" successful agers based upon a median split of their combined Life Satisfaction and Psychosocial Maturity scores. They were designated "average" and "high" because, overall, the participants in this study had higher scores than other groups that have been used for comparison.

The correlates of successful aging, such as activities of the past and present, the continuity of patterns of activity of the past into present, and traumatic situational conditions of the past were the other variables of the study. They were measured by the first half of the "Your Activities and Attitudes" scale designed by Burgess, Cavan, and

Havighurst (1948) to collect situational and biographical data and to determine levels of activity. In addition, objective and factual questions about the participants' earlier lives and present religious and travel activities were included in the questionnaire.

The average and highly successful aging groups were compared on self-ratings of four different sets of items: activities of the past and present (12 items), continuity of activity from past to present (8 items), traumatic conditions of the past (16 items), and accomplishments and successes (5 items).

As shown in Tables 5.6 through 5.9, remarkably few of the items discriminated between the average and highly successful aging groups. None of the past and current activities (Table 5.6), including visits to children, participation in religious activities, leisure activities, or friendship activities, were significantly different for average or highly successful agers. In the list of past activities that were carried into the present (Table 5.7), only one item out of eight was significant. Specifically, people who saw their families more now than they did in the past were more likely to be in the average rather than the

Table 5.6
Activities of the Past and Present for Average and Highly Successful Aging Groups

| Activity | Group Mean | | t | χ^2 |
	Average (n = 31)	High (n = 30)		
How often you see your family now	1.84	1.80	.16	
Number of confidential friends (df = 33)	3.72	5.58	−1.03	
Regular leisure activities	12.77	12.60	.16	
A trip is planned	.68	.57	.88	
Religious services monthly	6.06	6.07	.00	
Home religious activity	21.19	22.97	− .52	
Total present religious activity	27.26	29.03	− .52	
Religious services before retirement (df = 58)	9.22	11.07	− .68	
Total friends, leisure, religious, and paid activities now	23.00	24.63	− .71	
Leisure activities before retirement	10.03	10.10	− .05	
Taking care of home (df = 3)				.29
Happy with present activities (df=3)				2.73

NOTE: Adapted from Albaum (1985); *df* = 59 unless otherwise indicated.

Table 5.7
Continuation of Activities of the Past into the Present for
Average and Highly Successful Aging Groups

| Activity | Group Mean | | t | χ^2 | df |
	Average (n = 31)	High (n = 30)			
See family more or less now				6.03*	2
See friends more or less now				.35	2
Attend religious services more or less now				.28	2
More or less organizations now				.57	2
More or less leisure activity now				.46	2
Change in number of activities	3.84	4.67	−.86		59
Total friends, organizations, and religious services more or less now	1.94	2.00	−.54		59
Continue vocation into retirement				.71	1

NOTE: Adapted from Albaum (1985).
*$p < .05$.

highly successful aging group, contrary to our expectations. In the list of 16 items that dealt with "traumatic conditions of the past" (Table 5.8), only one item—death of a sibling during childhood—significantly separated average and high groups. Those participants whose brother or sister had died when they were children were significantly more likely to be in the lower of the two satisfaction groups. Finally, among the five separate items measuring accomplishments and successes (Table 5.9), only "consider life happy" and positive "feelings about accomplishments" (and the total accomplishment score) were significantly associated with high satisfaction.

These statistical results must be interpreted within the context of the lives of this unusual sample of retired people, all of whom were generally satisfied with their lives and participated in a supportive community with a strong ideological orientation and commitment to social and ethical values. Nevertheless, the relatively few significant findings provide little support for the activity hypothesis about successful aging. The kind or number of activities a person engaged in after retirement showed little power to predict life satisfaction.

Table 5.8
Traumatic Situational Conditions of the Past and Present for Average and Highly Successful Aging Groups

| Trauma | Group Mean | | t | Number |
	Average (n = 31)	High (n = 30)		Experiencing
Sibling died during subject's childhood	.42	.10	2.75**	15
Father died during subject's childhood	.16	.16	– .06	10
Mother died during subject's childhood	.06	.10	– .50	5
Suffered childhood illness longer than six months	.06	.17	–1.25	7
Suffered midlife illness longer than six months	.06	.10	– .50	5
Spouse died in subject's early or midlife	.13	.13	– .05	8
Children died in subject's early or midlife	.13	.20	– .74	10
Firsthand experience of war	.42	.33	.68	23
Loss of wealth or possessions	.29	.17	1.07	14
Loss changed life-style	.06	.13	– .94	6
Life's work destroyed	.06	.03	.53	3
Other early traumas	.90	.70	.85	34
Death of spouse since retirement	.29	.23	.43	12
Death of child since retirement	.06	.10	– .54	5
Death of siblings since retirement	.23	.38	–1.20	17
Other traumas since retirement	.06	.10	– .50	5
Total trauma score	3.42	3.13	.56	

NOTE: Adapted from Albaum (1985); *df* = 58 or 59.
**$p < .01$.

However, the basic premise of the continuity hypothesis did appear to be supported: that is, that people who maintain their basic lifestyle with its attendant psychological attitudes, values, and gratifications from pre- to postretirement will most likely experience high levels of life satisfaction.

Table 5.9
Accomplishments and Successes for Average and
Highly Successful Aging Groups

Variable	Group Mean Average (n = 31)	High (n = 30)	t	χ^2	df	r with Life Satisfaction (N = 61)
Honors	.74	1.03	– .95		59	.20
Happiness of last marriage				1.54	3	.07
Success of children				2.72	3	.19
Consider life happy				3.72*	1	.37*
Feelings about accomplishments						.51**
Total number of accomplishments	10.74	12.10	–1.88		59	.32*

NOTE: Adapted from Albaum (1985).
*$p < .05$; **$p < .001$.

A Study of Executives

The second study was an investigation by Clifford Alexander (1986) of retirement planning practices and adjustment to retirement among retired senior executive officers (SEOs) and their spouses living in retirement communities in Claremont. From a total population of 1,750 retired people who met the study's criteria for former occupation, income, and control over the work environment or employees, 250 married couples were randomly selected for inclusion in the study. Of this number, 235 (94%) agreed to participate and 228 (91%) completed lengthy questionnaires which were included in the data analysis. Of the 228 who completed questionnaires, 50 couples were randomly selected for interviews, and 47 (94%) of these agreed.

Because these couples were, by definition, retired executives, they tended to be much higher than average in income, education, and socioeconomic status, with long personal histories of leadership and professional accomplishments. In most cases, the wives had shared their husbands' success by acting as the husbands' professional partners, rather than by seeking their own work careers separate from their husbands. Thus, while these wives were often actively involved in their husbands' work lives, the husbands tended to be the clear leaders in the marriages and often made significant life decisions without the wives' counsel.

The primary data were gathered from a 64-item questionnaire called the Retirement Adjustment Profile (RAP), which was designed by C. Alexander for this study. The RAP measures the variables of retirement adjustment, time of retirement, involvement in retirement planning, activities with family and within community, life satisfaction, number of social activities, income, health, and other demographic data. While 46 of these items were rated on a five-point scale from "strongly agree" to "strongly disagree," 18 were answered by "yes" or "no."

From the analysis of 228 questionnaires, the following results seem most important:

(1) Whether the husband retires early (before age 62), on time (between ages 62 and 65), or late (after age 65) seems to have no bearing on measures of adjustment or life satisfaction; however, early retirees report lower levels of physical health than on-time or late retirees.

(2) The objective living conditions and activity levels of these couples do not seem to have an important effect upon postretirement life satisfaction. This result must be qualified by the reminder, however, that all of these subjects live in relative comfort and security in well-managed retirement communities; yet it seems less likely that the retirement community creates life satisfaction than that the high life satisfaction of the individual residents collectively creates a secure and happy community.

(3) Retirement planning seems to have a significant positive impact upon postretirement life satisfaction. This is particularly true when the wife participates with her husband in the retirement planning process and when the retirement planning process is supported by the employer. Those couples who enjoy the highest levels of life satisfaction planned their retirement together and had the support of their employers, usually in the form of a company-sponsored retirement planning seminar or series of workshops.

Implications for Future Research and Public Policy

In conclusion, life satisfaction is a social psychological construct that is likely to be with us for a long time, and continued work to improve its operationalization is needed. It is remarkable that such a commonsense notion as life satisfaction with its rather simplistic operationalization has stood the test of time so well. Such resiliency speaks well for the validity of the concept. At the same time, it is important that we continue to improve the measures themselves, and recent efforts at factor analysis of various measures of life satisfaction and measures of well-being, using data from different sex and ethnic groups, show considerable promise (Costa et al., 1987; Liang & Bollen, 1983, 1985; Liang, Lawrence, & Bollen, 1987; Liang, Tran, & Markides, 1988; Liang & Warfel, 1983).

The factors that promote life satisfaction among old people, or among people of any age, remain largely a mystery. The early hypotheses about life satisfaction that focused on older individuals' disengagement from social roles have given way to more sophisticated ideas about continuities in peoples' lives and the study of patterns of social role activity across the life span. These data all point to a complex set of forces that act in any particular person's life, and future studies should direct themselves to trying to sort out these differential effects.

Studies of retired people have helped to dispel earlier ideas about the nature of retirement itself. It now seems clear that retirement means very different things to different people, depending upon their work history, marital status, sex, and commitment to a work identity. As we begin to understand these individual differences better, we will be able to formulate better hypotheses not only about the effect of retirement but also about the impact of other normative life changes, such as the death of a spouse, moving one's place of residence, and forming new social networks of one's peers in later years. For many individuals, such events represent not only losses that must be "adjusted to" but also significant opportunities for new growth and continued development.

Finally, it is time that we begin to integrate traditional ideas from social psychology with the particular needs of older people. Here I return to my introductory remarks about the need to distinguish between research that is "developmental" and that which studies the "psychology of an age group." I would make a special plea to social psychologists to begin to test their favorite hypotheses within a "developmental" framework and not just by gathering data from samples of older subjects. Research within such a framework may help them both to discover new social psychological phenomena and also to answer theoretical questions that have puzzled them for years.

References

Albaum, J. (1985). *Factors which are related to successful aging in retired Christian workers.* Unpublished doctoral dissertation, Claremont Graduate School, Claremont, CA.

Alexander, C. (1986). *An examination of the effect of retirement planning on senior executive officers (SEO's) and their spouses.* Unpublished doctoral dissertation, Claremont Graduate School, Claremont, CA.

Burgess, E., Cavan, R., & Havighurst, R. J. (1984). *Your activities and attitudes.* Chicago: Science Research Associates.

Cavan, R., Burgess, E., Havighurst, R., & Goldhamer, H. (1949). *Personal adjustment in old age.* Chicago: Science Research Associates.

Clark, M., & Anderson, B. G. (1967). *Culture and aging: An anthropological study of older Americans.* Springfield, IL: Charles C Thomas.

Constantinople, A. (1969). An Eriksonian measure of personality development in college students. *Developmental Psychology, 1,* 357-372.

Costa, P. T., Zonderman, A. B., McCrae, R. R., Cornoni-Huntley, J., Locke, B. Z., & Barbano, H. E. (1987). Longitudinal analysis of psychological well-being in a national sample: Stability of mean levels. *Journal of Gerontology, 42,* 50-55.

Cumming, E., & Henry, W. (1961). *Growing old: The process of disengagement.* New York: Basic Books.

Erikson, E. (1959). Identity in the life cycle [Special issue]. *Psychological Issues. 1*(1).

Gesell, A. (1928). *Infancy and human growth.* New York: Macmillan.

Gibson, R. C. (1987). Reconceptualizing retirement for Black Americans. *Gerontologist, 27,* 691-698.

Glasmer, F. D., & DeJong, G. F. (1985). The efficacy of preretirement preparation programs for industrial workers. *Journal of Gerontology, 30,* 595-600.

Glick, P. C., Heer, D. M., & Beresford, J. C. (1973). Family formation and family composition: Trends and prospects. In M. B. Sussman (Ed.), *Sourcebook in marriage and the family.* New York: Houghton Mifflin.

Green, M. R. (1969). *Pre-retirement counseling, retirement adjustment, and the older employee.* Eugene: University of Oregon.

Havighurst, R. J., Neugarten, B. L., & Tobin, S. S. (1968). Disengagement and patterns of aging. In B. L. Neugarten (Ed.), *Middle age and aging* (pp. 161-172). Chicago: University of Chicago Press.

Hunter, W. W. (1968). *A longitudinal study of pre-retirement education.* Ann Arbor: University of Michigan Press.

Kellams, S. E., & Chronister, J. L. (1987, November 22). *Life after early retirement.* Paper presented at the meeting of the Association for the Study of Higher Education, Baltimore, MD.

Kimmel, D. C. (1980). *Adulthood and aging: An interdisciplinary, developmental view* (2nd ed.). New York: John Wiley.

Kimmel, D. C., Price, K. F., & Walker, J. W. (1978). Retirement choice and retirement satisfaction. *Journal of Gerontology, 33,* 575-585.

Kozma, A., & Stones, M. J. (1987). Social desirability in measures of subjective well-being: A systematic evaluation. *Journal of Gerontology, 42,* 56-59.

Lawton, M. P. (1975). The Philadelphia Geriatric Center morale scale: A revision. *Journal of Gerontology, 30,* 85-89.

Liang, J. (1982). Sex differences in life satisfaction among the elderly. *Journal of Gerontology, 37,* 100-108.

Liang, J., & Bollen, K. A. (1983). The structure of the Philadelphia Geriatric Center Morale Scale: A reinterpretation. *Journal of Gerontology, 38,* 181-189.

Liang, J., & Bollen, K. A. (1985). Sex differences in the structure of the Philadelphia Geriatric Center Morale Scale. *Journal of Gerontology, 40,* 468-477.

Liang, J., Lawrence, R. H., & Bollen, K. A. (1987). Race differences in factorial structures of two measures of subjective well being. *Journal of Gerontology, 42,* 426-428.

Liang, J., Tran, T. V., & Markides, K. S. (1988). Differences in the structure of Life Satisfaction Index in three generations of Mexican Americans. *Journal of Gerontology, 43,* S1-S8.

Liang, J., & Warfel, B. (1983). Urbanism and life satisfaction among the aged. *Journal of Gerontology, 38,* 97-106.

Lowenthal, M. F. (1964). *Lives in distress: The paths of the elderly to the psychiatric ward.* New York: Basic Books.

Lowenthal, M. F., Berkman, P. L., et al. (1967). *Aging and mental health in San Francisco: A social psychiatric study.* San Francisco: Jossey-Bass.

Maddox, G. (1968). Persistence of life style among the elderly: A longitudinal study of patterns of social activity in relation to life satisfaction. In B. L. Neugarten (Ed.), *Middle age and aging* (pp. 181-183). Chicago: University of Chicago Press.

Maddox, G., & Eisdorfer, C. (1962). Some correlates of activity and morale among the elderly. *Social Forces, 41,* 254-260.

Mead, M. (1978). *Culture and commitment: The new relationships between the generations in the 1970's.* Garden City, NY: Anchor Press/Doubleday.

National Center for Health Statistics. (1981). *Monthly Vital Statistics Report* (DHHS Pub. no. [PHS] 81-1120), *29*(13).

Neugarten, B. L. (1973). Personality change in late life: A developmental perspective. In C. Eisdorfer & M. P. Lawton (Eds.), *The psychology of adult development and aging* (pp. 311-338). Washington, DC: American Psychological Association.

Neugarten, B. L., & Datan, N. (1973). Sociological perspectives on the life cycle. In P. B. Baltes & K. W. Schaie (Eds.), *Life-span developmental psychology: Personality and socialization* (pp. 53-71). New York: Academic Press.

Neugarten, B. L., Havighurst, R. J., & Tobin, S. S. (1961). The measurement of life satisfaction. *Journal of Gerontology, 16,* 134-143.

Neugarten, B. L., Havighurst, R. J., & Tobin, S. S. (1968). Personality and patterns of aging. In B. L. Neugarten (Ed.), *Middle age and aging* (pp.173-177). Chicago: University of Chicago Press.

Neugarten, B. L., & associates. (Eds.). (1964). *Personality in middle and late life.* New York: Atherton.

Palmore, E. B. (1970). *Normal aging: Reports from the Duke longitudinal studies, 1955-1969.* Durham, NC: Duke University Press.

Palmore, E. B. (1974). *Normal aging II: Reports from the Duke longitudinal studies. 1970-1973.* Durham, NC: Duke University Press.

Piaget, J. (1951). *Play, dreams, and imitation in childhood.* New York: Norton.

Piaget, J. (1954). *The construction of reality in the child.* New York: Basic Books.

Piaget, J., & Inhelder, B. (1969). *The psychology of the child.* New York: Basic Books.

Schaic, K. W. (1970). A reinterpretation of age-related changes in cognitive structure and functioning. In L. R. Goulet & P. B. Baltes (Eds.). *Life-span developmental psychology: Research and theory* (pp. 486-508). New York: Academic Press.

Schaie, K. W. (1977). Quasi-experimental research designs in the psychology of aging. In J. Birren & K. W. Schaie (Eds.), *Handbook of the psychology of aging* (pp. 39-58). New York: Van Nostrand Reinhold.

Simon, A., Lowenthal, M. F., & Epstein, L. (1970). *Crisis and intervention: The fate of the elderly mental patient.* San Francisco: Jossey-Bass.

Streib, G. F., & Schneider, C. J. (1971). *Retirement in American society: Impact and process.* Ithaca, NY: Cornell University Press.

U. S. Bureau of the Census. (1984). *Statistical abstract of the United States: 1985* (105th ed.). Washington, DC: Government Printing Office.

Williams, R. H., & Wirths, C. G. (1965). *Lives through the years.* New York: Atherton.

Wood, V., Wylie, M., & Sheafor, B. (1969). An analysis of a short self-report measure of life satisfaction: Correlation with rater judgments. *Journal of Gerontology, 24,* 464-469.

6

Environmental Proactivity and Affect in Older People

M. POWELL LAWTON

T he development of an environmental psychology of later life has involved theoretical frameworks and research that have in turn fostered the growth of applied techniques for planning housing, institutions, neighborhoods, transportation, and other settings for older people. The goal has been to provide environments that are congruent with the needs and capabilities of the older user, under the hypothesis that congruence will, in turn, be associated with a favorable outcome in terms of psychological well-being. The application of such knowledge is now flourishing, with planners, architects, designers, and administrators being sensitized to such user needs in a way that seemed impossible 20 years ago. On the other hand, there has been a lull in the recent growth of both environmental theory and research. It is possible that a renaissance of such activity must await the filling of gaps in the conceptual frameworks that have been utilized in this area to date.

This chapter addresses the topic of affectivity in aging to elaborate better some of the mechanisms by which transactions between the person and the environment occur. One can, to be sure, say that person-environment transactions involve merely all that has ever been called psychology: the motivation to interact with the environment, cognitive representation of the environment, affective response to the environment, and behavior in relation to the environment. What else is there in our field? However, as is true in so many instances, gerontological research has not caught up with general psychological research, so that the richness of research findings in gerontology regarding such phenomena as need for achievement, intrinsic motivation, attribution, or stress and adaptation does not match that in general psychology. More detailed consideration of how older people are motivated to interact with their social and physical environments seems to be an area in which new knowledge is required, which, if available, might advance general person-environment research.

This chapter also considers further the consequences of person-environment transactions. A good bit of existing effort like that of Kahana (1982), Windley and Scheidt (1982), Carp and Carp (1984), and myself (Lawton, 1982) has used the hypothesis that the outcome of these transactions may be viewed in the rather global terms of life satisfaction, morale, or indicators of mental health. There is considerable need for differentiation within such an omnibus hypothesis. That is, what is the nature of the affective component of what is referred to as "psychological well-being," and how do contemporaneous affective experiences relate to longer-term states, dispositions, or manifestations of mental health? Especially important is the recognition that the link of person and environment to behavior and psychological well-being is far more complex than portrayed in the usual linear and unidirectional causal model. In particular, we need to concern ourselves with how affective experiences motivate behavior designed to manipulate or create environments.

As illustrated in Figure 6.1, the usual person-environment (P-E) system views person and environment as joint determinants of behavior, with the indirect path from person to behavior through environment representing the appraisal, or environmental cognition, element of the transaction. The left-to-right recursive process is virtually all that has heretofore been considered in our P-E research. Person characteristics such as temperament or stable traits influence psychological well-being and the recurrent affective experiences of the person, as do environmental factors. Person-environment transaction thus can be seen as the usual antecedent of emotion.

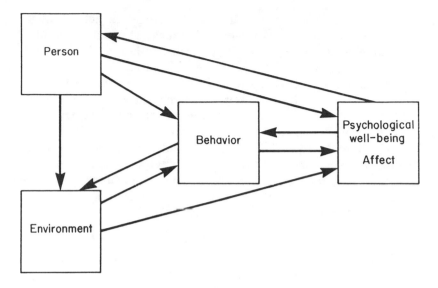

Figure 6.1. Person-environment transactional model

The reversed causal pathways of Figure 6.1 suggest, however, that affective responses may in turn constitute the motive power for adjusting behavior, for modifying the environment, and for personal growth. Discussion of these effects involves such processes as affective self-regulatory mechanisms, the affective quality of the environment, and the effect of emotional states on the environment. These processes and many others are discussed by Russell and Snodgrass (1987) in the first formal attempt to relate affect and environment systematically, and they are relevant to people of any age.

Autonomy Versus Security

The specificity of the relationship between affect and environment in later life can be approached through consideration of a dialectic with obvious human-developmental implications: the dialectic between autonomy and security. This dialectic may be viewed as a life plan (Miller, Pribram, & Galanter, 1960) that is continuously modified, one in which the balance between autonomy and security changes in keeping with both personal development and environmental context. Tracing the dynamics of this basic dialectic through later life leads to the discussion of such issues as adaptation, stimulus seeking versus stimulus avoidance, self-regulation of affect, and the affective qualities of home and neighborhood.

The autonomy-security dialectic is best portrayed in the ecological model about which I have written extensively (Lawton & Nahemow, 1973). Figure 6.2 was originally designed to portray the interaction between the competence of the person and environmental demands (or "press" in Murray's, 1938, terms) in determining the quality of the outcome. The surface of Figure 6.2 between the nonparallel diagonals represents positive outcomes of the person-environment transaction, outcomes that may be either in the behavioral-competence realm or in the psychological well-being realm.

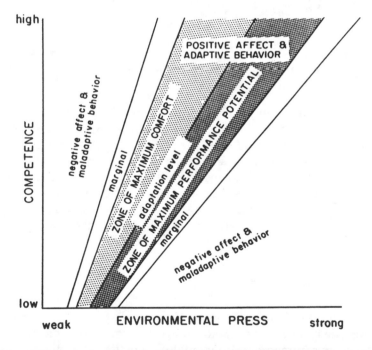

Figure 6.2. Ecological model of adaptation and aging. Source: Lawton, M. P., & Nahemow, L. (1973). Ecology and aging. In C. Eisdorfer & M. P. Lawton (Eds.), *The psychology of adult development and aging* (p. 661). Washington, DC: American Psychological Association. Copyright 1980 by the American Psychological Association. Reprinted by permission.

The portion of the model particularly cogent for the present purpose is the section to the right of the line marking the center, or the "adaptation level." This area depicts outcomes where the degree of environmental demand is incrementally greater than the competence of the behaving individual. Nahemow and I suggested that such a situation is one where the person's performance is paced by an external demand. A great deal of the practice of rehabilitation medicine is based on the idea that motivation is highest, and positive feedback most likely, when a performance goal is set above the current level but within reach. Provided the mismatch between demand and competence is relatively small, this situation is one where new learning and novel experience occurs, sometimes with the outcome of elevating the person's competence in that area (Lawton & Nahemow, 1973).

The segment on the left of the central line is labeled "zone of maximum comfort" and is meant to portray the situation where the strength of environmental demand is below the level that is usually managed by a person of a particular level of competence. This zone is characterized by the maintenance of appropriate behavior, together with a favorable level of psychological well-being consisting of restfulness, relaxation, or pleasant lassitude.

As either zone departs from the point of balance (adaptation level—AL), a further degree of mismatch between competence and demand is likely to result in maladaptation. Beyond the zone of maximum performance potential lies an excess of demand— environmental stress. Beyond the zone of maximum comfort lies boredom and atrophy of skills.

Both zones derive their attributes from comparison with the adaptation level (Helson, 1964), which represents the theoretical line containing all points of exact balance between competence and demand. Most everyday behavior falls within the most central area near AL and is relatively effortless. The adaptation level for a given individual is in a constant state of flux, being disturbed repeatedly by new demands and new retreats. Incorporating each such disturbance involves establishing a new adaptation level, which is stable only until the next disturbance.

Environmental Docility and
Environmental Proactivity

More recently I have added the agency of change away from AL as another element of the model. The model as depicted in Figure 6.1 lends itself to a conception of environment as a cause of the person's behavior and psychological state, the person being the passive recipient of the environment's demand characteristics. In fact, one of the first elements of the theory underlying this model was my statement of the "environmental docility hypothesis," which suggested that, as competence declined, environment would account for an increased proportion of the variance in outcome. However, the opposite direction of action and agency—the person's competence as a determinant of environment—clearly requires inclusion. Thus I suggested the "environmental proactivity hypothesis," which suggests that, as the person becomes more competent, the environment affords increasing resources relevant to the person's needs (Lawton, in press). Proactivity in seeking such resources thus represents the behavioral manifestation of achieved autonomy.

It is necessary to emphasize that the reality of person-in-environment is far more complex than portrayed by Figure 6.2 and its elaborations. Competences are many and they change, environments are highly volatile, and the direction of the P-E transactions is constantly shifting. This open system must be kept in mind as autonomy and security are discussed. In traditional fashion, these are viewed as needs, or motivations—person attributes as depicted in the upper-left box of Figure 6.1. Although they are basic and universal, they are above all in a constant state of redefinition. Viewed in relation to Figure 6.2, any change in "press" away from adaptation level may be instigated by the person or by the environment. Sometimes a relaxation of demands makes satisfaction of the need for security more likely, but in reaction this move may bring the need for autonomy into consciousness. For example, housing that provides meal service may seem luxurious. If a person is not impaired, however, the lack of ability to choose one's own food and prepare it to one's idiosyncratic taste may be a "cost" that makes the person reconsider whether the luxury of being waited on is worth it. An increase in environmental press (the demand to shop and cook) makes satisfaction of the need for security more problematic but may provide an opportunity for the satisfaction of the need for autonomy.

Positive Affect and Negative Affect

The outcomes are likely to be quite different when the agent is the self rather than an environmental demand. This situation represents one nexus of environment and affect. Zautra, Reich, and their colleagues have engaged in a program of research regarding these relationships. They differentiated between the two general affective dimensions, positive affect and negative affect, as outcomes. Some of their most interesting findings were that among younger people negative affect was, as expected, a consequence of negative life events (Zautra & Reich, 1980) and that externally caused events were associated with negative affect. Positive events, positive affect, and personally caused events were similarly related. The literature also contains suggestions that negative events for which the person assumed responsibility had less negative outcomes than those that came about without perceived personal causation—one such instance was Bulman and Wortman's (1977) study of people with traumatic spinal cord injury. Reich and Zautra (1981) also found that positive events that the person did not initiate (pawn events) were associated with negative affect. Those that the subject produced, by contrast, elevated positive affect. However, later research directed toward older subjects indicated an absence of a direct relationship between either pawn or origin events and either type of affect. Taking action in relation to either environmentally or self-initiated events was associated with favorable outcomes, however (Reich & Zautra, 1983). The findings indicate, first, the complexity of the subject and the prudence of testing relationships separately by age. However, the finding that "doing something" (whether reactively or proactively) was associated with well-being is itself consistent with the idea that an active stance in beneficial.

It is undoubtedly true that biological aging reduces older people's ability to choose as widely among behavioral alternatives as they had in earlier-adult years. There is a substantial literature about the barriers to behavioral freedom arising from a physical environment constructed for a more youthful society (see Regnier & Pynoos,

1987, for the most recent work in this area). And the constraints introduced by ageist social norms and institutions constitute yet another limitation on the opportunity for proactivity. If autonomy is thus restricted and the opportunity for proactivity decreased, this should mean a lower overall level of positive affect among older people. That situation is exactly what has been found in a number of different cross-sectional age comparisons of positive affect: Older groups usually are lower in positive affect (Bradburn, 1969; Campbell, Converse, & Rodgers, 1976; Costa et al., 1987).

One can also make a good case for a reduction in security as an intrinsic aspect of aging in our society. Biological aging is apt to increase concern over what might happen if a health need occurs and help happens not to be handy. Physical illness in itself has a well-known association with depression. Economic loss appears to become a growing problem during the years after retirement. Death takes its toll of spouse, other relatives, and friends. The prototype of subjective response to insecurity is anxiety. Despite such negative age trends in biological and social events, paradoxically, negative affect and other operationalizations of subjective distress show a *decrease* with age (Bradburn, 1969; Campbell et al., 1976; Costa et al., 1987). Thus what appears a very reasonable expectation for affective experience on the up side is confirmed, while the reasonable expectation on the down side is not confirmed.

Recently Costa et al. (1987) examined data from a very large nationally representative sample of people of all ages, the National Health and Nutrition Examination Survey (NHANES; National Center for Health Statistics, 1973). The cross-sectional data on a five-item negative affect scale and a three-item scale related to positive affect (but not the same scales as Bradburn, 1969) showed the age differences noted earlier. However, the 1981 replication of the NHANES involved both follow-up of surviving subjects from the 1971 NHANES and a sample of new subjects so that longitudinal and cross-sequential analyses could be performed (Cornoni-Huntley et al., 1983). In general, in the longitudinal perspective, the age-related narrowing of affective range (i.e., lower positive and negative affect) was far less perceptible than it was in cross-sectional comparisons. Although narrowing was not absent, these results underline the probability that cohort-related influences are potent determinants of people's readiness to identify and report subjective states.

It is worthwhile to consider at this point what it is that people are reporting in response to questions of the type that are referred to as "positive affect," "negative affect," and other indicators of psychological well-being. The Bradburn scales, the questions asked in the NHANES, and others have a relatively recent time referent, such as "the past few weeks" or "during the past month." This short-term focus is distinguished from the long-term or unspecified temporal referent that is encountered in the frequently used measures of morale, life satisfaction, and many mental health measures. It is notable that few such measures of stable well-being have been shown to be related to chronological age at all. Costa and McCrae (1980) have argued repeatedly that the most potent influences on happiness are the basic personality traits: Happiness is reported by people high in extraversion and low in neuroticism, and unhappiness by the opposite groups. Because extraversion and neuroticism have been shown to be very stable, Costa et al. (1987) suggest that happiness and positive and negative affect are relatively resistant to influence by environmental and maturational events, even health-related events; it is enduring personality traits that lead to the report of positive or negative feelings at any given time. These authors even suggest that, while there is such a state as "momentary happiness" with "situational determinants that vary more or less randomly [and] tend to cancel each other out" (Costa & McCrae, 1980, p. 676), such moments are insignificant in the longer range.

These are difficult relationships to disentangle. We clearly need to design better ways of measuring feeling tone. The further we depart from a feeling of the moment, the more opportunity there is for the superimposition of a cognitive judgment of "typical affect," derived from long-term personality traits. Personality can be viewed as the longest-term representations of recurrent subjective states. Such traits have been shown by Epstein (1983) to be reproduced as the number of repeated measures of daily feelings are aggregated. To accept this fact is not the same as suggesting that every day is the same, however.

The theory of affective states, as well as considerable research, such as that of Lazarus and associates on states termed "daily hassles" and "uplifts" (Kanner, Coyne, Schaefer, & Lazarus, 1981), affirms the importance of shorter-term feelings in people's quality of life. Such diverse findings as people's responses to life events

(Murrell & Norris, 1984), the lower psychological well-being observed among caregivers of impaired older people (George & Gwyther, 1986), and the favorable subjective responses of people to improved living conditions (Lawton & Cohen, 1974) attest to the fact that external conditions can affect subjective state.

Capturing a feeling of the moment is not an easy task for the researcher. Psychologically naive subjects do not easily focus on their current mood and often can comprehend a contemporary feeling only within the schema of a long-term personality disposition. Many emotions are fleeting and apt to be evinced at times other than at a research session. I am doing one research project on the fluctuations in affect rated by nursing home residents daily for 30 days. Although 70 people have completed this task of doing daily five-point ratings on 10 adjectives, a substantial number of their ratings of some particular mood adjectives were invariant over 30 days. In attempting to relate environmental events to these ratings, we have similarly found it difficult to elicit reports of potentially salient daily events. One thing has become clear, however: that some people's reported affect is more stable and others' more labile across this short period of time. For example, a group of psychiatric normals and a group of nursing home residents with major depression showed about equal amounts of variability on positive affect, while residents with dysphoria, or minor depression, showed greater variability. However, as one might expect, major depressives were relatively invariant in reporting an absence of positive affect, while normals were invariant in reporting the frequent presence of positive affect. The dysphorics were the most labile on both types of affect. Thus we learned at least that the up-and-down daily affect state is most characteristic of the milder depression group. We have not yet put our event data into the mix to determine whether the dysphorics are also more reactive to the environmental events. However, we do have evidence of short-term variability and, therefore, a reason to search out explanations for the variation.

As to whether chronological aging entails a narrowing of affective range, further answers to this question must involve the much more fine-grained study of specific affects and their elicitors. One study found over 2,000 affect terms in an English dictionary (Wallace & Carson, 1973). The present state of the art regarding the structure of affect suggests that people can readily identify semantically, environmentally, or by self-rating a number of discrete affect states.

These states can be hierarchically placed in a two-factor model of affective states (Russell, 1980; Watson & Tellegen, 1985). Thus there is much more to affective life than global positive and negative affect. But there is relatively little research to tell us about older people's experiences with this great variety of feelings. It may well be, for example, that the breadth and variety of emotions experienced may vary independent of the net balance of positive and negative emotions. The manner of experiencing emotions constitutes another uncharted area, either for older people alone or for age comparisons.

Manners of Experiencing Emotions

Schulz (1985) called attention to several formal qualities of affective experience that require research attention in the study of adult development: affective intensity, duration, and types of instigators. Since that article, Diener, Sandvik, and Larsen (1985) investigated affective intensity as a quality independent of the type of emotion experienced and found that older people did, indeed, report a lower intensity of affect than those of younger ages or generations. However, this finding was cross-sectional and is subject to the same ambiguity regarding age versus historical cohort as the cross-sectional findings regarding positive and negative affect. Duration and its related dimensions—speed of onset and decay—have had less satisfactory investigation, our knowledge generally being based on physiological indicators of activation, rather than the subjective experience of emotion. It has been suggested that older people have a higher threshold for autonomic activation than do younger people (i.e., a state of chronic underarousal), but that once activated, their return to resting state is slower (for a review, see Woodruff, 1985). However, the evidence for slower arousal and slower deactivation is not always consistent and is limited to laboratory situations. The types of instigators of affect have not been the subject of age comparisons. Indeed, the variety of possible instigators is so great and responses so idiosyncratic that it seems unlikely that age functions can be teased out of the complex interaction of the many determinants that evoke emotion.

Self-Regulation of Affect

It is possible to view these and other aspects of the experience of affect within the framework of proactivity and autonomy. To a certain extent, the study of emotion in general has often seemed to cast the person in the passive, receptive role: Emotional stimuli from within or without evoke affective responses that are handled by various defense or coping mechanisms. A contrasting, complementary view would see emotions as the potential result of self-regulation, in the same way that proactivity can characterize person-environment transactions. The process can be understood as a dialectic between biological or environmental forces that evoke affect from a reactive person versus the person as proactive self-regulator, that is, one who both controls the level of desired stimulation and the environmental contexts that are the source of stimulation. There are possible developmental aspects of affective self-regulation. That is, one can learn techniques for regulating and controlling affect over a lifetime; one may adjust earlier-life modes of affect management in response to changing health and energy; and one may change choices and actively shape external environments that are differentially appropriate to the physical, social, and psychological circumstances of later life.

Wide individual differences in the operation of such regulatory mechanisms have been documented in research on adult populations, although most of the research has not specified affect as the object. Thus people have been shown to differ on such control mechanisms as augmentation-reduction (Larsen, 1985; Petrie, 1967), which is an internal tendency to amplify or dampen the impact of external stimulation. "Amplifiers" need to seek low levels of environmental stimulation in order to maintain a manageable CNS activation level, while "reducers" require higher levels.

There is also a substantial literature on sensation seeking and the need for novelty (Zuckerman & Link, 1968). What little age-related research has been done does suggest that older people are lower in this pursuit than are younger people. Stimulus moderation is associated with affect moderation, and because sensation seeking represents a proactive type of behavior, sensation avoidance may similarly be part of a general strategy of affective self-management.

The opponent-process theory of motivation. A more general

theoretical model of motivation and affect suggested by Solomon (1980), the "opponent process" model, deserves extended consideration in terms of its age relevance. Solomon posits a cortical regulatory process for maintaining moderate levels of affective experience. For every emotion-generating stimulus, a primary response and an affectively opposite secondary or "opponent" response occur, their algebraic sum representing the experienced affective level. With continued repetition of the stimulus, the well-known phenomenon of habituation, or adaptation to the stimulation, occurs. Solomon suggests that habituation occurs because the magnitude of the secondary, or opponent, process increases over time. Figure 6.3 depicts this process. What happens with habituation is that the same level of stimulation produces a relatively milder net

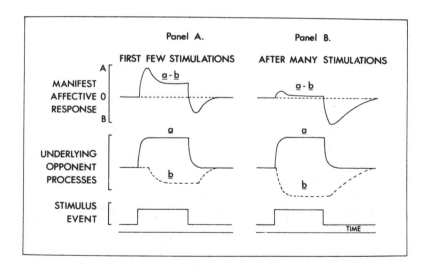

Figure 6.3. The opponent process. Schematic representation of the unconditioned stimulus (stimulus event), the primary ($\underline{a}$) and opponent ($\underline{b}$) process, and the resultant or manifest affective response ($\underline{a\text{-}b}$), when the stimulus is novel and after habituation has occurred. Source: Solomon, R. L. (1980). The opponent process theory of acquired motivation. The costs of pleasure and the benefits of pain. *American Psychologist, 35,* 691-712 (Figure 7, p. 700). Copyright 1980 American Psychological Association. Reprinted by permission.

affective experience; conversely, if a more intense affective experience is sought, the stimulus level must increase, and this causes a corresponding magnification of the opponent response with another resulting decrement in the manifest affective response. Perhaps the most critical feature of the opponent-process model is what happens when the stimulus is withdrawn: The primary process ceases and the opponent process becomes the sole determinant of manifest affect. The opponent-produced manifest affect decays much more slowly than it would have before habituation in the continued absence of the eliciting condition. Recent research in brain laterality and the action of neurotransmitters is consistent with this model, although the two processes have not been directly measured (Tucker, 1981; Tucker & Williamson, 1984).

Addiction and its withdrawal symptoms are also accounted for by this model. The earliest experiences with a psychoactive substance can produce extreme euphoria, which remains for some period of time, and the cessation of the substance is associated with a mild letdown. With continued use, adaptation to the drug occurs, with use of the substance no longer producing a rush of positive feeling but only a mildly positive experience as the craving is reduced. As adaptation occurs, the strength of the opponent process builds to a higher (negative) asymptote than prior to habituation. Solomon suggests that it is the strength of the opponent process that causes the subjective experience of withdrawal. That is, the mild positive primary response initially suppresses the highly negative opponent process, which remains strong after the positive primary response ceases.

The opponent-process model has been used to account for many naturalistic and experimental observations. For instance, the course of romantic love over time can be explained by the opponent process. The continued presence of the loved one results in habituation and attenuation of the euphoria of new love. If the love object is absent or lost, the opponent process is released with often unanticipatedly intense grief and anxiety. Instances where the original stimulus produces negative primary affect are also interesting. The study of parachutists through their training careers has documented the initial affective experience as one of extreme terror during the first few falls (Epstein, 1967, discussed by Solomon, 1980). After landing, a period of numbed relief follows. With continued jumps, however, terror disappears and the anticipation and act of jumping takes on the form of a thrilling job with relatively low anxiety. In correlated fashion, however, the postjump period becomes one of elation and animated socialization. This positive opponent process becomes the motivation to repeat the jumping, the reinforcement being the highly positive affect that follows the cessation of the jump and fall. It is important to note that the experienced affective strength of the response to the opponent process is much more intense after habituation than it was when the stimulating situation was novel. Recovery of the secondary process to baseline level is also much slower after habituation. Heavy exercise or running may be cited as other examples whose phases fit nicely into the opponent-process structure.

No attempt has been made to apply this model to aging, either conceptually or empirically. It would seem to have considerable relevance, however, to some questions about the relationship between environment and affective experience for this age group. The following discussion considers possible opponent-process operations that occur among older people, as they might among younger people, as well as those that might be specific to later life. Several questions are raised:

(1) Is aging associated with changes in the mix of positive and negative events (stimuli) or in the mix of novel and everyday events?
(2) To what extent is there proactivity and reactivity among older people in the regulation of internal states?
(3) What are the implications of the opponent process and lifelong adaptation for well-being in old age?

Events in Later Life

Despite the obvious salience of events like retirement and bereavement to the quality of later life, all research that has counted life events has determined that older people report fewer major life events (Chiriboga & Cutler, 1980; Goldberg & Comstock, 1980). Most such research has dealt only with negative events. Few empirical age-comparative data focusing explicitly on positive events are available. Age comparisons of minor events are also few. "Daily hassles" (DeLongis, Coyne, Dakof, Folkman, & Lazarus, 1982) occur less frequently in older than in middle-aged people (Folkman, Lazarus, Pimley, & Noracek, 1987). The incidence of positive events ("uplifts") does not appear to have been reported in terms of age comparisons.

Thus we can only note the need for such research while discussing the issue with qualitative and speculative information. Is *novelty* differentially likely at different ages? It seems improbable that a definitive answer will be obtainable for such a broad question. However, if there is a finite list of major experiences that account for the great preponderance of all human experiences, it is reasonable to suppose that a decreasing proportion of all such events will be experienced for the first time as one ages. Among the positive events, falling in love, marriage, having a child, advancement in a job, improving one's housing, and the like are often thought of as peaks, are usually experienced in earlier life, and may be unrepeatable in later life. The situation is not so clear with respect to major negative events. Schulz (1985) has observed that the major negative events of later life are also novel: bereavement, major health problems, a move after a long period of stability, and institutionalization. He suggests that such factors should, therefore, lower overall affective well-being in old age. It is worth noting further, however, that such states tend to be chronic, and adaptation thus will occur to some extent. To the extent that the eliciting events are intermittent (for example, in ups and downs of a chronic health condition), the negative primary affect may be relieved by periods of positive affect. In the case of bereavement following the long illness of a spouse, the death of the spouse has sometimes been noted to be followed by a period of unexpectedly able coping—accompanied by grief, to be sure, but sometimes with surprisingly favorable mental health. This sequence is made more understandable by the opponent-process theory. In this case, the opponent process is of positive valence, often overtly construed as relief that the suffering is over. The point is not to sugarcoat these losses but to point out the intrinsic regulatory process by which extremes of emotional experience are moderated.

That there could be a finite pool of *minor* positive and negative experiences that would all gradually become experienced, therefore depleting the ability of the person to experience novelty, hardly seems worth a thought. Yet a common observation is that there is a scarcity of novel, small, positive events in older people's lives. This conclusion is implied in Kastenbaum's (1980-1981) concept of "aging as habituation," Langer's application of "mindlessness" (Langer, Blank, & Chanowitz, 1978) to the course of life of some older people, and the elaboration of these and other observations by Scheidt and Norris-Baker (1987) into a generalized view of "hyper-habituation" as a point of intervention to help the aged. Reich and Zautra (1987) describe the process of "routinization" as one without the implications for mental health implied by the previously mentioned authors, but still one for which under some conditions intervention might be appropriate. That is, habituation to repetitive patterns of behavior, thought, and emotion does constrict experience, and it could well be that overly patterned behavior fills up life so that neither new events nor new internal experiences occur with the frequency they once did.

Does the same putative reduction of minor negative events occur as age increases? One could certainly argue that adherence to habituated patterns of behavior fills gaps that might otherwise increase the likelihood of exposure to unknown environmental situations where negative events could occur. One piece of indirect evidence on this issue came from a study of housing satisfaction of older residents of a suburban city (Golant, 1982). Among the predictors of high satisfaction were low rate of leaving the home and low scores on a measure of stimulus seeking. Allowing oneself the freedom to explore, in a sense, risked disturbing the comfort of perceived quality of the housing environment.

Thus passive regulatory processes undoubtedly serve to restrict the range of potentially stimulating negative and positive events. Allowing oneself to put simple satisfaction ahead of exploration of the environment limits the richness of experience. Although I know of no evidence (other than the cross-sectional findings on negative and positive affect) of constriction of event exposure with age, there are clearly environmental situations where this could occur. One example is settings that are naturally resource-poor, such as a poor and unsafe neighborhood. The event texture of some environments is deliberately leveled in the interest of minimizing the probability of negative events, the medical institution being the prototype of this. Further, it is clear that many of the ways our society constructs life for older people are likely to reduce their range of experience: retirement, low income, diminished social opportunities, and general ageism. Certainly for these people, their manifest affective response is apt to be at adaptation level more often than not.

Regulation of Events

Once again the duality of proactivity and reactivity needs to be considered as it relates to the production of events and the regulation of affective life. Sandvik, Diener, and Larsen (1985) reasoned that positive quality of life could be enhanced either by an excess of positive events or by the positive withdrawal effects associated with the end of a negative stimulus to which one had become habituated. The knowledge regarding the positive aspects of proactive behavior reviewed earlier suggests further that, if these effects are produced by the active agency of the person, their positive value should be enhanced.

Creating positive events. Three ways to create positive events come to mind. The first way is to choose environments that have a probability of yielding more novel positive events. Migrating to a recreational area of the country or to a resource-rich area of town are examples. Another route to the same goal is to create such events wherever one is; examples include walking in one's locality, attending an activity center, or resuming an old friendship. Still another route is to change the focus of the lens with which one looks at an objectively constant environment. This neglected phenomenon is clearly a proactive maneuver often engaged in by people immobilized by an illness. The hospitalized person differentiates among the people, the sounds, the activities, and the changing textures of the day to a far greater extent than does the casual observer. Rowles's (1980) housebound rural elderly created such environments, where one of the major sources of variation was the views afforded from different windows.

It is easier to advocate such self-created environments and events than to create them. A barrier to proactivity undoubtedly arises from the fact that situations with apparent positive affective valence, if novel, may begin as negatively valenced—minor versions of the parachuter example. Particularly if some period of isolation and social skill disuse has occurred, or if personal competence is eroded through poor health, an older person may find the perceived press level of a new task or new environment or new household object enough greater than adaptation level to produce a spike of manifest negative affect when the behavior is performed the first time. It may take some special level of intrinsic motivation or the personality trait of sensation seeking, or encouragement from a peer, for the person to take the risk of early coping with newness. Can such skills be trained? There has been some evidence that younger people who identified desirable events and were asked to make them happen over a several-week period were able to do so (Reich & Zautra, 1981).

Ending habituation to negative states. Ending a state of habituation to a negative situation may well be even more problematic. First, this state of adaptation is likely to be noxious at only a relatively mild level. Second, the way one construes this state of habituation may well involve compensatory value: "I have demonstrated my strength of character by learning how to live in this terrible neighborhood." Some such states of adaptation allow for breaks that can demonstrate to the person the strength of the positive opponent process. Thus vacations, exposure to sources of information about other ways to live, and other self-initiated cessations of the negative stimulus may affirm the person's feeling of competence to substitute a somewhat risky positive situation for the negative one.

To complete the picture, a contrasting view of the meaning of adaptation to apparent negative environments may be offered. We are all familiar with attachment to locality, neighborhood, home, and possessions, which is proverbial among older people. There are also wide individual differences among people in their degree of such attachment. Rubinstein (1987), Rowles (1978), Kamptner (this volume), and others have elaborated on the various functions subsumed by the term *attachment.* They include the emotional associations of the environment with spouse and children, with nostalgic memories, as the symbol of personal achievement; the concrete evidence that a home provides of one's proactivity of the past, its function as the current preserve where autonomy is maximized, and its function as a haven of security. Although, as professionals, we may assess the objective quality of such environments as deplorable, we also should have a ready understanding of the positive meaning for the inhabitants. But the affective links to home and other environments are not always positive. Some think of their homes as drab, their neighborhoods as threatening, their localities as a bitter replacement for their childhood homes or the retirement area of their dreams. Yet they remain habituated, as it were, to that negative environment.

Familiarity is often offered as an explanation for acceptance of such negative environments by older people. The tenacity with which some older people cling to a long-occupied home or neighborhood, an old appliance, a threadbare furnishing, has been observed by all of us. Even where no positive attachment may be evident, the person may have developed a cognitive schema involving the environmental object that provides an immediate guide to how it operates, what one should do with it, how it relates to other aspects of the person's life, and so on. In other words, the many facets of that environment have meaning for the person; and meaning affords control, even if the affective valence is negative. The opponent process can offer some further understanding here: Over time, the initially positive stimulus value of the surrounding engenders adaptation in the intensity of the resident's primary feeling of attachment to the residence. Awareness of the attachment dissipates, but just enough of the primary response (marginal satisfaction, with positive affect) remains to keep the opponent process at a subthreshold level. The marginal suprathreshold satisfaction may simply be due to the fact that one *knows* the environment, rather than loves it. Relocation or the prospect of relocation means the removal of the steady, low-level reinforcement provided by the stable environment. The negative opponent process then increases manifest negative affect to a more intense level. Thus viewed, the hold that a familiar element of the environment has over the person may be better understood.

I am not aware of the question having been raised as to the degree of control one might have over the opponent process. Certainly in Solomon's (1980) exposition, the opponent process is a stimulus-response sequence. There is no mention of agency, which is very relevant to the way one begins early experiences with a novel stimulus. The need associated with habituation clearly puts the person in a passive role with respect to internal physiological processes. Neither is there discussion of whether the dynamisms of the opponent process are within subjective awareness.

With such a total absence of data, speculation becomes relatively safe. First, it seems likely that people are aware of some aspects of the process. Doing something exciting to pick oneself up or anxiously looking for the fall after a high are commonplace occurrences. Second, with cumulating experience, why should not awareness increase? Third, with cumulated awareness, why should not personal control also increase?

The Opponent Process, Self-Regulation, and Well-Being

A hypothesis worthy of consideration is that over a lifetime the person gains familiarity with his or her own affective dynamisms and, in the interest of maximizing positive affect and minimizing negative affect, learns some mechanisms for regulating both exposure to and response to affect-eliciting situations.

Moderation of extremes seems to be the way of the nervous system. It happens. Yet volitional activity practiced over time may make the person more successful in selecting environmental elicitors of feelings. Some possible instances of self-regulation include the following:

- Avoidance of a known highly positive state in order to guard against the opponent negative process, particularly one succeeding the cessation of a habituated stimulus—an example is given by many people in saying that they are more cautious about forming intense new relationships in old age because something could so easily disturb the relationship.
- Clinging to the familiar, as discussed above—it is likely that people do so with some recognition of the strength of the opponent response and its potential for producing distress should the familiar be abandoned.
- Accepting challenge in anticipation of the turn toward exhilaration following successful completion of the challenge—in research now under way with participants in Elderhostel, we observe very clearly how first-time attenders are often anxious about the return to an academic environment. Even more striking is the general euphoria that results from completion of the experience. This is proactivity as discussed in connection with the Lawton and Nahemow (1973) model.
- Building coping skills for negative situations—it is somewhat more farfetched, but nonetheless possible, that people deliberately build up habituation to negative stimuli as a bank account of expected later

benefit due to release of the positive opponent process. Our research among public housing residents (Lawton & Cohen, 1974) has sometimes identified an older person who had been the victim of a street crime but nonetheless compulsively insisted on continuing to traverse the unsafe neighborhood. Theoretically at least, the feeling of relief on returning home safely might constitute a reinforcement for continuing the exposure.

- Selectively searching for differentiated types of affective experiences for their own sake—of course, the term *positive affect* includes love, peace, admiration, self-esteem, pride, and so on. Do people have "favorite" affects? Do they pursue them more effectively as they grow older, or choose new ones? Are negative affects sometimes enjoyed, such as "bittersweet" nostalgia? Some of the functions of reminiscence may be to savor affects of the past.

Competence, Affect, and Self-Regulation

Although an attempt has been made in passing to indicate how health and other aspects of competence affect some of the hypothesized processes, before concluding it is necessary to state positively that proactivity and self-regulation are within the power of all people to exert. However, the forms can clearly be different, and the mix of security maneuvers and autonomy maneuvers will be richer on the security side for those whose competences are low.

The Lawton and Nahemow (1973) model in Figure 6.2 portrays how adaptive behavior and positive affective outcomes are possible regardless of how low personal competence is. Yet the range of environmental press strength over which positive outcomes can occur is very narrow for the least competent individuals. A similar situation exists with respect to affective experience. It seems likely that the range of affective experience for the least competent may be restricted, in the interest of conserving energy and personal resources. Research is clearly needed to address this issue, however, because poor health has been shown repeatedly to be associated with stronger negative affect (see the meta-analysis of this relationship by Okun, Stock, Haring, & Witter, 1984); does poor health also reduce positive affect? It may be that the range of *intensity* of affect is less restricted among those in poor health than is the range of *elicitors* of affect and the *frequency* with which affects are expressed.

This chapter has not dealt with the interesting issue of the proportion of all available time during which any affective response occurs, that is, significant departures from affective adaptation level (the opponent-process theory does not deal with this question either). It is possible that it is more important for people of low competence to remain at baseline level than it is for those of average or high competence. If true, a consequence would be that elicitors (positive and negative events) and risks of stress would also be minimized in the interest of security.

As the environmental docility hypothesis would predict, however, impaired people are differentially vulnerable to environmental events, events to which the person is likely to be in the recipient role, rather than the initiator role. The deprivation that goes with impairment is also likely to restrict the incidence of positive events, and the impairment is likely to increase the incidence of negative events. Thus there is a natural tendency among observers to assume that poverty of life-style and receptiveness in the interest of security are intrinsic to the lives of impaired older people.

Even given the most extreme case—that is, the reduction of variety of positive events and affect elicitors, of intensity of affect, of frequency of affect, and of the proactive mode—a range of self-regulatory capability still exists, which needs to be recognized. I have written elsewhere about the proactive behavior of housebound older people who alter a microaspect of their home environment to create a "control center" (Lawton, 1985). The control center is designed to yield maximum knowledge of the external environment by orienting a chair occupied most of the time to window, door, television, telephone, and personal possessions. The control center also may yield positive events and affects by affording entertainment (television), interest (outdoor activity of others), social involvement (telephone), and emotional ties to the past (photos, prized possessions). I mentioned earlier the finer differentiation of an unchanging environment into novel features. Thus autonomous behavior and affective richness can be available at very low levels of competence.

Such remaining degrees of freedom exist within the severe confines imposed by illness and other decrements of competence. Habituation is a necessary element of this picture and is in fact a control mechanism necessary for the achievement of basic security. Thus it is not appropriate to view habituation as an inevitable villain; only when habituation is misapplied can it account for the negative aspects of life portrayed by Kastenbaum (1980-1981) and others. Competence, of course, is a continuum, and the principles outlined for people of low competence apply throughout the continuum. Where personal need, biological limitation, or environmental demands require, constriction of experience is appropriate for security.

Interventions

Interventions based on these principles require detailed discussion not possible in this chapter. As a guidepost to future exploration, however, the chapter ends with the suggestion that both environmental change and person change are routes to enhancement of positive affect and reduction of negative affect.

Environmental Change

A great deal of the literature on designing environments for the aged has been devoted to producing environments rich in positive-event possibilities (Carstens, 1985; Howell, 1980; Lawton, 1975). Less frequent has been any attempt to distinguish between built environments that impose favorable experiences on people versus those that provide maximum choice for a larger array of experiences to occur and be chosen by the older person. The single-solution design presumably is a research-based statistical generalization or an "expert" judgment that a majority of people will benefit from that solution. An example of a single solution is forcing all traffic entering a building to go through a lobby (a high-density social space that maximizes social contact) on the way to the elevator. A contrasting approach would be to provide that high-density space but also allow for an alternative side entrance for those whose privacy needs lead them to prefer a thinly populated route. Having alternatives not only increases person-environment congruence, but it adds an increment of self-regulation by providing the choice. Thus, while all environmental design to some extent forces people into a receptive mode, sensitization to the issues discussed in this chapter can, first, deliberately build in enriching features and, second, provide them in a way that affords choice and possible modification in response to individual need.

Person Change

"Person change" includes all the modalities of intervention directed toward the individual: psychotherapy, counseling, casework, administrative oversight, family advice, and peer interchange. These channels exist now, and there is no suggestion here for developing a new variety, such as "proactivity counseling." Rather, what is suggested is the incorporation of knowledge regarding the value of positive events, reduction of negative events, affective self-management, and proactivity into environmental programs and clinical practice. Training and continuing education in these fields can develop a repertoire of techniques by which to teach people how to recognize in themselves excessive reliance on security-inducing mechanisms, habituation, avoidance of novelty, and other elements. Further, any technique of intervention can be applied to the older person's learning of new ways of self-regulation. Person change can be coupled with environmental change by eliciting or teaching older people to act as experts in providing design-relevant information to professionals (Lawton, 1987). Regnier (1987) based the design of a total retirement housing complex on the carefully organized discussions of potential consumers. Parr and Green (1987) have accumulated a data bank of consumer preference data on variations within housing. People can also be taught or counseled to redesign their own households. There is no reason why in-home service agencies could not incorporate instruction on improving control centers and making other adaptations for disability, and on accomplishing such changes through self-directed means.

Overcoming dysfunctional habituation to negative states and initiating exposure to novel elements may require trained clinicians. However, habituation of this type is certainly not always associated with psychopathology. Experimentation with training groups devoted to improving the balance of positive and negative events might be worthwhile.

Summary

In conclusion, it seems that security and autonomy constitute a dialectic whose ascendant member at a given moment depends on the many facets of personal competence and environmental context. Considering the social deprivations inherent in an ageist society and our consequent tendency to disempower older people (sometimes in the name of enhancing their security), it seems very likely that some expansion of affective range might well occur for older people with continued efforts to upgrade the richness of available environments. If homes, neighborhoods, or institutions are resource-poor, almost by definition this will mean a reduction in the opportunity for positive affective experience. Overattention to the provision of a secure environment may, to be sure, reduce negative affect; but using the example of the institution, risks are few and pleasures are few in a highly secure environment. Regardless of the level of competence of the person, appropriately expanding the opportunities for choice and other forms of environmental flexibility is likely to give the older person an increased chance to be behaviorally proactive and affectively self-regulating and, therefore, to be most successful in enhancing positive affect. Such environmental enhancement will be selectively beneficial to the more competent, as suggested by the environmental proactivity hypothesis. The same enhancements may simply be irrelevant to those of lowest competence. While it is possible that an overrich environment may be threatening to such people, this fact has not been demonstrated. Therefore, for the time being, a useful working principle would seem to be to provide more opportunities for both environmental proactivity and affective self-management. These goals may be achieved both by enriching our person-made environments and by using our clinical and training skills to help older people move an increment beyond their adaptation level toward enhanced self-management.

References

Bradburn, N. M. (1969). *The structure of psychological well-being.* Chicago: Aldine.

Bulman, R. J., & Wortman, C. B. (1977). Attributions of blame and coping in the "real world." Severe accident victims react to their lot. *Journal of Personality and Social Psychology, 35,* 351-363.

Campbell, A., Converse, P. G., & Rodgers, W. (1976). *The quality of American life.* New York: Russell Sage.

Carp, F., & Carp, A. (1984). A complementary/congruence model of well-being on mental health for the community elderly. In I. Altman, M. P. Lawton, & J. F.

Wohlwill (Eds.), *Elderly people and their environment* (pp. 279-336). New York: Plenum.

Carstens, D. Y. (1985). *Site planning and design for the elderly.* New York: Van Nostrand Reinhold.

Chiriboga, D. A., & Cutler, L. (1980). Stress and adaptation: Lifespan perspectives. In L. W. Poon (Ed.), *Aging in the 1980s* (pp. 347-362). Washington, DC: American Psychological Association.

Cornoni-Huntley, J., Barbano, H. E., Brody, J. A., Cohen, B., Feldman, J. P., Kleinman, J. C., & Madans, J. (1983). National Health and Nutrition Examination I—Epidemiologic followup survey. *Public Health Reports, 98,* 245-251.

Costa, P. T., Jr., & McCrae, R. R. (1980). Influence of extraversion and neuroticism on subjective well-being: Happy and unhappy people. *Journal of Personality and Social Psychology, 38,* 668-678.

Costa, P. T., Jr., Zonderman, A. B., McCrae, R. R., Cornoni-Huntley, J., Locke, B. Z., & Barbano, H. E. (1987). Longitudinal analyses of psychological well-being in a national sample: Stability of mean levels. *Journal of Gerontology, 42,* 50-55.

DeLongis, A., Coyne, J. C., Dakof, G., Folkman, S., & Lazarus, R. S. (1982). Relationships of daily hassles, uplifts, and major life events to health status. *Health Psychology, 1,* 119-136.

Diener, E., Sandvik, E., & Larsen, R. J. (1985). Age and sex effects for emotional intensity. *Developmental Psychology, 21,* 542-546.

Epstein, S. M. (1967). Toward a unified theory of anxiety. In B. A. Maher (Ed.), *Progress in experimental personality research* (Vol. 4, pp. 1-89). New York: Academic Press.

Epstein, S. (1983). Aggregation and beyond: Some basic issues on the prediction of behavior. *Journal of Personality, 51,* 360-392.

Folkman, S., Lazarus, R. J., Pimley, S., & Noracek, J. (1987). Age differences in stress and coping processes. *Psychology and Aging, 2,* 171-184.

George, L. K., & Gwyther, L. P. (1986). Caregiver well-being: A multi-dimensional examination of family caregivers of demented adults. *Gerontologist, 26,* 253-259.

Golant, S. M. (1982). Individual differences underlying the dwelling satisfaction of the elderly. *Journal of Social Issues, 38*(3), 121-133.

Goldberg, E. L., & Comstock, G. W. (1980). Epidemiology of life events: Frequency in general populations. *American Journal of Epidemiology, 111,* 731-752.

Helson, H. (1964). *Adaptation level theory.* New York: Harper & Row.

Howell, S. C. (1980). *Designing for aging: Patterns of use.* Cambridge: MIT Press.

Kahana, E. (1982). A congruence model of person-environment interaction. In M. P. Lawton, P. G. Windley, & T. O. Byerts (Eds.), *Aging and the environment: Theoretical approaches* (pp. 97-121). New York: Springer.

Kanner, A. D., Coyne, J. C., Schaefer, C., & Lazarus, R. (1981). Comparison of the modes of stress measurement: Daily hassles and uplifts versus major life events. *Journal of Behavioral Medicine, 4,* 1-39.

Kastenbaum, R. (1980-1981). Habituation as a model of human aging. *International Journal of Aging and Human Development, 12,* 159-170.

Langer, E. J., Blank, A., & Chanowitz, B. (1978). The mindlessness of ostensibly thoughtful action. *Journal of Personality and Social Psychology, 36,* 635-642.

Larsen, R. J. (1985). *The role of affect intensity in augmenting or reducing stimula-*

tion level. West Lafayette, IN: Purdue University, Department of Psychological Sciences.

Lawton, M. P. (1975). *Planning and managing housing for the elderly.* New York: Wiley-Interscience.

Lawton, M. P. (1982). Competence, environmental press, and the adaptation of older people. In M. P. Lawton, P. G. Windley, & T. O Byerts (Eds.), *Aging and the environment: Theoretical approaches* (pp. 33-59). New York: Springer.

Lawton, M. P. (1985). The elderly in context: Perspectives from environmental psychology and gerontology. *Environment and Behavior, 17,* 501-519.

Lawton, M. P. (1987). Strategies in planning environments for the elderly. *Journal of Independent Living, 1*(3), 1-14.

Lawton, M. P. (in press). Behavior-relevant ecological factors. In K. W. Schaie & C. Schooler (Eds.), *Social structure and the psychological aging process.* Hillsdale, NJ: Lawrence Erlbaum.

Lawton, M. P., & Cohen, J. (1974). The generality of housing impact on the well-being of older people. *Journal of Gerontology, 28,* 194-204.

Lawton, M. P., & Nahemow, L. (1973). Ecology and the aging process. In C. Eisdorfer & M. P. Lawton (Eds.), *Psychology of adult development and aging* (pp. 619-674). Washington, DC: American Psychological Association.

Miller, G. A., Pribram, K. H., & Galanter, E. (1960). *Plans and the structure of behavior.* New York: Holt, Rinehart & Winston.

Murray, H. (1938). *Explorations in personality.* New York: Oxford University Press.

Murrell, S. A., & Norris, F. H. (1984). Resources, life events, and changes in positive affect and depression in older adults. *American Journal of Community Psychology, 12,* 445-464.

National Center for Health Statistics. (1973). *Plan and operation of the Health and Nutrition Examination Survey, 1971-1973.* Washington, DC: U.S. Department of Health, Education, & Welfare.

Okun, M. A., Stock, W. A., Haring, M. J., & Witter, R. (1984). Health and subjective well-being: A meta-analysis. *International Journal of Aging and Human Development, 19,* 111-132.

Parr, J., & Green, S. (1987). *Consumer factors in facility programming.* Clearwater, FL: Foundation for Aging Research.

Petrie, A. (1967). *Individuality in pain and suffering.* Chicago: University of Chicago Press.

Regnier, V. (1987). Programming congregate housing: The preferences of upper income elderly. In V. Regnier & J. Pynoos (Eds.), *Housing the aged* (pp. 207-226). New York: Elsevier.

Regnier, V., & Pynoos, J. (Eds.). (1987). *Housing the aged.* New York: Elsevier.

Reich, J. W., & Zautra, A. (1981). Life events and personal causation: Some relationships with satisfaction and distress. *Journal of Personality and Social Psychology, 41,* 1002-1012.

Reich, J., & Zautra, A. (1983). Demands and desires in daily life: Some influences on well-being. *American Journal of Community Psychology, 11,* 41-58.

Reich, J. W., & Zautra, A. J. (1987, July). *An event-based approach to personality mediation of subject well-being.* Paper presented at the Conference on Subject Well-Being, Bad Homburg, West Germany.

Rowles, G. D. (1978). *Prisoners of space?* Boulder, CO: Westview.

Rowles, G. D. (1980). Growing old "inside": Aging and attachment to place in an Appalachian community. In N. Datan & N. Lohmann (Eds.), *Transitions of aging* (pp. 153-170). New York: Academic Press.

Rubinstein, R. L. (1987). *The home environments of older people: Psychosocial processes relating person to space.* Philadelphia: Phildelphia Geriatric Center.

Russell, J. A. (1980). A circumplex model of affect. *Journal of Personality and Social Psychology, 39,* 1161-1178.

Russell, J. A., & Snodgrass, J. (1987). Emotion and the environment. In D. Stokols & I. Altman (Eds.), *Handbook of environmental psychology* (Vol. 1, pp. 175-204). New York: John Wiley.

Sandvik, E., Diener, E., & Larsen, R. J. (1985). The opponent process theory and affective reactions. *Motivation and Emotion, 9,* 407-418.

Scheidt, R. J., & Norris-Baker, C. (1987, November). *Kastenbaum's habituation theory of aging: Implications for environment-aging research.* Paper presented at the annual meeting of the Gerontological Society of America, Washington, DC.

Schulz, R. (1985). Emotion and affect. In J. E. Birren & K. W. Schaie (Eds.), *Handbook of the psychology of aging* (2nd ed., pp. 531-543). New York: Van Nostrand Reinhold.

Solomon, R. L. (1980). The opponent-process theory of acquired motivation: The costs of pleasure and the benefits of pain. *American Psychologist, 35,* 691-712.

Tucker, D. M. (1981). Lateral brain function, emotion, and conceptualization. *Psychological Bulletin, 89,* 19-46.

Tucker, D. M., & Williamson, P. A. (1984). Asymmetric neural control systems in human self-regulation. *Psychological Review, 91,* 185-215.

Wallace, A. F. C., & Carson, M. T. (1973). Sharing and diversity in emotion terminology. *Ethos, 1,* 1-29.

Watson, D., & Tellegen, A. (1985). Toward a consensual structure of mood. *Psychological Bulletin, 98,* 219-235.

Windley, P. G., & Scheidt, R. J. (1982). An ecological model of mental health among small-town rural elderly. *Journal of Gerontology, 37,* 235-242.

Woodruff, D. S. (1985). Arousal, sleep, and aging. In J. E. Birren & K. W. Schaie (Eds.), *Handbook of the psychology of aging* (2nd ed., pp. 261-295). New York: Van Nostrand Reinhold.

Zautra, A., & Reich, J. (1980). Positive life events and reports of well-being: Some useful distinctions. *American Journal of Community Psychology, 8,* 657-670.

Zuckerman, M., & Link, K. (1968). Construct validity for the Sensation Seeking Scale. *Journal of Consulting and Clinical Psychology, 32,* 420-426.

7

Personal Possessions and Their Meanings in Old Age

N. LAURA KAMPTNER

This chapter is about personal possessions—the meanings and functions they have for older adults, and their role in adaptation to old age. My interest in this area began several years ago, while undertaking a review of the literature on attachment throughout the life span. I came across theoretical and empirical work on the attachments that infants and young children develop to certain objects, which noted that these objects (i.e., soft objects such as teddy bears and blankets) function primarily as soothers and "substitutes" for certain characteristics of "mothering." When I sought information on this topic for the later stages of life, I found that little attention had been paid to studying this phenomenon in the years following early childhood. The lack of available information in the psychological literature on this topic became the impetus for beginning an investigation into personal possessions and their meanings in adulthood and old age.

This question appears worth asking, given that possessions are such a salient part of everyday life. As noted by Graumann (1974), most activities, including one's goals, means, circumstances, social interaction, habits, and motives are integrally connected to everyday things in the environment. Also, much of adult life revolves around the acquisition and maintenance of material possessions. For example, holidays, birthdays, and religious ceremonies involve the giving or exchanging of objects. Heirlooms are passed down through generations of families. Souvenirs and mementos of places visited or events experienced are picked up and saved through the years. Being a collector of dolls, stamps, books, or porcelain serves as an avocation for many individuals; and while scrapbooks, photo albums, religious relics, old letters, and keepsakes may yellow with age, they become more valued by their owner as time passes.

The available information on this topic suggests that personal belongings have a more meaningful place in adults' lives than they have been credited with. Writings from a variety of disciplines throughout the past century collectively suggest at least two major functions of possessions for individuals: instrumental and symbolic (e.g., Prentice, 1987). *Instrumental* functions of possessions are those that in some way enable individuals to manipulate or control their environment, allowing their owners to meet a specific objective or need. *Symbolic* functions, on the other hand, are those in which objects become symbols of some desirable state or relationship for their owner. More specifically, this literature suggests that possessions play a meaningful role in people's lives by acting as sources of control and mastery, moderators of affect, cultivators of the self, symbols of ties with others, and memories of the past (e.g., Csikszentmihalyi & Rochberg-Halton, 1981; Furby, 1978; Kron, 1983; Rochberg-Halton, 1984). These meanings of personal possessions for individuals would appear to be particularly salient for older adults, because they closely parallel many of the psychosocial tasks and challenges of late adulthood—such as the preservation of personal control and autonomy, the maintenance of self-identity, the integration of the past self with the present self (and the perception of continuity of self over time), and the maintenance of a socially supportive network of interpersonal ties (e.g., Butler & Lewis, 1983; Erikson, 1968; Erikson, Erikson, & Kivnick, 1986; Lieberman & Tobin, 1983; Neugarten, 1979).

In this chapter, these parallels are elaborated upon while personal belongings and their meanings in old age are examined more closely, with special emphasis placed on their role in adaptation to late adulthood. Following a discussion of the instrumental and symbolic meanings of possessions in old age, possessions that are especially valued by the elderly are examined. In addition, a section on homes and their meanings is included, because in my current research it became evident that homes are not only viewed as possessions (and as "keepers" of possessions)—they also embody the same kinds of meanings as do other (smaller) possessions.

Methodological Approach

Recent empirical findings from my own research on possessions and their meanings in old age are integrated within the above framework. This work is part of an ongoing series of studies on possessions and their meanings in adulthood and old age. The respondents in the findings reported below were 72 predominantly White, middle-class adults (36 males, 36 females) who ranged in age from 60 to 89 years (M = 70.3 years). These individuals were recruited from two *nonresidential* senior centers in a suburban community in Southern California, and all were living independently and were ambulatory and sufficiently well-oriented to respond to the questionnaire items. The questionnaire from which these data were gathered contained mostly open-ended items. It was designed to address the question of what possessions are salient under the following conditions (and what meanings such objects have for individuals): (a) "treasured" possessions, (b) "most important" possessions, (c) what (five) possessions one would rescue if one's house caught fire, (d) family heirlooms, (e) most "comforting" possessions, and (f) what things one prefers most to receive as gifts. Because the focus of this study was on inanimate possessions, respondents were specifically asked not to consider people, plants, or pets as possessions. The questionnaire took approximately one hour to complete, and it was self-administered for most respondents. (The analysis of the data resulted first in the development of classification categories for the objects and the object meanings named. These are listed in Table 7.1.)

Table 7.1
Object and Object Meaning Categories

Categories of objects*

1. Stuffed animals
2. Dolls
3. Pillows-blankets
4. Books
5. Clothing (clothes, hats, purses, shoes, and so on)
6. Childhood toys (trikes, wagons, toy cars, models, bikes, "toys," toy soldiers, toy weapons, dress-up items, and so on)
7. Sporting equipment (sports equipment and accessories, guns, knives)
8. Motor vehicles (cars, motorcycles, boats, planes)
9. Phonograph records-music (phonograph records and tapes, music, musical instruments)
10. Photos (photos, photograph albums, portraits)
11. Memorabilia (diaries, journals, yearbooks, pennants, souvenirs, scrapbooks, old cards, and letters)
12. Personal accomplishment (awards, trophies)
13. Furniture (furniture pieces, antiques, rugs, lamps)
14. Dishware-silverware (dishware, china, glassware, silverware)
15. Jewelry
16. Religious items (Bible, Torah, rosary, and so on)
17. Collections (stamp, coin, shell, or rock collections; "collection")
18. Small appliances (TVs, stereos, VCRs, cameras, typewriters, computers, phones, clocks, and so on)
19. Important documents (important documents, records, or papers)
20. Money (money, investments, savings)
21. Artwork (artwork, including handmade items such as handcrafts and woodwork)
22. Tools (tools, scientific equipment, handcraft equipment)
23. Personal items (jewelry boxes, perfume, wallets, flowers, "trinkets," eyeglasses, keys)
24. Homes
25. Other

Categories of object meanings

1. Memories (recollection of a specific occasion, place, or event; noninterpersonal memories; "memories")
2. Interpersonal-familial associations (object reminds them of someone special; was given by, or belonged to, someone special; represents attachments to others or love; has been handed down in family)
3. Personification (object represents "someone to talk to," a "companion," or something to care for; is "reliable and always there"; "is something to love")
4. Cultural-religious associations (ethnic, cultural, or religious association)
5. Pleasant experience (enjoyment; positive feelings; object provides for feelings of "release" or "escape"; creates positive affect and mood; makes respondent feel good; is soothing or relaxing; provides feelings of comfort or security)
6. Utilitarian value (object provides convenience, saves time, or fills a need; is used for learning)
7. Intrinsic quality (descriptions of physical characteristics of object, including comments about its design, style, color, monetary worth, its irreplaceability, its being part of a collection, or its being "handmade" or "one of a kind")
8. Personal history (historical, personal, relationship of object to self—e.g., "had it for a long time," "is part of my past," "had it the longest," "is the first one I had," "always with me," "is a part of my life," or it marks the transition from one life stage to the next)
9. Self-expression (expression of self; "is part of me"; "looks like me")
10. Personal accomplishment (object represents a desired accomplishment or goal; is something that was always wanted; embodies or expresses personal values, goals, or ideals)
11. Freedom (object provides or represents freedom, independence, or autonomy)
12. Other

*Based, in part, on a scheme developed by Csikszentmihalyi and Rochberg-Halton (1981).

In the following sections, two primary functions of possessions are discussed. These include using possessions to accomplish a particular goal in the environment (i.e., "instrumental" functions) and using possessions as symbolic representations of oneself and one's ties with others. Each of these is discussed in detail, with particular attention paid to the relation between these functions and adaptation in old age.

Instrumental Functions of Possessions

Personal Control

Theories of motivation emphasize that individuals have a need to feel effective and interact competently with their environment (e.g., Brehm, 1972; Deci, 1975; Seligman, 1975; White, 1959). A challenge faced by many aging individuals is a decline in autonomy and personal control which may come about by changes or losses in one's work or family status, income, social network, and physical capacities, or through societal devaluation (Cox, 1984). Because the extent to which one is capable of effecting a desired outcome in one's environment becomes incorporated into one's self-concept, one's sense of self can be eroded, along with a decline of personal control, causing feelings of personal inadequacy, incompetency, and self-doubt (Cox, 1984). Conversely, environments that foster one's sense of autonomy and personal control may have a positive effect on individuals, for example, in recovery from illness (Pastalan, 1983).

Objects have been suggested as playing a vital role in the preservation of one's sense of control by enabling individuals to experience a sense of efficacy. Possessions make possible certain activities and conveniences, and may make people feel some mastery over nature because they can provide a margin of safety if one miscalculates future need (Litwinski, 1943-1944). According to Furby (1978), a contemporary researcher on possessive behavior, possessions are one means by which individuals can express a healthy degree of personal control, particularly in relatively uncontrollable environments like nursing homes or mental institutions. This line of reasoning is based on findings from her studies, which suggest that possessions are such by virtue of the degree of control one has over them. Also, objects may, in fact, *be* more controllable compared to other aspects of one's environment (Hong, 1978). The ability of objects to function in this manner may be why, in situations where personal control is limited but where personal possessions are allowed, a patient's attitude is more positive and rehabilitation tends to be more successful (e.g., Bot, 1968; Morgan & Cushing, 1966).

Objects may also function as a means of controlling (or at least influencing) the social environment by serving as sources of social status and social dominance. Such objects, according to Csikszentmihalyi and Rochberg-Halton (1981), are found in most cultures, and they may function to elicit the respect, consideration, and envy of others. Objects that are especially rare, expensive, or old are most apt to function as status symbols, by conveying to others who believe in their status that their owner possesses distinctive or superior qualities. (A good example of this in our culture is a rare, expensive, or very old car.) Possessions have even been described as being instruments for defining and controlling the relationship between two or more persons (Hallowell, 1943; Suttie, Ginsberg, Isaacs, & Marshall, 1935).

Influencing Affect

Possessions may also function as moderators of affect by acting as sources of security, enjoyment, or solace (Neal, 1985; Rochberg-Halton, 1984; Vlosky, 1979). Teddy bears and blankets are perhaps the most well-known objects that provide feelings of security, especially for young children (Horton, Louy, & Coppolillo, 1974; Passman, 1976, 1977; Stevenson, 1954; Winnicott, 1953). The use of objects in this manner is not confined to the young, however. Numerous reports support the notion that adults may extract these benefits from certain objects as well—for example, from teddy bears (Beck, Cooper, Dallas, Abramson, & McCormick, 1984; Horton et al., 1974; Stevenson, 1954), blankets (Van Buren, 1985), and rings, photographs, and books ("Adult Security Blankets," 1986). Feelings of security may also be evoked by possessions that embody the memories of, and connections to, one's past (Neal, 1985), which in some cases may be the only stable and unchanging component of one's environment (Taylor, 1981). This latter point may be particularly salient for older adults, for whom a high proportion of life changes may be occurring.

In addition to enhancing feelings of security, possessions may provide feelings of enjoyment. In a study by Csikszentmihalyi and Rochberg-Halton (1981) in which Chicago families were asked what things in their homes were special and why, one of the major themes that emerged as to why certain objects in the home were more meaningful than others (e.g., televisions and stereos) was that they provided enjoyment. Televisions, for example, were described by respondents as providing low-intensity experiences that were valued as enjoyment and release. Enjoyment has also been described as an outcome of reviewing reminders of one's past. Taylor (1981, p. 40), in describing the worth of her collections of various objects, stated that "indescribable pleasure can be derived from recalling the circumstances surrounding the acquisition of an item . . . such memories triggering other pleasurable associations as well." A few examples from my current research also illustrate this theme—a 64-year-old female remarked that her most important possession was her children's photo albums, because "I enjoy looking and remembering their growing-up years." Similarly, a 70-year-old male described his most treasured possession as a plaster plaque of a Sioux Indian in full dress that was "beautifully detailed and colored . . . it was a surprise gift from my wife . . . we were on a vacation . . . I saw it and admired it. Wife corresponded and arranged for purchase in secrecy. I enjoy looking at it . . . I remember the circumstances of its acquisition."

What objects offer solace or comfort to older adults? While the literature on the early years of life suggests that the tactile qualities of soft objects are most comforting, no information exists to date on what is comforting during the later stages of life. In my current research, I asked older adults what objects are especially comforting to them when they are lonely, upset, afraid, or anxious. As indicated in Table 7.2, these respondents named primarily small appliances (47%)—which included mainly televisions—and books (23%). Small appliances were far more salient than books for males compared to females, who seemed to turn to books as often as to television.

Table 7.2
Most Frequently Named "Comforting" Possessions
(percentage of each group naming object)

Object	Total Group (N = 72)	Males (n = 36)	Females (n = 36)
Small appliances	47	59	36
Books	23	14	32
Photographs	6	—	8
Religious items	4	9	—
Furniture	4	—	8
Phonograph records/music	4	9	—
Clothing	—	5	—
Dolls	—	—	4
Jewelry	—	—	4

Although respondents were not specifically asked about the meanings of the objects identified as "comforting," many offered variations of the following comment: "TV . . . it distracts me." This interpretation seemed to fit the objects named, in that they could be viewed as providing a temporary escape, release, or distraction that might, in turn, have the effect of altering one's current mood state. Thus, compared to the early years of life, where physical tactile comfort is effective in comforting one, solace in the later years of life seems to come from more "mental" strategies such as diverting one's attention.

Symbolic Functions of Possessions

In addition to objects functioning as a means of accomplishing some goal, possessions may also function as symbols of the self, of others, and of one's past.

The initial discussion linking possessions with the self dates back at least to William James (1890), who postulated a close—even indistinguishable—relationship between the self and one's possessions. He viewed possessions as important because part of the definition of self was the "material self," which included all that a person owned, including one's body and possessions. Subsequent writers have also noted that object ownership creates a feeling of "psychological nearness" to an object, with the object assimilated to and integrated with the self so that the two are essentially fused. Beaglehole (1932), for example, examined possession and ownership in many different cultures and concluded that people view personal property as somehow assimilated into the self. He suggested that there is a tendency to integrate part of the self with any object one uses or views as one's own, such that part of one's "life spirit" is united with the object. Interesting in this regard is a study by Irwin and Gephard (1946), who found that subjects preferred their own object even when presented with the same new (but unowned) object.

In addition to being viewed as "fused" with the self, objects have also been described as playing a significant role in the development of one's sense of self (during the early years of life) by "telling" individuals who they are and what they are to become (Rochberg-Halton, 1984). In other words, possessions are a part of the socializing environment from which the self emerges. Objects may also influence the development of one's concept of self by providing experiences of mastery and competency (or incompetency), or enhancing (or preventing) the expression of one's actions and thoughts. Possessions may later aid in the cultivation and maintenance of self as one grows older by "reminding" individuals of who they are or were (e.g., Csikszentmihalyi & Rochberg-Halton, 1981).

It is to the issues of self and possessions in later adulthood that we now turn. In the following sections, the relations between possessions and the maintenance of self, the life review process, and ties with others are examined.

Symbols of the Self:
Maintenance of Self-Identity

Many of the developmental tasks and challenges of late adulthood revolve around the self. The maintenance of one's self-identity (and integrity of one's self-system) is one such example, which, according to Erikson et al. (1986) and Lieberman and Tobin (1983), is considered to be the critical task of late adulthood. According to these researchers, there are a number of factors working simultaneously that can erode identity in late life, such as the loss of those things that have in the past confirmed one's sense of self, for example, physical deterioration, role losses or less clearly defined roles, fewer opportunities for validating experiences, social network losses, and devaluation by society. The results of a study by Lieberman and Tobin (1983) suggest that the viability of using current interactions with the social and physical environment as validating experiences for one's sense of self appears to decline with age (for the reasons listed above), and consequently the elderly may ignore the present and focus on the past to affirm their identity. Especially for the elderly, the past may be a storehouse of memories that ensure the maintenance of their sense of self even in an unsupportive environmental context. Reviewing the past, then, tells them, "I am who I always have been" (Lieberman & Tobin, 1983, p. 259). In support of this strategy, Erikson (1968) and Erikson et al. (1986) assert that perceiving continuity of self over time is one of the major components of a sense of self. The elderly's ability to do this, however, may depend on their ability to articulate what they have believed in, valued, and stood for over their entire lifetime (Erikson et al., 1986).

Possessions function to maintain one's sense of self by being concrete reminders of experiences, events, roles, relationships, and values that are important components of one's lifelong sense of self (Butler & Lewis, 1983; Csikszentmihalyi & Rochberg-Halton, 1981; deBeauvoir, 1973; Erikson et al., 1986). Rochberg-Halton (1984), in fact, suggests that transactions with possessions are really communicative dialogues with the self. One's personal belongings collected over a lifetime become, in a sense, artifacts of one's personal history. Objects evoke certain memories of the past—photos, for example, provide a record of one's life, and preserve the memory of personal ties and the lives of one's forebears. Events with loved ones as well as other experiences from the past can be relived, certain moods and emotions may be aroused, and comparisons of the past with the present may be evoked by photos or other artifacts of the past—such as souvenirs, mementos, gifts, photos, old letters, pressed flowers, bronzed baby shoes, journals, diaries, keepsakes, and furniture. These items are, in a sense, "snapshots" of the past that may trigger memories, feelings, and other associations. The ability of objects to be holders of memories was poignantly expressed in an essay by a young woman who described her feelings upon finding out that her parents were selling the house in which she grew up—she feared that, if all of the old objects, furnishings, and rooms were gone, her memories would disappear as well (Korelitz, 1986). Certain objects, particularly heirlooms and photos, may remind individuals of their ancestors, their own childhoods, and the roots of their personal and cultural origins (Erikson et al., 1986).

This ongoing "dialogue" with one's personal belongings appears to be important and even perhaps necessary for the maintenance of one's sense of self. Kron (1983), for example, suggests that identities "flicker and fade," and that one's belongings function as self-reinforcers that keep one from feeling disoriented. This notion is aptly illustrated in writings by Goffman (1961), who states that the loss or absence of one's possessions may result in "deselfing," an occurrence that typically happens in institutions and mental hospitals. According to Goffman, a patient's personal possessions are the material out of which he or she builds or maintains the sense of self. Personal possessions such as clothing, cosmetics, scrapbooks, photograph albums, mementos, souvenirs, and jewelry form an individual's "identity kit," which allows them to present their usual self to others (and that also embodies their own personal histories). The loss of such "identity equipment," according to Goffman, may cause personal defacement and the erosion of self because it literally strips the individual of the symbols and representations of self. Similarly, Frankl (1955) noted that in the concentration camps of World War II, when all possessions were taken away, people had nothing with which to make a connection with their former lives. This same effect was also evident in Carp's (1966) study of a government-planned apartment building in Texas called Victoria Plaza. There, the failure to take cherished possessions into account in relocating the elderly had the negative effect of the objects being missed not only as instrumental items, but also as reminders of family and personal history.

Possessions also often represent social ties or bonds. According to Csikszentmihalyi and Rochberg-Halton (1981), the self of older adults is to a certain extent structured around networks of past and present relationships. One elderly man in my study, for example, described his most important possession as being the family Bible because it has a record of his entire family's history. Csikszent-mihalyi and Rochberg-Halton (1981) suggest that a lack of personal possessions that function as symbols of others may lead to an erosion (or even destruction) of one's personal self.

Possessions not only function to maintain their owner's sense of self, but they may also enable one to communicate that self to others. In a study by Millard and Smith (1981), when older people in nursing homes were allowed to have personal belongings around them (e.g., photos, plants), medical students expressed more positive attitudes toward them than toward patients who were in bare surroundings. It was as if one's personal belongings nonverbally described or defined one's self to others, so that the owner of the possessions was more apt to be viewed as an individual with a self and not as a "non-person." An elderly man in my study reiterated this same theme when he was discussing his most treasured possession, family photographs: "Photographs . . . family history is in those photos . . . I like to show the great-grandchildren [our lives]."

Symbols of the Self:
The Life Review

Another developmental challenge of late adulthood that is related to the self in old age concerns the task of developing an integrated and coherent personal history, and reevaluating one's experiences in the perspective of time (Butler & Lewis, 1983; Erikson, 1968; Erikson et al., 1986). One of the ways in which this may be accomplished is through what has been called the "life review," in which older adults become preoccupied with going over the past in memory, pictures, or through conversing with others. According to Butler (1963, 1970), the life review is a natural and universal adaptive process where, by bringing one's past experiences back to consciousness, older adults are helped in solidifying and integrating their identities. By reexamining the past and reintegrating past unresolved conflicts, older adults may come to know themselves better, communicate to others who they were and are, and help themselves deal with their mortality (Butler, 1963).

Studies on the effects of the life review process have found that older individuals who reminisced experienced an increase in the consistency of their past and present self-concepts in comparison with those who did not reminisce (e.g., Lewis, 1971). Kiefer (1974), for example, found that constructing and reconstructing one's life and personal history assisted elderly Japanese Americans in explaining to themselves and others how they came to be who they were. According to Marshall (1980), the life review process may not only help bring meaning to one's life, it can also be particularly important to the elderly, who may be experiencing social and physical losses, by helping them preserve a sense of esteem based on their past status.

Personal belongings may function as objects of reminiscence by triggering or enhancing one's reflections on the past and by assisting one in integrating the various patterns around which the self is organized at different points in one's life (Csikszentmihalyi & Rochberg-Halton, 1981). Each belonging has a personal history; each object may be a part of one's identity that can, in turn, trigger other memories and segments of one's life history (e.g., Kellogg, 1985; Taylor, 1981). Certain possessions may also function in a more literal sense as documents or records (and reminders) of one's life, such as family trees and genealogy records, photograph albums, scrapbooks, diaries, journals, old letters, keepsakes, mementos, and souvenirs. Numerous examples of possessions functioning in this manner were evident in my study. One elderly woman, for example, stated that her most treasured possession was her photographs because "they are a part of my life history." Another elderly man treasured his genealogy records, which had become such an important hobby to him that he spent at least some part of each day working on them: "Genealogy records . . . they are important as a backup for what I am unable to remember." Another elderly man's most treasured possession was a set of pistols because "they remind me of my past and my accomplishments as a sharpshooter." An older woman regarded "family photographs of my [deceased] husband and children and grandchildren" as her most important possession, because "they remind me of former times." In a sense, then, certain personal belongings function as images or souvenirs of the past, and they may even be the last symbolic remnants of who and what a person once was (Unruh, 1983). As Kron (1983) eloquently states, possessions compose the fabric of one's experience (and, one could add, one's life).

Symbols of the Self:
Self-in-the-Future

In addition to one's self-in-the-past being salient to the integrity of the self for the elderly, so may be one's self-in-the-future—that is, the survival of the self beyond death (Erikson et al., 1986; Kahn & Antonucci, 1980; Unruh, 1983). According to Butler (1970), the desire to leave a trace or mark of oneself may result in older adults becoming more interested in posterity, history as written by others, or in the reading and writing of memoirs. Unruh (1983) suggests that perceptions of the nearness of death may also trigger the elderly to begin putting together and documenting their personal histories through autobiographies, journals, letters, diaries, stories, or poems. Butler (1970, p. 123) labels such attempts to transcend mortality as *historicity*—that is, "a search for identity beyond the grave."

How might the self be preserved after death? Again, one's personal belongings may play a role. They may function to remind others (including one's progeny) of the deceased (Unruh, 1983); and, by being handed down to progeny, they may have the effect of preserving the deceased person's sense of self in immortality and generational history (Erikson et al., 1986). Also, through wills specifying how one's personal belongings are to be distributed after death, the deceased can control which of their identities they want preserved and at the same time express their feelings toward others (Unruh, 1983).

In my research, I was interested in finding out which objects typically serve as heirlooms and what meanings their owners attribute to them. Heirlooms are unique in that they serve both of the functions described above—that is, they are "records" of family and personal history ("self-in-the-past") and they may also function as "self-in-the-future" because their current owner may decide to give them to someone through a will. As the top of Table 7.3 indicates, the objects named most frequently by the total group as heirlooms were dishware-silverware (30%), furniture (20%), and jewelry (15%). Dishware-silverware was named significantly more often by females compared to males ($\chi^2 (1) = 7.68, p < .006$). The meanings these objects carried for individuals were overwhelmingly (and it is not surprising) interpersonal-familial associations—and almost exclusively familial in nature. These data suggest that heirlooms tend to

Table 7.3
Most Frequently Named Heirlooms and Their Meanings
(percentage of each group naming object and meaning)

Category	Total Group (N = 72)	Males (n = 36)	Females (n = 36)
Objects:			
Dishware-silverware	30	15	39
Furniture	20	19	21
Jewelry	15	22	11
Artwork	10	—	11
Photographs	7	15	—
Small appliances	—	—	4
Religious items	—	11	—
Clothing	—	—	4
Meanings:			
Interpersonal-familial association	83	89	80
Utilitarian value	8	4	11
Intrinsic quality	6	4	7
Memories	1	4	—
Cultural-religious association	1	—	2

be household and personal possessions (ones that were typically used a great deal by their previous owners), which symbolized familial ties.

Symbols of Others

In addition to functioning as symbols of the self, possessions may represent others—the ties or bonds one has with others, as well as the self of others (Csikszentmihalyi & Rochberg-Halton, 1981; Sherman & Newman, 1977-1978). Possessions acquired as gifts, for example, have been described as being symbolic containers for the being of a donor, who, according to Schudson (1986), gives a part of him- or herself to the recipient in the process of giving a gift. Also, photos in one's home have been described as being the primary means by which people preserve the memories of personal ties, because they carry the actual image of a person (Csikszentmihalyi & Rochberg-Halton, 1981).

Possessions as symbols of others was a theme mentioned over and over again by my respondents. In fact, both my research and that of others (e.g., Csikszentmihalyi & Rochberg-Halton, 1981) demonstrated that this is one of the most salient meanings attributed to possessions, particularly for those objects that are especially valued. For example, wedding rings typically symbolize the bond between the two partners; a photograph may be a pictorial reminder of the tie that exists between friends or family; or a family heirloom may symbolize the bonds that link the generations of one's family.

Some examples of this function from the current study include the following comments by respondents: A 75-year-old woman who was describing her most important possessions as being two dresses and a slipper that had belonged to her mother stated that they were very special to her because "[they] remind me so of my mother . . . they give me warm feelings." A 79-year-old woman said a picture of the Holy Family was her current treasured possession, "because my uncle made and gave it to me . . . I was 11 years old, and it was my First Communion." In another instance, a 68-year-old woman treasured an antique-white "lemonade" china set with hand-painted designs, which had been given to her by her mother, because "it belonged to someone I loved very much and who loved me." A 73-year-old male, discussing an all-gold chain with an anchor on it, said that he received it at age 18 while on leave and that he treasured it "because my grandfather gave it to me . . . it reminds me of how much he loved me." A 71-year-old male named as his current treasured possession a lithographed wood print of a Welsh countryside. He treasured it because it was given to him after his grandfather's death, and it reminds him of his grandfather and of his family. A 77-year-old male named a lemon as his current treasured possession —he said that it had been given to him by his wife when he was leaving Warsaw with the Polish Army in 1939, and that he had saved it throughout the years because of its emotional and romantic value. Finally, a 79-year-old woman, describing a treasured pair of framed miniature portraits of her parents in their midfifties, said: "My father had them made 'while we still look good' . . . I even take them with me on travels . . . they are comforting. They were such perfect parents . . . the miniatures represent their presence to me."

According to Unruh (1983), the possessions of a deceased person, such as their collections, their favorite paintings, or their jewelry, may also symbolize the identity of that person and provide a means by which the survivors may reminisce about that person. A 75-year-old woman in my study illustrated this very well: In discussing her current most treasured possession, she described a set of golf clubs that had belonged to her husband, who had been a golfer before his death five years earlier. When he died, she kept them and took up golfing, which made her feel closer to him. (I got the feeling that the golf clubs embodied the self of her husband, and/or that by assuming his activities and possessions, she felt closer to him.)

Summary

Personal possessions appear to play a salient and meaningful role in many of the developmental tasks and challenges that old age may bring. One's belongings may enhance one's mastery and control in the face of losses; they may act as mood modulators; they may assist individuals in maintaining and preserving their identities in the face of events that erode their sense of self; they may trigger and enhance the life review process; and they may represent ties or bonds with others at a time of life when social losses tend to be greater.

What about possessions that are considered to be the *most* valued by their owners? While possessions may serve a variety of functions, such as those discussed above, what are the meanings associated with possessions that are especially valued? We turn to this issue next.

Valued Possessions in Old Age

Of all of one's personal belongings, what kinds of things are more valued by their owners than others? The few studies that have examined what possessions are considered to be the most "special" or cherished in late adulthood suggest that these possessions typically include photographs, books, artwork, religious items, jewelry, plateware and silverware, furniture, and television sets, which have meanings that refer primarily to affective ties and the self (Csikszentmihalyi & Rochberg-Halton, 1981; Morris, 1987; Sherman & Newman, 1977-1978). With increasing age, Csikszentmihalyi and Rochberg-Halton (1981) noted an increase in object meanings that referred to the past.

While these studies focused primarily on having older respondents identify special or cherished objects, my research was aimed at attaining a broader picture of valued possessions and their meanings. Part of the goal was to get a clearer understanding of what "cherished," or "special," means. Toward this end, I asked elderly respondents to consider possessions according to different value criteria (i.e., "treasured" possessions, "most important" possessions, what possessions would be rescued if one's house caught fire, and what objects they preferred to receive as gifts). The results of these inquiries are reported below.

Treasured Possessions

For the total group, the most frequently named treasured possessions were photos (17%), jewelry (16%), and small appliances (14%) (see Table 7.4). Males most often named small appliances, photos, motor vehicles, and artwork, while females named primarily jewelry, dishware-silverware, and photos. Females, more often than males, named dishware-silverware (χ^2 (1) = 8.10, $p < .005$) and jewelry (χ^2 (1) = 8.64, $p < .004$).

When respondents were asked why the object was considered to be "treasured," the most frequent responses involved interpersonal-familial associations (49%) and pleasant experience (24%), as indicated in Table 7.4. Females named interpersonal-familial associations proportionately more often than males did, although this difference was not statistically significant. Males named pleasant experience more often than females did (χ^2 (1) = 4.00, $p < .042$). These findings are fairly similar to those of Csikszentmihalyi and Rochberg-Halton (1981).

Table 7.4
Most Frequently Named "Treasured" Possessions and Their Meanings (percentage of each group naming object and meaning)

Category	Total Group (N = 72)	Males (n = 36)	Females (n = 36)
Objects:			
Photographs	17	17	17
Jewelry	16	—	25
Small appliances	14	26	6
Dishware-silverware	11	—	19
Artwork	7	11	—
Motor vehicles	—	11	—
Sports equipment	—	9	—
Collections	—	9	—
Religious items	—	—	6
Furniture	—	—	6
Meanings:			
Interpersonal-familial association	49	34	64
Pleasant experience	24	34	12
Utilitarian value	6	11	—
Memories	6	6	6
Personification	3	6	—
Intrinsic quality	3	—	6
Self-expression	3	—	3
Personal accomplishment	3	—	3
Cultural-religious association	—	—	3

"Most Important" Possessions

When asked what possessions they considered to be the "most important" of all that they owned, my respondents most frequently named homes (18%), motor vehicles (14%), and photos, dishware-silverware, and jewelry (each 10%). As indicated in Table 7.5, males named motor vehicles, homes, and small appliances most often, while females named homes, dishware-silverware, and jewelry most frequently. Once again, females named dishware-silverware more often, in comparison with males (χ^2 (1) = 6.13, $p < .013$).

Table 7.5
Most Frequently Named "Most Important" Possessions and
Their Meanings (percentage of each group naming
object and meaning)

Category	Total Group (N = 72)	Males (n = 36)	Females (n = 36)
Objects:			
Homes	18	17	19
Motor vehicles	14	22	—
Photographs	10	11	9
Dishware-silverware	10	—	19
Jewelry	10	—	14
Small appliances	—	14	—
Religious items	—	11	—
Artwork	—	—	9
Meanings:			
Interpersonal-familial association	35	23	44
Utilitarian value	22	19	24
Pleasant experience	12	15	9
Freedom	10	19	—
Intrinsic quality	8	12	6
Memories	—	—	9

As the bottom half of Table 7.5 indicates, the most frequently named meanings attributed to these objects were interpersonal-familial associations (35%), utilitarian value (22%), and pleasant experience (12%). Females named interpersonal-familial associations significantly more often than did males (χ^2 (1) = 3.86, $p <$ .047), while freedom was a nonsignificantly more salient meaning for males than for females.

Possessions to Be Rescued in a Fire

When respondents were asked what five possessions they would rescue if their houses caught fire, the most frequently mentioned were

Table 7.6
Most Frequently Named Possessions That Would Be
Rescued in a Fire and Why (percentage of each group
naming object and meaning)

Category	Total Group (N = 72)	Males (n = 36)	Females (n = 36)
Objects:			
Photographs	17	14	20
Important documents	13	15	11
Clothing	12	13	11
Jewelry	10	8	12
Personal items	8	—	8
Small appliances	—	10	—
Meanings:			
Intrinsic quality	42	50	32
Interpersonal-familial association	22	18	26
Utilitarian value	12	8	16
Freedom	7	—	16
Self-expression	4	8	—
Pleasant experience	—	—	7
Cultural-religious association	—	3	—
Personal accomplishment	—	3	—

photos (17%), important documents (13%), and clothing (12%). Males most often named important documents, photos, and clothing, while females named photos, jewelry, important documents, and clothing most often (see Table 7.6).

When asked why these particular objects would be rescued, the group named intrinsic quality (42%)—which in this case referred primarily to the irreplaceability of the objects—interpersonal-familial associations (22%), and utilitarian value (12%) as indicated in Table 7.6. The meanings attributed to these objects by males and females were fairly similar.

Table 7.7
Most Frequently Named Preferred Gifts
(percentage of each group naming object)

Object	Total Group (N = 72)	Males (n = 36)	Females (n = 36)
Clothing	29	38	22
Personal items	17	10	18
Artwork	11	—	18
Jewelry	10	—	16
Books	9	13	6
Money	—	8	—
Tools		8	
Memorabilia	—	8	—

Preferred Gifts

As indicated in Table 7.7, when asked what things they preferred to receive as gifts, respondents most frequently mentioned clothing (29%), personal items (17%), and artwork (11%). Females named jewelry (χ^2 (1) = 4.00, $p < .043$) and artwork (χ^2 (1) = 4.90, $p < .025$) significantly more often than did males.

Discussion

Treasured possessions, especially for females, symbolized mainly interpersonal ties and, secondarily, enjoyment. "Most important" possessions, on the other hand, seemed to be considered as such because of their interpersonal associations and their utilitarian value (i.e., their usefulness). Regarding the latter, one elderly individual wrote, "Business papers, because I am retired and [have] no income so [I] must be able to control funds, pensions, and annuities I now have." Of particular interest is the fact that the most frequently named "most important" possessions were homes—a topic addressed in the next section.

The major features defining possessions that respondents said they would rescue if their houses caught fire seemed to be their irreplaceability and, second, their associated interpersonal ties. Although this questionnaire item was initially included as a behavioral assessment of possessions designated as "most important," the results of the two items were quite different, suggesting that what older adults say is important is not necessarily what they would try to rescue if their houses caught fire. For these to-be-rescued objects, their irreplaceability really does not explain the objects' true value or meaning—that is, it does not explain why the fact that they are irreplaceable is important.

The meanings evident in these three categories of valued possessions reflected the instrumental and symbolic meaning categories described earlier. For all three categories, a salient meaning of objects was as a symbol of interpersonal ties. Two of the three object categories also had instrumental associations—for treasured possessions, affect (i.e., pleasant experience) was a salient meaning; for "most important" possessions, mastery and control could be interpreted as being the underlying meaning of utilitarian value.

Why was interpersonal-familial associations the most consistently salient meaning? Research suggests that interpersonal ties are particularly salient in late adulthood—they are related to life satisfaction, provide social support benefits, and play a role in identity preservation. Research has found that subjective well-being and family life satisfaction are strongly related to life satisfaction as a whole (Medley, 1976). Friendships may compensate for the loss of other social roles and may thus increase in importance in late adulthood (Hess, 1972). Close kin relations have been found to be more common in older than in middle-aged adults (Dickens & Perlman, 1981), and adult children are typically the main providers of emotional support for their parents, especially for parents who are widowed (Lopata, 1973). Also, older people turn to their families first when in need, and are most likely to name a family member as the person closest to them (Lopata, 1975; Lowenthal & Robinson, 1977; Troll & Bengtson, 1982). In addition, the self of the older individual has been said to be structured around networks of past and present relationships (Csikszentmihalyi & Rochberg-Halton, 1981), with the social group functioning to maintain an individual's sense of self and personal identity during later life (Myerhoff, 1978).

Several other characteristics of the elderly may contribute to the increased salience of interpersonal ties with age. Stevens-Long (1984), for example, has suggested that, as instrumental roles become less urgent (as they generally do with increasing age), expressive ones may become more salient. Also, Butler and Lewis (1983) suggest that the change in one's perspective of time that typically occurs with aging causes older people to experience more of a sense of immediacy, with the elemental things of life (e.g., intimacy, plants, nature, and human relationships) assuming a greater significance in their lives.

In my study, the most often mentioned preferred gifts were initially rather surprising—clothing was named most frequently by both males and females—and the responses for this item deviated from the other three object categories. However, the salience of clothing is consistent with my findings of preferred gifts for young and middle-aged adults (Kamptner, 1988) and with Caplow's (1982) analyses of Christmas gift-giving, in which he found clothing to be the most common type of gift given to both males and females. He suggested that the preference for clothing over other gifts was probably accounted for by the automatic individualization of items of clothing, in that they readily describe the receiver by age, sex, appearance, and style. This may also be the reason that personal items were the second most preferred gift in the current study. From a practical standpoint, it may also be that the high cost of clothing may make it a preferred gift, that is, a luxury that one may not indulge on one's own.

One other important observation is the gender differences noted in the objects and the object meanings named. Although in many instances these differences were not significant, they were relatively consistent with those noted by Csikszentmihalyi and Rochberg-Halton (1981), who found that the males (and children) in their study of special objects in the home cared more for action objects and tools, while females cared more for objects of contemplation and ones that reminded them of their families. These authors suggested that women and men pay attention to different things in the environment and may even value the same things but for different reasons. The findings in my research on object preferences fell along rather traditional lines (e.g., females named dishware and jewelry more often than males, whereas males named motor vehicles and small appliances more often), as did the object meanings (i.e., females exhibited a greater interpersonal orientation than did males).

These differences are probably due to the differential sex-role socialization experiences of males and females in our culture.

Homes and Their Meanings

One of the interesting findings that came out of my inquiries was that respondents included their homes as possessions, particularly as "most important" possessions. Both instrumental and symbolic meanings were attributed to them, and they were described in much the same manner as the other possessions.

A number of researchers have described homes as becoming increasingly salient to the elderly, and remaining in one's home becoming more important as one becomes older (Atchley, 1983; Cooper, 1976). Housing for the elderly is more than a place to live—it can become a symbol of independence; a focal point for family get-togethers; a source of pleasant memories, family sentiments, and traditions (Atchley, 1983; Cox, 1984; Kron, 1983); a place of security (Cooper, 1976); and a "cultivator" of the self (i.e., assisting in maintaining the integrity of the self through constantly reminding one of who one is—Cooper, 1976; Kron, 1983). Regarding the latter, Csikszentmihalyi and Rochberg-Halton (1981, p. 144) have commented, "The home is a shelter for those persons and objects that define the self; thus it becomes . . . an indispensible symbolic environment." The furnishings of one's home, the decor, and the many personal belongings collected over a lifetime serve to remind individuals of loved ones, of travels, and of other events and value systems that are part of their own personal histories. Thus these environments become extensions of one's self (Cooper, 1976; Csikszentmihalyi & Rochberg-Halton, 1981; Howell, 1983). Homes may, in fact, be the most reinforcing environment for one's self because one is surrounded by belongings that cultivate the self and thus provide one with a sense of "belongingness," a feeling of relatedness to the environment (e.g., Fromm, 1955; Kalish, 1975).

For the elderly, homes may be some of the last remaining sources of self-esteem and self-identity, with decor and personal belongings in their homes standing for themselves and their personal life histories (Cooper, 1976; Kron, 1983). With less validation for the self coming in from the environment, housing may be an important means by which older adults can retain their valued identities. In addition to cultivating one's sense of self, homes may serve as reminders or symbols of one's economic and physical independence, an important component of one's self-concept. One elderly woman in our study spoke to this issue, emphasizing the notion of personal control symbolized by her home, when she wrote, "My home . . . I bought it myself . . . I'm comfortable here; I hope to remain here as long as I have the physical and mental ability to care for myself." Another stated, "Home . . . it is important to me because of the freedom of movement." Homes may be the single environment where individuals experience the greatest amount of control.

The privacy afforded by one's own living space is said to be an important factor in cultivating one's sense of self, in that it both enhances and protects the self (Kron, 1983). For example, the privacy of one's home allows a context for emotional release, self-evaluation, psychological (and self-identity) protection, a sense of control, and the expression and reinforcement of one's self and goals without interference or ridicule from others (Csikszentmihalyi & Rochberg-Halton, 1981). One elderly woman in my study remarked, "Home . . . it is my own private little world." Another stated simply, "My home [is my most important possession] because I enjoy it the most."

Security is another theme in the literature on symbolic meanings of homes. One individual in my study wrote, "Home . . . you can return from the noisy outside world, and relax. . . . My home makes me feel secure." A sense of security may come from being surrounded by possessions that remind one of who one is, who loves one, what one believes in, and what experiences one has had (Kron, 1983). An older woman in my study, describing her home as her most important possession, stated, "My home . . . the furniture and objects within it give me security." Security may also be derived from viewing one's home as a "fortress" or emotional refuge in which to retreat from a threatening or depleting external environment (Cooper, 1976; Kron, 1983). According to Cooper, the greater the extent to which persons view themselves as living in a hostile and dangerous world that is threatening to the self, the more likely the home is to be viewed as a protective "fortress." The notion of a house as a symbol of mother or womb (i.e., "protector") and place of birth of the self is a fairly common one in literature (see Cooper,

1976). An elderly woman who described her home in the mountains as her most important possession wrote, "It is comforting, soothing, and makes me feel secure."

Summary and Conclusions

The theoretical and empirical work reviewed in this chapter suggest than an individual's belongings are an important and perhaps necessary part of the self (at least in Western culture), and can potentially play a vital role in the successful adaptation to old age. As described above, many of the instrumental and symbolic meanings of personal belongings parallel and help to resolve the psychosocial issues and challenges of late adulthood. They may help preserve one's perceived mastery and control over aspects of the environment, enhance positive affect, enhance or trigger the life review process by embodying the rich life histories of their owners, cultivate and, therefore, help people maintain their self-identity, and remind them of their place within a social network by symbolizing ties with others. Possessions, then, in a sense communicate what's important (and what's not) about older adults' lives.

The meanings of possessions outlined here collectively suggest that objects symbolize the self—its expression (e.g., as in perceived control and fluctuating affective states), and the preservation of self-identity by personal, social, and historical means. In fact, particularly in old age, possessions may be *the* primary source of self-maintenance.

If this is the case, why objects become imbued with the self (and take on its developmental issues and expressions) becomes a fascinating question. Cooper (1976) speculates that humans' quest for a rational explanation of the self leads them to grasp at physical concrete forms or symbols that are close by, meaningful, physical, and definable. Furby (1978, p. 319), on the other hand, suggests that the more we control something, the more it becomes a part of (and synonymous with?) the self: "If it's not mine, it's not me." A third suggestion as to why objects may become synonymous with the self is because they play such a significant role in the development and maintenance of the self throughout the course of one's lifetime. Further investigations into the relation between people and things are needed to bring greater insight to this issue.

Curiously, mention of personal possessions and their role in late-life adaptation is noticeably absent from the gerontological litera-ture. Attributes of the physical environment that have typically been scrutinized as affecting the behavior, adaptation, and well-being of older adults include the location of one's residence (e.g., the proximity to and availability of needed services), social network characteristics (e.g., the density and accessibility of, and proximity to, one's social network; the effects of design of space on social in-teraction), comfort, physical accessibility, and safety (e.g., degree of barrier-freeness, sturdiness and safety of fixtures, and fixtures that minimize the need to lift objects), sensory qualities (e.g., beauty and aesthetics, readability of environmental cues, degree of sensory stimulation, lighting, color schemes, sound and noise control, and temperature), and privacy (i.e., the ratio of private to public spaces) (e.g., Altman, 1975; Lawton; 1974; Proshansky, Ittelson, & Rivlin, 1970). However, if the following premises are true—that self-identity is a central task throughout the life span (Erikson, 1968; Erikson et al., 1986; Neugarten, 1979), that the integrity of the self is a critical issue such that without it personal disintegration and disorientation occur (Frankl, 1955; Goffman, 1961), and that per-sonal belongings play a critical role in cultivation of the self—then the aspects of the physical environment listed above as critical features of the elderly's surroundings must be expanded to include personal belongings as a necessary and valued component of late-adulthood lives.

The theoretical and empirical work described here has far-reaching implications, especially for situations in which the elderly are typically separated from their belongings. Consider, for exam-ple, changes in living arrangements (i.e., institutionalization, mov-ing from one's home where a lifetime of memories exist, and/or moving from larger to smaller living quarters that cannot accommo-date all of one's possessions), being a victim of a natural disaster (e.g., earthquakes, floods, or fires) or of a robbery or burglary. These events become more than just the loss of material things—they in-volve loss of part of the fabric of one's life and one's self, a fabric that has been carefully woven over the course of an entire lifetime.

References

Adult security blankets take strange forms. (1986, March 31). *The San Bernardino Sun.*

Altman, I. (1975). *The environment and social behavior.* Belmont, CA: Wadsworth.

Atchley, R. C. (1983). *Aging.* Belmont, CA: Wadsworth.

Beaglehole, E. (1932). *Property: A study in social psychology.* New York: Macmillan.

Beck, M., Cooper, N., Dallas, R., Abramson, P., & McCormick, J. (1984, December 24). Looking for Mr. Good Bear. *Newsweek,* pp. 66-71.

Bot, B. W. (1968). The nursing home patient and his environment. *Gawein, 16,* 163-186.

Brehm, J. W. (1972). *Responses to loss of freedom: A theory of psychological reactance.* Morristown, NJ: General Learning Press.

Butler, R. (1963). The life review: An interpretation of reminiscence in the aged. *Psychiatry, 26,* 65-75.

Butler, R. N. (1970). Looking forward to what? *American Behavioral Scientist, 14,* 121-128.

Butler, R., & Lewis, M. (1983). *Aging and mental health.* New York: Mosby.

Caplow, T. (1982). Christmas gifts and kin networks. *American Sociological Review, 47,* 383-392.

Carp, G. (1966). *A future for the aged: Victoria Plaza and its residents.* Austin: University of Texas Press.

Cooper, C. (1976). The house as symbol of the self. In H. M. Proshansky, W. H. Ittelson, & L. G. Rivlin (Eds.), *Environmental psychology: People and their physical settings* (2nd ed., pp. 435-448). New York: Holt, Rinehart & Winston.

Cox, H. (1984). *Aging.* Englewood Cliffs, NJ: Prentice-Hall.

Csikszentmihalyi, M., & Rochberg-Halton, E. (1981). *The meaning of things: Domestic symbols and the self.* Cambridge, MA: Cambridge University Press.

deBeauvoir, S. (1973). *The coming of age.* New York: Warner.

Deci, E. L. (1975). *Intrinsic motivation.* New York: Plenum.

Dickens, W. J., & Perlman, D. (1981). Friendship over the life cycle. In S. Duck & R. Gilmour (Eds.), *Developing personal relationships* (pp. 91-122). London: Academic Press.

Erikson, E. H. (1968). *Identity: Youth and crisis.* New York: Norton.

Erikson, J. M., Erikson, E. H., & Kivnick, H. (1986). *Vital involvement in old age.* New York: Norton.

Frankl, V. (1955). *The doctor and the soul.* New York: Bantam.

Fromm, E. (1955). *The sane society.* New York: Rinehart.

Furby, L. (1978). Possessions in humans: An exploratory study of its meaning and motivation. *Journal of Social Behavior and Personality, 6,* 49-65.

Goffman, E. (1961). *Asylums.* New York: Anchor.

Graumann, C. F. (1974). The neglect of things in psychology. *Journal of Phenomenological Psychology, 4,* 389-404.

Hallowell, A. (1943). The nature and function of property as a social institution. *Journal of Legal and Political Sociology, 1,* 115-138.

Hess, B. (1972). Friendship. In M. W. Riley, M. Johnson, & A. Foner (Eds.), *Aging and society* (pp. 357-393). Beverly Hills, CA: Sage.

Hong, K. (1978). The transitional phenomena. *Psychoanalytic Study of the Child, 3*, 47-49.

Horton, P. C., Louy, J. W., & Coppolillo, H. P. (1974). Personality and transitional relatedness. *Archives of General Psychiatry, 30*, 618-622.

Howell, S. C. (1983). The meaning of place in old age. In G. D. Rowles & R. J. Ohta (Eds.), *Aging and milieu: Environmental perspectives on growing old* (pp. 97-107). New York: Academic Press.

Irwin, F. W., & Gephard, M. E. (1946). Studies in object preferences: The effect of ownership and other social influences. *American Journal of Psychology, 59*, 633-651.

James, W. (1890). *The principles of psychology*. New York: Dover.

Kahn, R. L., & Antonucci, T. C. (1980). Convoys over the life course: Attachment, roles, and social support. In P. B. Baltes & O. G. Brim (Eds.), *Life-span development and behavior* (Vol. 3, pp. 253-286). New York: Academic Press.

Kalish, R. A. (1975). *Late adulthood perspective on human development*. Monterey, CA: Brooks/Cole.

Kamptner, N. L. (1988). *Personal possessions and their meanings in young, middle, and late adulthood*. Unpublished manuscript.

Kellogg, M. (1985). My lost luggage. *Glamour, 83*(4), 204.

Kiefer, C. W. (1974). *Changing cultures, changing lives*. San Francisco: Jossey-Bass.

Korelitz, J. H. (1986). The house I grew up in. *Glamour, 84*(9), 256.

Kron, J. (1983). *Home-psych: The social psychology of home and decoration*. New York: Clarkson N. Potter.

Lawton, M. P. (1974). Coping behavior and the environment of older people. In A. N. Schwartz & I. Mensh (Eds.), *Professional obligations and approaches to the aged* (pp. 67-93). Springfield, IL: Charles C Thomas.

Lewis, C. N. (1971). Reminiscing and self-concept in old age. *Journal of Gerontology, 26*, 240-243.

Lieberman, M. A., & Tobin, S. (1983). *The experience of old age*. New York: Basic Books.

Litwinski, L. (1943-1944). Is there an instinct of possession? *British Journal of Psychology, 33*, 28-39.

Lopata, H. Z. (1973). *Widowhood in an American city*. Cambridge, MA: Schenkman.

Lopata, H. Z. (1975). Widowhood: Societal factors in life-span disruptions and alternatives. In N. Datan & L. Ginsburg (Eds.), *Life-span developmental psychology: Normative life crises* (pp. 217-234). New York: Academic Press.

Lowenthal, M. F., & Robinson, B. (1977). Social networks and isolation. In R. H. Binstock & E. Shanas (Eds.), *Handbook of aging and the social sciences* (pp. 432-456). New York: Van Nostrand.

Marshall, V. W. (1980). *Last chapters: A sociology of aging and dying*. Monterey, CA: Brooks/Cole.

Medley, M. L. (1976). Satisfaction with life among persons sixty-five years and older: A causal model. *Journal of Gerontology, 31*, 448-455.

Millard, P. H., & Smith, C. S. (1981). Personal belongings: A positive effect? *Gerontologist, 21*, 85-90.

Morgan, R., & Cushing, D. (1966). The personal possessions of long-stay patients in mental hospitals. *Social Psychiatry, 1*, 151-157.

Morris, B. (1987, November). *Elderly women and their cherished personal posses-*

sions. Paper presented at the Gerontological Association meeting, Washington, DC.

Myerhoff, B. (1978). *Life's career: Aging.* Beverly Hills, CA: Sage.

Neal, P. (1985, February 11). My grandmother, the bag lady. *Newsweek,* p. 14.

Neugarten, B. (1979). Time, age, and the life cycle. *American Journal of Psychiatry, 136,* 887-894.

Passman, R. H. (1976). Arousal reducing properties of attachment objects: Testing the functional limits of the security blanket relative to the mother. *Developmental Psychology, 12,* 448-459.

Passman, R. H. (1977). Providing attachment objects to facilitate learning and reduce distress: Effects of mothers and security blankets. *Developmental Psychology, 13,* 25-28.

Pastalan, L. A. (1983). Environmental displacement: A literature reflecting old-person-environment transactions. In G. D. Rowles & R. J. Ohta (Eds.), *Aging and milieu: Environmental perspectives on growing older* (pp. 189-204). New York: Academic Press.

Prentice, D. A. (1987). Psychological correspondence of possessions, attitudes, and values. *Journal of Personality and Social Psychology, 53,* 993-1003.

Proshansky, H., Ittelson, W., & Rivlin, L. (1970). *Environmental psychology: Man and his physical setting.* New York: Holt, Rinehart & Winston.

Rochberg-Halton, E. (1984). Object relations, role models, and cultivation of the self. *Environment and Behavior, 16,* 335-368.

Schudson, M. (1986, December). The giving of gifts. *Psychology Today,* pp. 27-29.

Seligman, M. (1975). *Helplessness.* San Francisco: Freeman.

Sherman, E., & Newman, E. (1977-1978). The meaning of cherished possessions for the elderly. *Journal of Aging and Human Development, 8,* 181-192.

Stevens-Long, J. (1984). *Adult life.* Palo Alto, CA: Mayfield.

Stevenson, O. (1954). The first treasured possession: A study of the part played by specially loved objects and toys in the lives of certain children. *Psychoanalytic Study of the Child, 9,* 199-217.

Suttie, I., Ginsberg, M., Isaacs, S., & Marshall, T. (1935). A symposium on property and possessiveness. *British Journal of Medical Psychology, 15,* 51-83.

Taylor, L. (1981, April). Collections of memories. *Architectural Digest,* pp. 36-42.

Troll, L. E., & Bengtson, V. (1982). Intergenerational relations throughout the life span. In B. B. Wolman (Ed.), *Handbook of developmental psychology* (pp. 890-911). Englewood Cliffs, NJ: Prentice-Hall.

Unruh, D. (1983). Death and personal history: Strategies of identity preservation. *Social Problems, 30,* 340-351.

Van Buren, A. (1985, September 13). Don't lose sleep over security blanket. *Los Angeles Times,* p. 18.

Vlosky, M. (1979). Adults' transitional objects. *Dissertation Abstracts International 41* (2-B), 703.

White, R. W. (1959). Motivation reconsidered: The concept of competence. *Psychological Review, 66,* 297-333.

Winnicott, D. W. (1953). Transitional objects and transitional phenomena: A study of the first not-me possession. *International Journal of Psychoanalysis, 34,* 89-97.

8

Aging and Public Policy: Psychological Perspectives

J. THOMAS PUGLISI
LARRY D. RICKARDS

America is growing older. The "aged" now number 29 million persons and comprise almost 12% of the American population (Special Committee on Aging, 1987-1988). By the year 2030, their numbers will rise to over 64 million, with more than 21% of all Americans aged 65 or older. Moreover, the elderly population is itself getting older. The fastest growing subgroup of aged are individuals over the age of 85. By 2050, this group will include 16 million persons, or about 5% of America's overall population. Clearly, these dramatic increases in the number and proportion of older persons in our society will present significant challenges for policymakers. Ultimately, these demographic changes will require profound choices on the part of the American people, entailing the reevaluation of existing social programs as well as the development of new programs to meet changing social needs.

AUTHORS' NOTE: We contributed equally to this manuscript, and the order of authorship is alphabetical.

What roles can psychologists play in meeting the challenges presented by an aging society? The traditional roles of psychologists have been as research scientists and clinical practitioners. In these roles, psychologists can offer policymakers sound empirical data to help them better understand both individual and societal behavior, and to help them evaluate the effectiveness of existing programs and develop new courses of action. In an era when resources are limited and there is competition for funding, policymakers are looking for evidence that social programs address the real needs of older persons in a financially responsible and cost-effective fashion. By virtue of psychology's scientific approach to data collection, the profession is in a strong position to influence the framing of social issues and the development of social programs.

In addition to the traditional roles of scientist and practitioner, psychologists in the arena of aging increasingly function as social critics, community-level interventionists, and advocates. These new activist roles apply multidisciplinary research findings and clinical experience to address societal-level problems. As social critics, psychologists are challenging policymakers and questioning the basic tenets, assumptions, and effectiveness of social policies and programs in meeting the needs of older persons. Examples of this are the criticisms lodged against a mental health care system that neglects services to the aged (Flemming, Rickards, Santos, & West, 1986) and ignores prevention efforts (Klein & Goldston, 1977).

As community-level interventionists, psychologists focus on the community and its systems, rather than on the individual, as the source of problems and solutions. At this level, for example, psychologists might work to have a professional with a background in geriatric mental health included on the community mental health board. Similarly, as a way to improve service delivery, psychologists might help to develop coordination agreements between departments and agencies that provide services to the elderly. Addressing the need for mental health services for older persons not only entails obtaining care for particular individuals but also involves assuring that the mental health system is responsive to the needs of the elderly, that there is an adequate number of mental health practitioners trained to provide geriatric treatment, and that Medicare provides adequate reimbursement for outpatient mental health care.

In the role of advocate, psychologists have focused on political agendas and on the needs of such special populations as children, those with physical and mental handicaps, minorities, and the aged. As part of this role, the particular needs and concerns of these populations are emphasized to policymakers and a course of remedial and programmatic action is proposed. The specific activities involved in advocacy are ones with which psychologists have generally had little experience, such as public relations, developing and presenting congressional testimony, developing grass-roots lobbying support, developing and participating in special interest coalitions, and presenting research data in a way that can be used by nonpsychologists (DeLeon, Frohboese, & Meyers, 1984). While psychology has been involved in the political process for over a decade, the public interest focus of this activism (as opposed to activism focused only on the guild interests of the profession) is relatively recent.

Unfortunately, most policymakers have only a vague understanding of what psychologists do and what the profession can offer in the development of scientific and social programs. As a profession, psychology is not generally seen as addressing broad social issues, yet psychologists are actively involved in the policy research activities conducted by the Alcohol, Drug Abuse and Mental Health Administration, the Office of Technology Assessment, the U.S. General Accounting Office, and the Veterans Administration. As a field, psychology should work to encourage effective communication between psychologists, who function within the realms of science and/or practice, and policymakers, who function within the very different and fairly well-defined constraints of American politics. This will require a two-pronged educational effort. Policymakers must be educated about the value of psychological research, and individual psychologists must be encouraged to recognize and disseminate the policy implications of their work.

Conflicts between psychologists and policymakers may arise due to differences in orientation and values. One problem that can arise is that psychologists recognize the complexity of human behavior and seek to develop interventions accordingly, whereas policymakers are often driven by the financial "bottom line." Psychologists have not traditionally been concerned with the costs of treatment or programs. A challenge for psychologists lies in learning to address pertinent policy issues in a manner that is not only intellectually rigorous and professionally sound but also understandable to, and relevant to the concerns of, nonpsychologists. At the very least, psychologists must be ready to clarify the conceptual links between their work and the social issues to which policymakers respond. Policymakers will not seek out psychology until they become convinced that psychology has something useful to offer and can address their needs and concerns.

The theme of this chapter is that psychology has the potential to make a variety of important contributions in the public policy arena, not only in the field of aging but also in many other areas. These contributions can arise both from psychologists' traditional roles of scientist and practitioner as well as from the emerging roles of social critic, community-level interventionist, and advocate. In this chapter, we discuss ways in which psychologists can contribute to the development of public policy affecting three different, specific aspects of aging—health and long-term care, the special needs of aging women, and mental health. We give special attention to the latter area because it is the one where psychology probably has its most immediate opportunity to affect public policy.

Aging and Public Policy: Psychology's Role

One need only review the reference section of any current text on the psychology of aging to grasp the depth and breadth of psychology's contribution to the study of aging. From a conceptual perspective, Schaie's (1965) elucidation of age, cohort, and time of measurement as basic factors in developmental change are fundamental to an understanding of the aging process. Edited volumes published by the American Psychological Association directly address aging-related topics as diverse as methodology, clinical intervention and assessment, interpersonal relations, cognition, and environmental influences on behavior (Poon, 1980, 1986). Indeed, the most recent Master Lecture Series in Psychology (American Psychological Association, 1988) focused on the adult years and included presentations on basic cognitive processes, health psychology, personality, and clinical psychology; it even included a presentation on policy issues. Clearly, psychological research has produced a wealth of information that should be relevant to the development of sound public policy relative to aging.

Psychology's potential in this area could be virtually unlimited, given the numerous ways in which psychological methods, principles, and data can contribute to the understanding of the aging process. For example, psychology, more than any other discipline, has recognized the importance of individual differences in behavior. Considering the pervasive stereotypes that surround aging in our society, it is critical to recognize the great variation among older persons on almost any psychological, social, or physical variable that one might care to examine. As students of research methodology know, it can be quite misleading to characterize groups on the basis of central tendency without also examining variability. Yet, it is just such one-dimensional characterizations that too often find their way into debates concerning public policy and aging.

A superficial examination of poverty rates, for example, might lead to the conclusion that older persons (with a 12.4% poverty rate) are relatively well-off compared to the nonelderly (with a poverty rate of 13.7%—Special Committee on Aging, 1987-1988). Indeed, *Newsweek* recently published an article titled "The Elderly Aren't Needy," which pointed out that "the elderly's poverty rate is lower than the non-elderly's" in calling for a reexamination of age-based programs like social security and medicare (Samuelson, 1988, p.68). While the fairness and cost-effectiveness of age-based categorical entitlement programs are important issues that do warrant thoughtful examination and debate, the *Newsweek* article (and many like it) failed to acknowledge the variability among the elderly when it comes to income. It ignored the fact that the elderly are much more likely than younger people to be among the near-poor (20.5% of the elderly have incomes below 125% of the poverty level), or that 24.7% of female elderly fall in this category, as do 30.6% of persons over age 85, 32.9% of Hispanic elderly, and 44.7% of Black elderly (Special Committee on Aging, 1987-1988).

An appreciation for scientific observation and careful quantitative analysis are also basic skills that psychologists can bring to the policy area. Moreover, psychologists have led the way in the use of sophisticated quantitative approaches designed to assess the interactive effects of multiple variables over long periods of time (e.g., Nesselroade & Reese, 1973). These quantitative skills are necessary for program evaluation and thus are especially valuable because current policy debates cry out for good program evaluation research. One example where good program evaluation research would be helpful involves the claim that many federal programs for the elderly are costly and ineffective, especially compared to some of the federal programs targeted at children (e.g., WIC, the supplemental nutrition program for women, infants, and children), which have been demonstrated to be highly cost-effective. Beyond this methodological expertise, there are a variety of specific substantive areas of current policy debate to which psychologists are particularly qualified to contribute.

In the public mind, psychology tends to be most readily identified with the area of mental health/mental illness. Although sophisticated observers may realize that psychologists have a wide range of other interests and expertise, few persons outside the discipline really understand the differences between the various specialty areas of psychology. For this reason, it is perhaps easiest to convince policymakers that psychologists can make a contribution when it comes to the development and delivery of mental health services, and so we concentrate heavily on it in this chapter. But first we discuss health and long-term care of the aged and the special problems of elderly women.

Health Policy and Aging

Among the most controversial issues that America faces today, and one that especially affects the elderly, is a health-care system that seems to be financially out of control. Health-care expenditures, both in terms of dollar amounts and as a percentage of the gross national product, have skyrocketed from $41.9 billion (about 6% of GNP) in 1965 to a projected $647.3 billion (12% of GNP) by 1990, and $1.53 trillion (15% of GNP) by the year 2000 (Special Committee on Aging, 1988). In spite of these increases, 37 million people under the age of 65 remain uninsured against the threat of serious illness, 200 million people of all ages remain underinsured against the costs of long-term care (Select Committee on Aging, 1987), and the quality of health-care services remains a serious area of concern (Special Committee on Aging, 1988).

Elderly persons are particularly vulnerable to policy decisions affecting health care. One-third of all the health-care expenditures in the United States go to the care of older persons. Of this amount, about 49% is paid by medicare, 13% is paid by medicaid, 7% is paid by private insurance, and 25% is paid "out of pocket" by the elderly themselves. Incredibly, this "out-of-pocket" spending for health care (which does not include the premiums older persons pay for Part B of medicare or for private health insurance) represents 15% of elderly income, "the same as before Medicare and Medicaid were enacted" over 20 years ago (Special Committee on Aging, 1987-1988, p. 130).

Despite the common perception that medicare covers all of the elderly's health-care needs, medicare leaves serious gaps in coverage that many elderly persons (and their families) only discover when they are faced with serious health problems. Available to all persons aged 65 or older who are eligible for Social Security benefits (as well as to certain other persons, including the disabled), medicare consists of a "Part A" Hospital Insurance Program and a "Part B" Supplementary Medical Insurance Program (Committee on Ways and Means, 1987). Although benefits have been extended under the Medicare Catastrophic Coverage Act of 1988 (P.L. 100-360), medicare still fails to provide complete protection against medical and financial catastrophe.

Briefly, Part A covers inpatient hospital services (subject to an annual deductible, set initially in 1989 at $564) as well as 150 days per year of skilled nursing home care (subject to a coinsurance charge for the first eight days). Part B covers "reasonable" charges for physician services and certain other medical services (charges in excess of what medicare considers "reasonable" must be paid by the patient). Part B is a voluntary program for which enrollees pay a monthly premium, an annual deductible, and various coinsurance charges. Beginning in 1990, there will be an annual "catastrophic limit" (set initially at $1370) on these deductibles and copayments, beyond which medicare will pay 100% of allowable charges. A new benefit will provide assistance with prescription drug charges once a substantial annual deductible ($600 in 1991) has been met.

Medicare's primary shortcoming is that is focuses on acute care needs while ignoring the great need among the elderly for long-term care. Current estimates indicate that as many as 7 million people now need long-term care and that persons reaching age 65 "face a 43 percent risk of entering a nursing home during their remaining lifetime" (Select Committee on Aging, 1987, p. 5). Yet, no benefits are provided under medicare for skilled nursing home care beyond 150 days, or for less skilled forms of institutional care, which are often necessary for chronic conditions common to the elderly. Moreover, home-care benefits under medicare, even as extended beginning in 1990, are severely limited, consisting only of (a) home health services provided to homebound individuals either on an "intermittent" basis or for up to 38 consecutive days, and (b) 80 hours per year of in-home care for chronically dependent individuals who have met the Part B catastrophic limit or the prescription drug deductible.

"The reality is that virtually all long-term care is paid for from two sources, patients and their families (44 percent) or Medicaid (40 percent)" (Select Committee on Aging, 1987, p. 3). Although medicaid does provide long-term nursing home care, it requires impoverishment in order to establish eligibility. Moreover, medicaid benefits for home and community-based services are minimal in most states, even though about 80% of elderly persons needing long-term care do not live in nursing homes but in the community (Special Committee on Aging, 1988).

The above facts demonstrate that the area of health policy could benefit from the kind of research and analysis that psychology can provide. Efficient service delivery, cost control mechanisms, and quality control are health system characteristics that policymakers are now eager to foster and that are literally wide open for rigorous and creative researchers. In addition, more traditional psychological research is needed to investigate the effects of the health-care system on the people who must negotiate it. Patients, caregivers, and extended family members are involved in complex interactions not only with each other but also with the health-care system itself. Moreover, the professionals, paraprofessionals, and other service providers working within the system are "real" people, too, subject to the same, very human, feelings and concerns as the elderly and their families. Researchers need to examine these complex human interactions in a scientific fashion to help policymakers understand how the health-care system affects people who are confronted with their own illnesses, with the illnesses of their family members, or with the illnesses of the people they serve.

Unfortunately, psychologists interested in health issues have only recently begun to recognize the challenges presented by an aging society. Indeed, a systematic and comprehensive literature in this area has yet to be developed (Siegler & Costa, 1985). Nevertheless, the potential for creative research in this area is great, and the possible contribution of health psychology to the development of sound aging policy could be substantial.

Women and Aging

A second important, and timely, area of concern involves the particular experiences of older women. Indeed, the Select Committee on Aging of the U.S. House of Representatives recently launched a series of hearings to address the "Quality of Life for Older Women." Testimony presented to the committee has highlighted the demographic, economic, and social realities that cause most women to have very different experiences in old age compared to men (Davis, 1988). Because of longer life expectancies, for example, women are much more likely than men to outlive their spouses, their siblings, and even their children. As a result, about 6.5 million elderly women live alone, compared with fewer than 2 million elderly men. These elderly women living alone are much more likely to live in poverty than are elderly men or elderly couples. It is not surprising that elderly persons living alone (over 75% of them women) have more tenuous support networks than other elderly, and display the highest levels of dissatisfaction with their lives (Davis, 1988; Kasper, 1988).

Elderly women, especially those living alone, are particularly vulnerable to the growing shortage of decent, affordable housing in the United States today, and "are disproportionately represented among low-income renters, low-income home-owners, and among public housing residents" (Jones, 1988, p. 4). According to the Special Committee on Aging (1988), elderly women living alone can expect to spend almost half of their incomes on housing, and in spite of wide recognition that there is a tremendous need for housing assistance, federal programs in this area have been decimated since 1981. Because decent housing has never been considered an entitlement in this country, only about 25% of those eligible for housing assistance can actually be served, and it has been estimated that almost 40% of elderly renter households with incomes below the poverty level live in substandard housing (Special Committee on Aging, 1988).

Psychologists are particularly qualified to address the social and psychological implications of substandard housing and to document the importance of physically, socially, and emotionally supportive living environments (Moos & Lemke, 1985; Scheidt & Windley, 1985). In addition, psychologists should be at the forefront in making policymakers aware of the great need among frail elderly persons for supportive living arrangements, a need that will rise dramatically over the next several decades with increasing numbers of the very old. However, psychology's role should not be limited to documenting need, but should be expanded to the design of such environments and the documentation of their utility. Returning to the specific issue of older women, psychologists must recognize the demographic reality that the vast majority of the very old are, and will continue to be, women and must take care to conceptualize environmental research in a way that acknowledges the differential needs of older women.

Older women also have health-care needs that are different from those of older men. More likely than men to suffer from chronic conditions requiring long-term home health care, homemaking assistance, or nursing home care, women are especially disadvantaged by medicare's emphasis on acute hospital care. In addition, the financial, emotional, and physical burden of in-home caregiving for infirm elderly is more likely to fall upon elderly and middle-aged women than upon men (Roybal, 1988c). In fact, women make up about 72% of the caregivers of disabled older persons. Of these women caregivers, 33% (with a mean age of 69 years) provide care for their spouses, and 40% (with a mean age of 52 years) provide care for a parent (Special Committee on Aging, 1988). The unfortunate result is that these female caregivers are left in old age with little in the way of financial or emotional resources to help cope with their own increasing medical and social needs.

From the House Aging Committee's hearings came the acknowledgment that researchers, policymakers, and administrators have often assumed that the circumstances of aged men characterize the aged population as a whole, even though there are only 68 men for every 100 women over the age of 65 (Roybal, 1988c). Psychologists are in an excellent position to examine empirically the similarities and differences in the social settings and life cycles of aging women and to analyze critically the development and implementation of social policies affecting them. Rodeheaver (1987), for example, maintains that social policies for the aged have been developed largely from a masculine perspective that dichotomizes dependence and independence while disregarding the importance of interdependence and social relatedness. Certainly, older women face a kind of "double jeopardy arising from social, economic, and psychological conditions surrounding aging and gender" (Rodeheaver & Datan, 1988, p. 648), which policymakers must be encouraged to recognize and confront.

Researchers interested in the psychology of aging and researchers interested in the psychology of women have made significant contributions to their fields. We are now faced with the important challenge of strengthening the interface between these traditionally distinct areas in order to achieve a more thorough understanding of aging women. Moreover, we must make a conscious effort to formulate this understanding in ways that have specific policy implications so that those who develop and administer social programs will not be tempted to ignore the very real differences in the circumstances and perspectives of older women and men.

Health policy and the concerns of older women are but two of many current areas in which psychology can make a substantial contribution to policy development. We turn, now, to a detailed discussion of federal mental health policy in order to illustrate what we believe is psychology's most immediate opportunity to affect the policy arena.

Mental Health and Aging: Influencing Public Policy

While most older persons are healthy and stable individuals, disorders such as depression, misuse of alcohol and prescription drugs, and various forms of cognitive impairment occur with alarming frequency among the aged (Abrams & Alexopoulos, 1988; Kermis, 1986; U.S. Congress, 1987). Indeed, it has been estimated that as many as 10% to 28% of today's community elderly suffer from mental health problems serious enough to warrant professional attention (Flemming, Rickards, Santos, & West, 1986; Gatz, Smyer, & Lawton, 1980; George, Blazer, Winfield-Laird, Leaf, & Fischback, 1988).

Older persons who are in need of mental health services are a heterogeneous population, but they may be grouped into three broad categories (Frazier, Lebowitz, & Silver, 1986). These categories may represent different etiological factors for mental disorders and different service needs. In the first category are individuals with a history of chronic mental impairment who have reached old age (e.g., those with schizophrenia or severe character disorders). The second category includes older persons who have developed mental disorders later in life with no prior history of mental impairment (e.g., those with generalized depression or Alzheimer's disease). The third category includes individuals with mental disorders associated with physical health problems, such as the depression that is frequently linked with cardiac disease (Butler & Lewis, 1982; Cohen, 1985).

Although research and clinical experience have demonstrated that older persons do respond well to appropriate psychotherapeutic, psychopharmacological, behavioral, and social interventions (Birren & Sloan, 1980; Gatz, Popkin, Pino, & VandenBos, 1985), the mental health needs of the elderly largely go unmet in present-day American society (U.S. General Accounting Office, 1982). As many as 80% of the elderly in need of mental health services do not receive them (German, Shapiro, & Skinner, 1985; Kramer, Taube, & Redick, 1973). Moreover, in spite of the findings that therapeutic interventions can often be effectively provided for elderly persons in a variety of outpatient settings, including community mental health centers, senior centers, and health clinics (Cohen, 1983; Knight, 1983; Lowy, 1980; Raschko, 1985), and that the elderly will use such services when they are made available to them (Lebowitz, 1988; Lebowitz, Light, & Bailey, 1987), fewer than 6% of community mental health center clients and fewer than 2% of private therapy clients are elderly (MacDonald, 1987; U.S. General Accounting Office, 1982).

Clearly, there is now a tremendous need among the elderly for mental health services, and this need will continue to grow as the size of the elderly population increases. In the face of such need, it is important to understand why elderly persons in our society are not receiving the mental health treatment they deserve so that we can begin to create a more responsive mental health system. Psychologists have already played an important role in providing such an understanding, and they should play an equal role in helping to design a more responsive system. Unfortunately, remedying the unmet mental health needs of the elderly will not be a simple task as there are a variety of factors that contribute to the system's lack of effectiveness when it comes to older persons.

These factors, which have been discussed in detail by other authors (Butler & Lewis, 1982; Gatz et al., 1985; Roybal, 1988a), include a constellation of both negative and positive stereotypes about aging and the elderly (Gatz & Pearson, 1988; Kimmel, 1988); a lack of training in geriatric mental health on the part of physicians, psychologists, and other service providers (German et al., 1987; Kermis, 1986; Lebowitz, 1988; Waxman, Larner, & Klein, 1984); and a reluctance on the part of the present cohort of elderly persons to seek the help of mental health professionals. Another problem is a lack of specialized programs and outreach, including programs for racial and ethnic minority elderly individuals (Fellin & Powell, 1988; MacDonald, 1987) and for rural elderly (Rosenberg, 1986).

A central aspect of the problem, however, is the fact that federal programs affecting elderly mental health have failed, in a series of ways, to encourage an effective service delivery system for elderly mental health. Medicare mental health benefits are inadequate, medicaid regulations do not strongly encourage mental health treatment, and federal HMO regulations virtually ignore mental health. In addition, the issue of long-term care, which has important implications for victims of disorders like Alzheimer's disease, has yet to be addressed in a substantive fashion.

The Development of Mental Health Policy

In order to understand how this unfortunate situation has developed, and how it might be addressed effectively, it is important to consider how mental health policy (and public policy in general) is developed. Federal mental health policy comes from several sources: from the administration through stated policy and agency regulations, from the Congress through legislation and oversight, and from court decisions. It is increasingly affected by the actions and policies of state legislatures, county government, and local communities. It is stimulated by the lobbying activity of interest groups and the advocacy activity of grass-roots citizens organizations. Clearly, then, mental health policy is not a coherent, unified entity to which all parties agree. Moreover, it is a political process as much as, or more than, it is a professional process.

The elusiveness of consistent public policy concerning mental health becomes better appreciated with the understanding that within the administration alone there are several agencies and offices developing policy affecting mental health and the aged, including the Health Care Financing Administration, the Administration on Aging, the Alcohol, Drug Abuse, and Mental Health Administration, and the Office of Management and Budget, and these bodies often fail to coordinate their activities with one another. A similar array of input is also true of Congress, where there are ten committees and six subcommittees that have jurisdiction of direct concern to mental health and aging (not including committees and subcommittees concerned with related issues such as income, nutrition, housing, or crime). To add to the complexity, the mental health policies of these sources may be at variance with each other, and the policies of a particular source may or may not be consistent over time.

The lack of clarity and consistency in addressing the needs of the elderly has resulted in a de facto policy of neglect on the part of the federal government in providing for the mental health needs of older persons. This policy of neglect can be demonstrated by the nonenforcement of congressional directives, cost-reduction plans that decreased funding for geriatric service programs, and the failure to develop funding mechanisms that encourage delivery of mental health services to the aged. Nowhere is this policy of neglect more evident than in the area of community mental health.

Community Mental Health
Services for the Elderly

The Community Mental Health Centers Act of 1963 (P.L. 88-164) is the primary federal initiative for the provision of community-based mental health care. When the program was launched, the community mental health centers (CMHCs) were envisioned by the Kennedy-Johnson administrations and Congress as the desired alternative to institutional care. While CMHCs were initially organized as comprehensive care centers to provide services to individuals regardless of age, during the 1970s there emerged a trend toward the provision of services for specialized targeted populations.

Although older persons were mandated for specialized services in both the 1975 (P.L. 94-63) and the 1978 (P.L. 95-622) reauthorizations of the CMHC Act, there has never been adequate administration interest or funding of CMHCs to provide incentives for full implementation of the congressional directives. While the percentage of older persons served by CMHCs increased nationally between 1975 and 1978 from 3.8% to 4.3%, this was still well below the estimates of service need (Gatz et al., 1980; George et al., 1988). The Carter administration expressed interest in improving mental health services to older persons, and specific recommendations from the President's Commission on Mental Health (1978) were incorporated in the Mental Health Systems Act of 1980 (P.L. 96-398—Levine, 1981). The glimmer of optimism that accompanied the passage of this act, however, was quickly extinguished by the Reagan administration's "new federalism" policy.

The Mental Health Systems Act was rescinded by the Omnibus Budget Reconciliation Act of 1981 (P.L. 97-35), which established the Alcohol, Drug Abuse, and Mental Health Services Block Grant as the mechanism of federal funding for mental health services. The philosophy behind the block grant was the Reagan administration's belief that these services should be planned and implemented by the states rather than by the federal government. Although the law directed states to use funds for the identification and assessment of mentally ill elderly individuals and for the provision of appropriate services to such individuals, there were no mandates for specialized geriatric services and no reporting requirements that held states and local agencies accountable for the delivery of services to meet the directive.

Concurrent with the implementation of the block grant in 1983, there was an immediate 25% decrease in federal expenditures for mental health, alcohol, and substance abuse services. Funding was reduced from $549 million in fiscal year (FY) 1981 to $439 million in FY 1983 (P.L. 97-377). Federal funding for mental health services has never returned to the 1981 level. Only $503 million was appropriated for FY 1989 (and this with an inflation rate of over 19% since 1981).

The Action Committee to implement the Mental Health Recommendations of the 1981 White House Conference on Aging (Flemming, Buchanan, Santos, & Rickards, 1984; Flemming et al., 1986 conducted a nationwide study of community mental health centers to determine the impact of the federal block grant system of funding on the delivery of mental health services to the aged. Surveys of CMHCs conducted in 1983 and 1985 found that the drastic reduction in federal support and the lack of federal direction in service provision had severe consequences for service delivery to older persons. Over one-third of CMHCs reported adverse effects of the reduced federal funding, including decreases in the number of clinical staff, particularly geriatric services staff, and decreases in outreach efforts and in the number of home visits, both of which are important in attracting the aged and providing services to them. Of the CMHCs, 45% reported having no specific programs for the aged, and 40% reported they did not have any clinical staff members trained to deliver geriatric services. In addition, there was almost no coordination in service delivery and little routine interaction between CMHCs and other geriatric service programs (such as Area Agencies on Aging).

Recent Federal Action on Elderly Mental Health

In the face of the federal government's neglect of elderly mental health needs, mental health professionals with expertise in aging must begin building a strong case for more effective mental health service delivery to older persons. Three recent developments on the federal level indicate that at least a few policymakers are beginning to be concerned about elderly mental health. These developments, described in turn below, could lay the groundwork for a more responsive mental health system for the elderly. Psychologists need to position themselves to influence and shape the evolution of this system.

1987 Older Americans Act Reauthorization. The first of these developments concerns the 1987 Reauthorization of the Older Americans Act (P.L. 100-175), which funds a wide array of locally operated human services programs designed to maintain older persons in their own homes and communities and to prevent unnecessary institutionalization (Select Committee on Aging, 1985). Faced with the reality that elderly mental health services have been reduced under the federal mechanism that funds mental health, an alternate strategy for enhancing elderly mental health is to provide such services under programs specifically targeted at the elderly. To this end, the 1987 Older Americans Act Reauthorization contained three major mental health provisions: (a) mental health is now specifically included under all sections of the act pertaining to health services; (b) mentally impaired elderly are specifically included among individuals "with greatest social need" to be targeted for services; and (c) Area Agencies on Aging are required to include provisions in their Area Plans to improve coordination between Older Americans Act services and Community Mental Health Center services.

While these provisions do not mandate delivery of mental health services for the elderly, they do serve to highlight such services as a legitimate health need of older persons that should be considered in the development of area service delivery plans. Moreover, the increased coordination of Older Americans Act services with those of community mental health centers directly addresses the fragmentation of services that has plagued effective service delivery to the elderly.

Unfortunately, these small advances for elderly mental health under the Older Americans Act are qualified by the fact that, with a relatively stable annual appropriation of about $725 million, increased mental health services can only be provided at the expense of other important services (see Binstock, 1987). As a result, it is highly unlikely that provision of elderly mental health services under the Older Americans Act will increase significantly unless appropriations increase. Nevertheless, the increased visibility given to elderly mental health under the 1987 reauthorization constitutes an important first step in the battle to reshape mental health policy for the elderly.

Omnibus Budget Reconciliation Act of 1987. A second small, but highly important, set of advances for elderly mental health came as a result of the 1987 Omnibus Budget Reconciliation Act (OBRA, P.L. 100-203), which included a number of reforms to federal entitlement programs such as medicare and medicaid. Among the less heralded of these reforms are three provisions that directly affect elderly mental health.

The first provision concerns the level of coverage for outpatient mental health services under Part B of medicare, which has been extended from $250, the level originally set over 20 years ago when medicare was first established, to $450 in 1988, and to $1,100 in 1989. Unfortunately, in spite of this increase, the outpatient mental health benefit remains inadequate and continues to be subject to a 50% copayment on the part of the beneficiary, compared to the 20% copayment required for other Part B services.

The second new provision is the recognition of psychologists as providers of mental health services under Part B of medicare, which represents a limited, but important, advance in the delivery of mental health services to elderly persons by qualified nonphysician providers. Under this reform, medicare will now provide direct reimbursement for mental health services provided by clinical psychologists when these services are delivered through community mental health centers and rural health clinics. This change will extend mental health services to many elderly persons, especially those in rural areas for whom access to such services has been extremely limited. Psychology should take maximum advantage of this limited recognition of psychologists as medicare service providers in order to demonstrate that psychologists offer high-quality, cost-effective mental health services that are comparable to, if not better than, the services offered by physician providers.

Finally, OBRA strengthened conditions of participation for nursing homes under medicare and medicaid. These conditions of participation mandate written plans of care for each resident that include psychosocial as well as medical needs, and they require that nursing homes conduct a comprehensive assessment of each resident upon admission and at least annually thereafter. While this increased attention to mental health among nursing home residents is a significant advance, preadmission screening for mental health problems could represent a double-edged sword if the process becomes a mechanism for controlling costs by keeping mentally impaired elderly out of nursing homes, and thus depriving them of care altogether.

Nevertheless, the OBRA nursing home provisions provide a concrete opportunity for psychologists to affect the implementation and further development of policy in at least three critical ways (Smyer, 1988). First, OBRA's emphasis on assessment is important for psychology because geriatric assessment is clearly an area in which psychologists have developed considerable expertise. Second, OBRA provisions mandate increased training for nurses' aides. Psychologists are already recognized as trainers of other human services personnel and could make a significant contribution to the training of nurses' aides. Psychologists also have a wide range of expertise in the development of training programs, which could be useful in designing comprehensive nurses' aide training programs. Finally, psychologists have developed considerable experience in program evaluation. Smyer (1988) suggests that psychology's expertise in program evaluation will become increasingly valuable as policymakers demand empirical verification of the effects of nursing home interventions, of job performance in nursing homes, and of the behavioral functioning of nursing home residents.

The Roybal Mental Health Initiative. The third significant development in the awakening of policymakers to the mental health needs of the elderly is the introduction in Congress of a comprehensive initiative (H.R. 4860) "to improve Medicare and Medicaid mental health benefits and to encourage the development of community based" mental health services for elderly persons, children, and families (Roybal, 1988b, p. E2069). Introduced by Representative Edward R. Roybal of California, chair of the House Select Committee on Aging, the Mental Health and Aging Act of 1988, if passed, would substantially expand federal funding for mental health services, research, and training.

Moreover, this legislation would reform medicare and medicaid to encourage outpatient and community-based mental health services, establish a mental health consumer bill of rights, and provide for direct medicare reimbursement of services provided by psychologists and other qualified mental health professionals. Although it is unlikely that such comprehensive elderly mental health legislation will be enacted in its entirety in the near future, Representative Roybal's efforts have helped raise the awareness of policymakers about the great mental health needs of the nation's elderly and have provided concrete ideas that may be incorporated into other legislation.

Indeed, two components of the Roybal mental health legislation were included in the bill to reauthorize the Alcohol, Drug Abuse, and Mental Health Block Grant passed by the 100th Congress. The first of these was an intergenerational provision that provided for a "set-aside" of funds to improve mental health services for children. Under this provision, states are immediately required to allocate 10% of their block grant mental health funds for programs for seriously emotionally disturbed children and adolescents.

The second provision established a National Mental Health Education Program designed to "create a national focus on mental health problems and mental health care" (Roybal, 1988b, p. E2070). This education program will have both symbolic and practical importance. On the symbolic level, the program will help increase national awareness of mental health and its critical impact on children, the elderly, and their families. In addition, the program will be given the concrete function of meeting two practical needs. First, the program will include a clearinghouse for efficient and timely dispersal of the most current information on mental health research and practice to individual families and practitioners who may be faced with addressing a specific mental health problem. Second, the program will provide technical assistance to service agencies and other organizations with mental health concerns.

Opportunities for Psychology in the Policy Arena

These three developments in federal mental health policy for the elderly (i.e., the 1987 Older Americans Act mental health amendments, the 1987 OBRA reforms, and the Roybal mental health and aging initiative) are modest, yet important, steps in improving the mental health system for the elderly. In addition, they provide psychology with a concrete opportunity to demonstrate what the profession has to offer in the policy arena. Psychologists with expertise in aging need to accept the responsibility for making the hope for improved mental health care a reality.

Once again, we must emphasize that substantial reform will not occur unless policymakers become convinced (a) that older persons have significant, unmet mental health needs, (b) that potentially available mental health services can really bring about positive outcomes, and (c) that these services can be delivered in a fiscally responsible, cost-effective manner. Practical and viable approaches to service delivery must be demonstrated, and these approaches must include strong mechanisms to ensure the quality of services rendered, as well as equitable and professionally sound mechanisms to control costs. Unless policymakers become convinced that such sound approaches exist and can be implemented, reform of the mental health system for the elderly will probably be haphazard and ineffective. It is important that psychologists forge a role for themselves in bringing about whatever reform is to take place.

Returning to the underlying thesis of this chapter, it is our belief that psychology has a significant contribution to make in addressing the needs and concerns of our aging society. However, in order for psychology to become fully involved in the policymaking process, it will have to engage in activities beyond the traditional roles of research scientist and clinical practitioner. We have suggested the new roles of social critic, community-level interventionist, and advocate as appropriate for the aging arena. In addition, it is important that psychology develop ways to situate itself more directly in the public debate surrounding a variety of aging issues. To the extent that psychology fails to understand the public policy process and fails to address policy issues effectively, the profession must bear some of the burden for the flawed policies that will inevitably result.

At the same time, we must not lose sight of the fact that psychology's credibility stems directly from the scientific approach that it can lend to the investigation of aging issues and from the empirically verifiable data it can generate concerning them. The challenges for psychology are to formulate policy-related questions in ways that lend themselves to empirical testing, to apply scientific findings to issues of social concern, and to work with policymakers in the development of solutions that have practical application. Psychology has a tradition of seeking solutions to difficult problems. We should do no less for the challenges of an aging society.

References

Abrams, R. C., & Alexopoulos, G. S. (1988). Substance abuse in the elderly: Over-the-counter and illegal drugs. *Hospital and Community Psychiatry, 39*, 822-823, 839.

American Psychological Association, Continuing Education Committee. (1988, August). *The adult years: Continuity and change.* Master Lecture Series presented at the annual meeting of the American Psychological Association, Atlanta.

Binstock, R. H. (1987). Title III of the Older Americans Act: An analysis and proposal for the 1987 reauthorization. *Gerontologist, 27,* 259-265.

Birren, J. E., & Sloane, R. B. (Eds.). (1980). *Handbook of mental health and aging.* Englewood Cliffs, NJ: Prentice-Hall.

Butler, R. N., & Lewis, M. I. (1982). *Aging and mental health.* St. Louis: C. V. Mosby.

Cohen, G. D. (1983). Psychogeriatric program in a public housing setting. *Psychiatric Quarterly, 55,* 173-181.

Cohen, G. D. (1985). Mental health aspects of nursing home care. In E. L. Schneider, C. J. Wendland, M. W. Zimmer, N. List, & M. Ory (Eds.), *The teaching nursing home* (pp. 157-164). New York: Raven.

Committee on Ways and Means, U.S. House of Representatives. (1987). *Compilation of the social security laws* (Committee Print 100-14). Washington, DC: Government Printing Office.

Davis, K. (1988, September 27). *Improving the quality of life among elderly women living alone.* Testimony of the Commonwealth Fund Commission on Elderly People Living Alone before the Select Committee on Aging, U.S. House of Representatives.

DeLeon, P. H., Frohboese, R., & Meyers, J. C. (1984). Psychologists on Capitol Hill: A unique use of the skills of the scientist/practitioner. *Professional Psychology, 15,* 697-705.

Fellin, P. A., & Powell, T. J. (1988). Mental health services and older adult minorities: An assessment. *Gerontologist, 28,* 442-447.

Flemming, A. S., Buchanan, J. G., Santos, J. F., & Rickards, L. D. (1984). *Mental health services for the elderly: A report on a survey of community mental health centers* (Vols. 1, 2). Washington, DC: Action Committee to Implement the Mental Health Recommendations of the 1981 White House Conference on Aging.

Flemming, A. S., Rickards, L. D., Santos, J. F., & West, P. R. (1986). *Mental health services for the elderly: A report on a survey of community mental health centers* (Vol. 3). Washington, DC: Action Committee to Implement the Mental Health Recommendations of the 1981 White House Conference on Aging.

Frazier, S. H., Lebowitz, B. D., & Silver, L. B. (1986). Aging, mental health, and rehabilitation. In S. J. Brody & G. E. Ruff (Eds.), *Aging and rehabilitation* (pp. 19-26). New York: Springer.

Gatz, M., & Pearson, C. G. (1988). Ageism revised and the provision of psychological services. *American Psychologist, 43,* 184-188.

Gatz, M., Popkin, S. J., Pino, C. D., & VandenBos, G. R. (1985). Psychological interventions with older adults. In J. E. Birren & K. W. Schaie (Eds.), *Handbook of the psychology of aging* (2nd ed., pp. 755-785). New York: Van Nostrand Reinhold.

Gatz, M., Smyer, M., & Lawton, M. P. (1980). The mental health system and the older adult. In L. W. Poon (Ed.), *Aging in the 1980s* (pp. 5-18). Washington, DC: American Psychological Association.

George, L. K., Blazer, D. G., Winfield-Laird, I., Leaf, P. J., & Fischback, R. L. (1988). Psychiatric disorders and mental health service use in later life: Evidence from the Epidemiologic Catchment Area Program. In J. Brody & G. L. Maddox (Eds.), *Epidemiology and aging.* New York: Springer.

German, P. S., Shapiro, S., & Skinner, E. A. (1985). Mental Health of the elderly: Use of health and mental health services. *Journal of the American Geriatrics Society, 33*, 246-252.

German, P. S., Shapiro, S., Skinner, E. A., Von Korff, M., Klein, L. E., Turner, R. W., Teitelbaum, M. L., Burke, J., & Burns, B. J. (1987). Detection and management of mental health problems of older patients by primary care providers. *Journal of the American Medical Association, 257*, 489-493.

Jones, M. G. (1988, September 27). *The quality of life for older women: Older women living alone.* Testimony of the Older Women's League before the Select Committee on Aging, U.S. House of Representatives.

Kasper, J. D. (1988). *Aging alone: Profiles and projections.* Baltimore: Commonwealth Fund Commission on Elderly People Living Alone.

Kermis, M. D. (1986). *Mental health in late life: The adaptive process.* Boston: Jones & Bartlett.

Kimmel, D. C. (1988). Ageism, psychology, and public policy. *American Psychologist, 43*, 175-178.

Klein, D. C., & Goldston, S. E. (1977). *Primary prevention: An idea whose time has come.* Rockville, MD: National Institute of Mental Health.

Knight, B. (1983). Assessing a mobile outreach team. In M. A. Smyer & M. Gatz (Eds.), *Mental health and aging* (pp. 23-40). Beverly Hills, CA: Sage.

Kramer, M., Taube, C. A., & Redick, R. W. (1973). Patterns of use of psychiatric facilities by the aged. In C. Eisdorfer & M. P. Lawton (Eds.), *The psychology of adult development and aging* (pp. 428-528). Washington, DC: American Psychological Association.

Lebowitz, B. D. (1988). Practical geriatrics: Correlates of success in community mental health programs for the elderly. *Hospital and Community Psychiatry, 39*, 721-722.

Lebowitz, B. D., Light, E., & Bailey, F. (1987). Mental health center services for the elderly: The impact of coordination with area agencies on aging. *Gerontologist, 27*, 699-702.

Levine, M. (1981). *The history and politics of community mental health.* New York: Oxford University Press.

Lowy, L. (1980). Mental health services in the community. In J. E. Birren & R. B. Sloane (Eds.), *Handbook of mental health and aging* (pp. 827-853). Englewood Cliffs, NJ: Prentice-Hall.

MacDonald, D. I. (1987, March 4). *Testimony of the administrator of the alcohol, drug abuse, and mental health administration before the Committee on Appropriations, Subcommittee on the Departments of Labor, HHS, and Education, U.S. House of Representatives.* Washington, DC: Government Printing Office.

Moos, R. H., & Lemke, S. (1985). Specialized living environments for older people. In J. E. Birren & K. W. Schaie (Eds.), *Handbook of the psychology of aging* (2nd ed., pp. 864-889). New York: Van Nostrand Reinhold.

Nesselroade, J. R., & Reese, H. W. (1973). *Life-span developmental psychology: Methodological issues.* New York: Academic Press.

Poon, L. W. (Ed.). (1980). *Aging in the 1980s: Psychological issues.* Washington, DC: American Psychological Association.

Poon, L. W. (Ed.). (1986). *Clinical memory assessment of older adults.* Washington,

DC: American Psychological Association.

President's Commission on Mental Health. (1978). *Panel report: Mental health of the elderly* (DHEW Publication no. PCMH/P-78/15). Washington, DC: U.S. Government Printing Office.

Raschko, R. (1985). Systems integration at the program level: Aging and mental health. *Gerontologist, 25,* 460-463.

Rodeheaver, D. (1987). When old age became a social problem, women were left behind. *Gerontologist, 27,* 741-746.

Rodeheaver, D., & Datan, N. (1988). The challenge of double jeopardy: Toward a mental health agenda for aging women. *American Psychologist, 43,* 648-654.

Rosenberg, J. (1986). *Summary report: Policy forum on the personal stress problems of farmers and rural Americans, sponsored by the National Institute of Mental Health and the Center for Agriculture and Rural Development of the Council of State Governments.* Rockville, MD: National Institute of Mental Health.

Roybal, E. R. (1988a). Mental health and aging: The need for an expanded federal response. *American Psychologist, 43,* 189-194.

Roybal, E. R. (1988b). Mental Health and Aging Act. *Congressional Record, 137*(91), E2069-E2076.

Roybal, E. R. (1988c, September 27). *Chairman's statement on the quality of life for older women: Older women living alone.* Select Committee on Aging, U.S. House of Representatives.

Samuelson, R. J. (1988, March 21). The elderly aren't needy. *Newsweek,* p. 68.

Schaie, K. W. (1965). A general model for the study of developmental problems. *Psychological Bulletin, 64,* 92-107.

Scheidt, R. J., & Windley, P. G. (1985). The ecology of aging. In J. E. Birren & K. W. Schaie (Eds.), *Handbook of the psychology of aging* (2nd ed., pp. 245-258). New York: Van Nostrand Reinhold.

Select Committee on Aging, U.S. House of Representatives. (1985). *Older Americans Act: A staff summary by the Subcommittee on Human Services* (Committee Publication no. 98-482). Washington, DC: Government Printing Office.

Select Committee on Aging, U.S. House of Representatives. (1987). *Long term care and personal impoverishment: Seven in ten elderly living alone are at risk* (Committee Publication no. 100-631). Washington, DC: Government Printing Office.

Siegler, I. C., & Costa, P. T. (1985). Health behavior relationships. In J. E. Birren & K. W. Schaie (Eds.), *Handbook of the psychology of aging* (2nd ed., pp. 144-166). New York: Van Nostrand Reinhold.

Smyer, M. A. (1988, August). Nursing homes as a setting for psychological practice: Public policy perspectives. In J. T. Puglisi (Chair), *Mental health and aging: Public policy perspectives.* Symposium presented at the annual meeting of the American Psychological Association, Atlanta.

Special Committee on Aging, U.S. Senate. (1987-1988). *Aging America: Trends and projections.* Washington, DC: U.S. Department of Health and Human Services.

Special Committee on Aging, U.S. Senate. (1988). *Developments in aging: 1987* (Vols. 1, 3, Report no. 100-291). Washington, DC: Government Printing Office.

U.S. Congress, Office of Technology Assessment. (1987). *Losing a million minds: Confronting the tragedy of Alzheimer's disease and other dementias* (Publication no. OTA-BA-323). Washington, DC: Government Printing Office.

U.S. General Accounting Office. (1982). *The elderly remain in need of mental health services* (Publication no. GAO/HRD-82-112). Washington, DC: Author.
Waxman, H., Larner, E., & Klein, M. (1984). Underutilization of mental health professionals by community elderly. *Gerontologist, 24,* 23-30.

Author Index

Subject Index

About the Authors

TORA K. BIKSON is a Senior Behavioral Scientist at the RAND Corporation, who holds doctoral degrees in psychology from UCLA and in philosophy from the University of Missouri. Her work currently focuses on understanding the social-psychological implications of computer-based information and communication technologies and on learning how their potential benefits can be more broadly distributed. She serves on the UN's Advisory Commission on the Coordination of Information Systems and on the NSF's Advisory Board for Industrial Science and Technological Innovation.

PHILIP H. DREYER is Professor of Education and Psychology and Director of the Center for Developmental Studies at the Claremont Graduate School. A life-span developmental psychologist educated at Harvard, Yale, and the University of Chicago, he is currently investigating processes of psychosocial development during adolescence and adulthood with emphasis on the interaction of individuals with major socializing institutions, such as the family, school, and the work group. He is a member of numerous professional organizations including the Gerontological Society, and has been a Spencer Fellow of the National Academy for Education.

JACQUELINE D. GOODCHILDS received her Ph.D. at Cornell University and is a social psychologist in the Department of Psychology at UCLA and a consultant at the RAND Corporation. Currently President of the Society for the Psychological Study of Social Issues, she has a major research interest in the problems of being an older man or an older woman in today's world. She previously collaborated with Tora Bikson in NSF-supported research on older adults' receptivity to new products and their ability to assimilate new information about old products.

ROBERT O. HANSSON earned his Ph.D. in social psychology at the University of Washington, and currently is Professor of Psychology at the University of Tulsa. His research interests focus on concerns of the aging

235

family, widowhood, relational competence, relationships, and adjustment in old age. His work on these topics has appeared in the *Journal of Gerontology, Journal of Personality and Social Psychology, Journal of Social Issues, Journal of Social and Clinical Psychology,* and *Applied Social Psychology Annual.*

N. LAURA KAMPTNER received her Ph.D. in developmental psychology from Michigan State University. She is currently Assistant Professor of Psychology at California State University, San Bernardino, and specializes in life-span developmental psychology. Her research interests include possessions and their meanings in adolescence through old age, sibling relations in adulthood, identity and self in adulthood and old age, and attachment across the life span.

M. POWELL LAWTON is Director of Research at the Philadelphia Geriatric Center. His research has concerned the environmental psychology of later life, mental health and aging, and affectivity and aging. He is a past president of the Gerontological Society of America and past chair of Division 20 (Adult Development and Aging) of the American Psychological Association. He is the founding editor of the APA journal *Psychology and Aging.*

MELVIN J. LERNER is Professor of Social Psychology at the University of Waterloo. Following a fellowship from the Social Sciences and Humanities Research Council of Canada (SSHRC) to study problems in "population aging," he has been engaged in research sponsored by SSHRC and the National Institute on Aging (NIA) focusing on sibling caretakers of the dependent elderly, and coping and growth among the elderly. He is editor of the multidisciplinary journal *Social Justice Review* and the book series *Critical Issues in Social Justice,* and also directs the Center for the Study of Social Justice at the University of Leiden, the Netherlands.

STUART OSKAMP is Professor of Psychology at Claremont Graduate School. He received his Ph.D. from Stanford University and has had visiting appointments at the University of Michigan, University of Bristol, London School of Economics and Political Science, and University of New South Wales. His main research interests are in the areas of attitudes and attitude change, behavioral aspects of energy and resource conservation, and social issues and public policy. His books include *Attitudes and Opinions* and *Applied Social Psychology.* He is a past president of the APA Division of Population and Environmental Psychology and is currently editor of the *Journal of Social Issues.*

J. THOMAS PUGLISI is Associate Professor of Psychology and Coordinator of the Interdisciplinary Program in Gerontology at the University of North Carolina at Charlotte. As a 1986-1987 APA Congressional Science Fellow, he served with the professional staff of the Select Committee on Aging of the U.S. House of Representatives, where his legislative issues included budget and appropriations for aging programs, health and long-term care, mental health and aging, and the Older Americans Act. Trained in developmental psychology, he holds a doctorate from the Ohio State University and has conducted basic and applied research in aging for over 10 years.

DAVID W. REID is Associate Professor of Psychology at York University, Toronto. He received his Ph.D. in social-personality psychology from the University of Waterloo and completed postdoctoral training in clinical psychology at the University of Washington. Since the 1970s, he has conducted research on the psychological adjustment and well-being of the elderly. More recently he has focused his studies on how the quality of human relationships—including those with health professionals and family—can facilitate adjustment to changes by giving the elderly person control over these changes.

LARRY D. RICKARDS is currently the assistant director for the National Association of Area Agencies on Aging. He has over 15 years of experience in the fields of health, mental health, geriatrics, and government relations. From 1982 to 1988, he served as legislative affairs officer for the American Psychological Association, where he had primary responsibility for policy issues pertaining to the aged, and as project director and co-principal investigator for a grant to implement the mental health recommendations of the 1981 White House Conference on Aging. His legislative issues have included the Older Americans Act, mental health, long-term care, homelessness, and civil rights. His previous publications have focused on aging and mental health, Alzheimer's disease, and the financing of mental health care. He has a doctorate in counseling and community psychology from the University of Maryland.

DARRYL G. SOMERS is a doctoral candidate in social psychology at the University of Waterloo, Canada. His research interests focus on people's responses to major life stresses and the processes they employ to maintain coherent constructions of reality. His M.A. research examined vulnerable self-concept domains and stress in college freshmen, and he is presently engaged in a prospective longitudinal study of employees' reactions to plant closure.

SHIRLYNN SPACAPAN is Associate Professor of Psychology at Harvey Mudd College and at the Claremont Graduate School. She received her Ph.D. from the University of Oregon in 1982, where she taught for two years before moving to Claremont. She is currently studying topics at the interface of environmental psychology and organizational behavior such as perceived control in the workplace and workplace design. She was a 1988 Haynes Foundation Faculty Fellow for her work on the social psychology of aging.

MARY C. TIERNEY is supervisor of all psychological services to elderly patients at the Sunnybrook Medical Centre in Toronto. Since 1982, she has been director of a large multidisciplinary prospective study of Alzheimer's disease. She received her Ph.D. in psychology from the University of Windsor.